DesignForLiving

DesignForLiving

Furniture and Lighting 1950-2000
The Liliane and David M. Stewart Collection

David A. Hanks and Anne Hoy
Edited by Martin Eidelberg

Flammarion

Paris - New York

Montreal Museum of Decorative Arts
Montreal Museum of Fine Arts

Notes on the Use of the Catalogue

Dimensions are in centimeters. Height precedes width precedes depth.
An asterisk following a donor's name indicates an object donated through
the American Friends of Canada.

Flammarion
26, rue Racine 75006 Paris

EDITORIAL DIRECTION
Suzanne Tise-Isoré

ART DIRECTION
Compagnie Bernard Baissait
Bernard Lagacé

COPY EDITING
Bernard Wooding

COLOR SEPARATIONS
Sele Offset, Italy

PRINTED AND BOUND
JCG, Spain

Numéro d'édition: FA 3672-01
ISBN: 2-0801-3672-0

Contents

Foreword

Twenty years ago, when the Montreal Museum of Decorative Arts welcomed its first visitor, it was Canada's first museum devoted exclusively to the decorative arts. Dedicated to acquiring and exhibiting outstanding examples of twentieth-century design, it has been unique among museums of North America for most of its life. Today it enjoys the rising tide of interest in the design of that period, an interest that it helped to create, and that has now become the focus of other institutions as well. The Montreal Museum of Decorative Arts, of which the Liliane and David M. Stewart Collection is the core, now boasts over five thousand objects, representing all media—furniture, lighting, glass, ceramics, jewelry, metalware, textiles, and graphic arts—and all forms, from one-of-a-kind handicrafts to industrial prototypes and mass-produced objects. These objects are celebrated for their aesthetic excellence and their pivotal roles in the evolution of the decorative arts.

Since the museum's opening in 1979, its programs have encouraged both the general public's appreciation and the specialist's study of design. Its traveling exhibitions and their scholarly catalogues have done much to familiarize international audiences with major monuments of modern design, as well as some provocative, less-known examples in the Stewart Collection. In the present book, drawn exclusively from its holdings, the MMDA demonstrates its continued commitment to acquiring major examples from the last five decades. *Design for Living* celebrates the museum's twenty years of collecting, a history made possible by the enlightened support of Mrs. David M. Stewart in the tradition she and her late husband inaugurated, and also by the generosity of many donors—notable collectors, the designers themselves, and manufacturers. Here are some of the classics of the past fifty years conceived by renowned leaders. These objects serve as guideposts to less familiar but no less fascinating works found at the MMDA—and they testify to the diversity, vitality, and surprise of design in these last five decades.

The works presented in this volume are the products of a half-century of tumultuous political, cultural, and technological change, which has altered world thinking as irrevocably as it has changed the world map. These objects reflect an international scene of extraordinary creativity, with designers of different temperaments and points of view. They bear witness to innovations in both technology and art; they reveal responses to new needs and tastes that have arisen with ever-increasing speed. In this book, these objects are presented by decade and according to kinships of form and fabrication. Together, they embody the high quality of design between 1950 and the present, and their parity with the best of contemporary architecture and fine art.

Design for Living also acknowledges the integration of the Montreal Museum of Decorative Arts with the Montreal Museum of Fine Arts, and its new location in the center of the city. In 1997, the collection of the MMDA was installed in galleries designed by Frank Gehry, and in 2001, it will be shown in the newly refurbished space to be known as the Liliane and David M. Stewart Galleries, along with the MMFA's collection of decorative arts ranging from the Middle Ages through the nineteenth century. Such a publication, like its predecessors at the MMDA, is the work of many hands. Foremost among them is our learned and indefatigable expert editor, the scholar Martin Eidelberg. We especially thank David A. Hanks, Curatorial Consultant to the museum since its founding, not only for the discerning essays he wrote for this book, but also for his wise counsel and for the ways in which he has helped guide the museum in its development and in so many of its important acquisitions and exhibitions. We are greatly indebted to Anne Hoy, the capable and insightful author of the catalogue entries for each object. Among the many in Montreal who were essential to this project, we are grateful to Diane Charbonneau, Coordinator of the MMDA collection, who undertook the many challenges of the publication with her usual grace, wisdom, and resourcefulness, and took on great burdens with calm intelligence. Our heart-felt thanks go to James Carroll for his able administrative assistance in all aspects of the project. Our cataloguer, Anne-Marie Chevrier, accomplished the painstaking task of verifying registrarial information. Linda-Anne D'Anjou cleared copyrights and Majella Beauregard secured archival photographs with patience and perseverance. As ever, we appreciate the great care with which Louise Giroux has read the manuscript and supervised the French edition. We are grateful to Marcel Marcotte, Suzanne Couillard, and Nadine Brien for their superb assistance and preparatory work, and for facilitating the new photography, which was undertaken by Denis Farley. At the MMFA, Christine Guest and Brian Merrett were also responsible for new photography, with the collaboration of Jeanne Frégault. At the office of David A. Hanks & Associates, publication coordinator Jill Grannan was responsible for numerous aspects of this book, including supervision of the production of the manuscript, procuring photographs, and pursuing factual data, all of which she accomplished with great skill. Intern Mina Takahashi helped in the initial stages of this book. Joan Rosasco provided graceful literary assistance. Dorys Codina oversaw administrative matters with her customary good nature and expertise.

At Flammarion, editorial consultant Suzanne Tise-Isoré proved once more how wise and supportive a collaborator and friend she is to the museum and to all of us. She was charged with the myriad and taxing details of production, and we are grateful for the time and energy she gave to this project. We appreciate the care of Sandrine Balihaut-Martin at Flammarion, who was responsible for the French edition of this book. We thank Montreal-born Bernard Lagacé for creating a design that is contemporary yet timeless, like the objects it spotlights.

Many of the designers and manufacturers of the objects presented here, as well as their colleagues and families, provided information essential to the texts and in some cases also lent transparencies for reproduction. In particular, we warmly thank Artemide; Val Bertoia; Andrea Branzi; Denise Scott Brown; Antonia Campi; Design Gallery Milano; Droog Design; Yoshiko Ebihara, Gallery 91; Ignazia Favata, Studio Joe Colombo; Anna Castelli Ferrieri; Robert Viol, Herman Miller Furniture Company; Joseph Helman Gallery; The Knoll Group; Nancy Knox, Issey Miyake USA; Jeffrey Manta, Arcosanti; Marianne Panton; Gaetano Pesce; Poltronova; Liana Cavallaro, Sottsass Associati; Charles Stendig; Studio 80; and Robert Venturi. We also thank Paola Antonelli of The Museum of Modern Art, David Arky, Richard Axsom, Jacqueline Nelson, Marianne Wegner Sørensen, and Charles Solin for their assistance in this regard.

Finally we thank Mrs. Stewart most gratefully for her vision, her generosity, and her faith in this project. Her support for this, as for past publications, has been indispensable.

Guy Cogeval
Director of the Montreal Museum of Fine Arts
and The Montreal Museum of Decorative Arts

Luc d'Iberville-Moreau
Former Director of the Montreal Museum of Decorative Arts
Advisor to the Montreal Museum of Fine Arts

fig. 1 ▲ Noël Coward with Alfred Lunt and Lynn Fontanne in the final scene of *Design for Living*, Ethel Barrymore Theatre, New York, 1933. Set design by Gladys E. Calthrop.

Preface

Looking back at the first twenty years of the Montreal Museum of Decorative Arts is a source of gratification and, admittedly, a certain wonder. When in 1976 Montreal's mayor, Monsieur Jean Drapeau, asked us to visit the majestic but then cavernously empty and partially vandalized twin mansions known as the Château Dufresne, we did not foresee where its restoration would lead or what it would eventually contain. From the grand Louis XVI style of Marius Dufresne's architecture of 1914-17 to Frank Gehry's exuberant plywood and fir-covered galleries for today's museum—what a marvelous leap!

My husband's love of New World history and of his native Montreal impelled us forward. Not long after we saw the Château Dufresne, we agreed to undertake returning the Dufresne brothers' home to what they had built. We also decided to give it a new public life: as a museum of decorative arts. With the astute counsel of an advisory board that was soon assembled, we determined to focus on mid-twentieth-century design—especially of the years between 1940 and 1960.

The first ambition, the restoration of the Château Dufresne, was realized with the talent and collaborative effort of skilled artisans. Fortunately, Mme. Marius Dufresne had carefully preserved many of the château's original furnishings, and they became available after her death in 1976. For the opening of the Montreal Museum of Decorative Arts on June 14, 1979, a number of the château's forty rooms were recreated with their Louis XV, Louis XVI, Tudor, and Gothic Revival interiors, and they were made complete with the restoration of the original murals, carvings, and plasterwork.

The second ambition, the acquisition and exhibition of mid-twentieth-century decorative arts, was not only initiated but soon enlarged. Consulting Curator David A. Hanks, and our distinguished Collections Advisory Board, composed of George Beylerian, Helen Drutt, Jack Lenor Larsen, and Toshiko Mori, had helped lead the museum to purchases and gifts from the postwar years. The mandate was extended to one of collecting objects from the years 1935 to 1965, and then it was ultimately expanded to include all decades from 1900 to the present. These redefinitions of our parameters were motivated by two provocative exhibitions drawn from the museum's collections and published in ground-breaking catalogues edited by the scholar Martin Eidelberg.

The growing collection was fated, however, to clash with the elegant but small Neoclassic Dufresne home. By the mid-1980s it was obvious that the museum would have to relocate. As early as 1985, new space was sought to accommodate our extensive collection and exhibitions program. In 1994, we leased unfinished space in the Jean-Noël Desmarais Pavilion of the Montreal Museum of Fine Arts, and we invited the acclaimed architect Frank Gehry to conceive a facility for us. His new galleries opened in 1997. Thus, after eighteen years, we regretfully left the Château Dufresne and its beautiful suburban setting near the Botanical Gardens, but we delightedly took up residence on Sherbrooke Street in the center of downtown Montreal. In January 2000, one more significant step was taken: the collection of the Montreal Museum of Decorative Arts was joined to those of the Montreal Museum of Fine Arts, one of Canada's most eminent museums. There it enjoys many services, from administration and conservation to education, and has the honor of being integrated into a splendid display of decorative and fine arts. The MMDA retains its name, its board of directors, its advisory committee, and its exhibition programs. In sum, it retains its identity within this new symbiotic relationship. From its origins at the Château Dufresne to its new home at the Museum of Fine Arts, the Montreal Museum of Decorative Arts has never lost focus on its commitment to acquire and present objects that speak of the century and of the moment.

Our focus on contemporary design is not that far removed from the urbane stagecraft of Noël Coward, whose 1933 *Design for Living* inspired the title of this book. In Coward's play, a *ménage à trois*—itself a shocking yet modern arrangement—takes place in Paris, London, and New York as the characters pursue one another through fashionably modern settings. When *Design for Living* was performed by Alfred Lunt, Lynn Fontanne, and Coward himself in New York, the three stars collapsed laughingly in the last scene onto a *moderne* sofa before a cocktail table covered with chromed Art Deco objects and Jean Luce dinnerware (fig. 1). Such chic, Syrie Maugham-style sets captured the witty, contemporary tone of the characters, a spirit this book also seeks to convey as it considers how design both mirrors and shapes the social patterns of contemporary life.

Where possible, *Design for Living* presents not only significant objects but also photographs of them in actual interiors to suggest how design truly intersects with our lives. Although the museum's collection encompasses a wide range of decorative arts, this publication focuses on furniture and lighting, objects whose demands of form and function have inspired the most innovative solutions.

The history of the Montreal Museum of Decorative Arts reflects the ever-widening attention paid to modern design worldwide. Much of the recognition that we have received thus far has been earned by numerous expert advisors, a dedicated and gifted staff, and the great generosity of both donors and the artists themselves. With deepest gratitude, we dedicate this book to all the friends and supporters we have come to know over the last twenty years.

Mrs. David M. Stewart
President, Montreal Museum of Decorative Arts

fig. 2 ▲ Frank O. Gehry and Associates, signage above the entrance to the MMDA from the Cultural Corridor, 1996.

Collecting and Exhibiting Twentieth-Century Design

In 1980, the Liliane and David M. Stewart Collection acquired its first example of decorative art, a classic *LCW Chair* designed by Charles and Ray Eames. At that time, interest in midcentury design was barely nascent; most museums and private collectors rarely pursued objects of the postwar period. For the Stewart Collection, however, obtaining not only postwar objects, but also examples of contemporary design was the mandate; the first purchase of a contemporary work was made in 1981, a celadon-glazed porcelain centerpiece designed that very year by the Quebec native Louis Gosselin and executed by the Sèvres Manufactory. This pattern of collecting both the recent "historic" past and contemporary work has continued at the Montreal Museum of Decorative Arts throughout the last two decades.

Aesthetic excellence is the primary goal of the Montreal Museum of Decorative Arts' collecting policy, but it also tries to maintain a broad perspective in its approach. Its vantage point is international, and its interests are shaped by an awareness of important developments in contemporary art and design.

In devoting itself to the twentieth century and emphasizing the postwar period, the Liliane and David M. Stewart Collection may seem quite specialized—especially in comparison with museum collections that span four thousand years. Yet the field of modern international design is vast and collecting can easily be arbitrary and unfocused. For the Montreal Museum of Decorative Arts, discipline and focus were achieved by two major exhibitions for which objects were specifically acquired. *Design 1935-1965: What Modern Was* (1991) sought to define Modernism and its legacies, while *Designed for Delight: Alternative Aspects of Twentieth-Century Decorative Arts* (1997) explored Modernism's antitheses in exuberant, eccentric, individualistic conceptions.

In addition, the logic of the Stewart Collection has gained strength by its stress on certain countries. Given the primacy of design in Scandinavia and the United States at midcentury, it was natural that emphasis was first placed on those geographical areas. In recent decades, the collecting focus has shifted to Italy and Japan, reflecting the growing importance of those countries. A further focus has been on major designers, many of whom the MMDA is fortunate enough to know and celebrate; pivotal figures such as Ettore Sottsass and Gaetano Pesce are represented by richly diverse, extensive holdings. Certain major designers such as George Nelson and manufacturers including Herman Miller have made generous gifts of their work to the MMDA. Also, special exhibitions have helped enrich the collection, as acquisitions are often made from shows organized by the museum.

In addition to the recognized examples of furniture and lighting highlighted in this book, the MMDA's collection has other strengths, particularly in the areas of textiles and jewelry—often neglected areas of design. Overall, the collection is notable for its encyclopedic breadth and the quality of individual objects. Time will tell whether all its accessions have been prescient. Nonetheless, they have been made with deliberation, passion, and a deep commitment.

Quality, of course, is the foremost criterion in the creation of any museum collection. But presenting that collection is also of great significance to its appreciation and understanding. To the Montreal Museum of Decorative Arts, an appropriate contemporary structure is

fig. 3 ▶ Moshe Safdie, Jean-Noël Desmarais Pavilion, Montreal Museum of Fine Arts, 1997, exterior showing exhibition banners.

especially important, for the architecture can express and extend the philosophy underlying our acquisitions, and unite them in a meaningful statement.

As has been described, the MMDA opened in 1979 in a historic mansion on the city's east side, but quickly outgrew its original Neoclassical home. A larger and more cohesive exhibition facility was soon felt essential, one that would enhance comprehension of these modern objects through its own contemporary design. As early as 1985, the MMDA sought appropriate new space for its collection and exhibition programs, space that could display with equal sensitivity objects as small as jewelry and as large as furniture. Between 1980 and 1990, several detailed studies regarding the MMDA's future were undertaken, and several sites were considered. In 1990, the MMDA approached the Canadian-born architect Frank Gehry with the idea of creating a new facility for its holdings. Well known as a museum architect today, he had not yet received a significant commission in his native country. Plans for a new museum facility progressed as the MMDA, working closely with the architect, organized the 1992 exhibition and catalogue *Frank Gehry: New Bentwood Furniture Designs.*[1]

A preliminary planning study had already provided schematics for a new building that would include twenty thousand square feet for exhibition space and six thousand square feet for storage.[2] An additional report confirmed that the museum should relocate to a more central area of Montreal if attendance was to increase.[3] By 1993, however, it became clear that the ambitious project would have to be postponed due to lack of funding, a consequence of the several years of recession in the Canadian (and global) economy. In 1994, in order to obtain both much-needed exhibition areas and proper climate control for its exhibitions and collection, the MMDA decided to move to a new location without creating a building of its own. It entered into an agreement with the Montreal Museum of Fine Arts to lease space in the museum's Jean-Noël Desmarais Pavilion (fig. 3), built in 1991 to designs by Moshe Safdie but never fully occupied. Gehry's original commission for an entirely new building was put aside, and he was invited instead to renovate part of this pavilion. If the solution was not ideal, the site was—a prime location on Sherbrooke Street, in the heart of the city. And there were other practical advantages, such as museum-quality climate control and services such as security and maintenance, all of which were included in the lease agreement. It was the first step toward a close, cooperative alliance between the two institutions. Most important was the assurance that the government funding originally sought for the separate Gehry building would be forthcoming for this more modest facility, despite the still-difficult economic situation. In 1993, Gehry initiated his plans for the MMDA. The distinctive and innovative gallery, constructed in association with the Montreal firm of Provencher Roy and Associates, was completed and opened in May 1997.

Based in Los Angeles, Gehry has had a long history of working with museums, beginning in 1965 with a series of installations for special exhibitions at the Los Angeles County Museum of Art.[4] The architect's earliest commission for an entire museum building was the Vitra Design Museum in Weil am Rhein, Germany, completed in 1989. Although initially intended as a corporate showcase of twentieth-century furniture, the Vitra Museum soon evolved into a very popular public attraction. In 1993, while plans for the Montreal Museum of Decorative Arts were evolving, Gehry's second art museum was completed—the Frederick R. Weisman Art and Teaching Museum in Minneapolis, Minnesota. In the same period, Gehry's most ambitious museum building, The Solomon R. Guggenheim Museum in Bilbao, Spain, was being erected, with over one hundred thousand square feet of exhibition space. Resembling a giant metal sculpture, the Bilbao Guggenheim opened in 1997 to tremendous critical acclaim, and it has become one of Europe's most popular destinations.

The project most similar to that of the MMDA, however, was Gehry's facility of 1983 for the Museum of Contemporary Art, Los Angeles. Although initially intended as a temporary exhibition space, Gehry's design for the so-called "Temporary Contemporary" delighted the public to such an extent that it continued to be used even after the completion of the museum's new building, and it is still functioning today. While the Los Angeles project is larger than the MMDA, both museums are renovations of existing spaces originally intended for other purposes. Gehry treated these interiors similarly, without altering or attempting to hide the industrial appearance of the shells.

Gehry's design for the MMDA provides approximately ten thousand square feet for permanent and temporary exhibitions, creating two halls (fig. 4). The museum is entered through a two-story, glass-enclosed atrium originally intended by Safdie as a public-access *allée* between Crescent and Bishop Streets. This space, known as the "Cultural Corridor," also connects to the rest of the Desmarais pavilion. One of the museum's specifications was to create a distinction between itself and the adjacent Museum of Fine Arts and to give the MMDA a strong, separate identity. To achieve this, Gehry provided monumental yet exuberant signage above the entrance (fig. 2), in which the MMDA's name in French is spelled out in green letters that project from plywood panels like a Cubist collage. Gehry also created two schemes to dramatize the entrances to the Cultural Corridor on Crescent and Bishop Streets: the first a caterpillar-like roof of wire mesh (fig. 7), the second a group of animated sculptural forms in sheet metal that are prophetic of the facade of the Guggenheim Museum in Bilbao (fig. 8). Unfortunately, neither of Gehry's schemes for entrance roofs could be constructed because of the restrictions posed by city codes mandated by Montreal's snowy winters.

When it came to display cases for Montreal, Gehry's imagination took flight. At the Los Angeles County Museum of Art, he designed only relatively simple units, but for the MMDA he conceived an elaborate system of sculptural towers, platforms, and vitrines. The museum's exhibition areas are distinguished by four striking cubistic compositions in Gehry's signature plywood—trapezoidal, strongly canted vitrines clustered like trees (figs. 5-6). These unusual

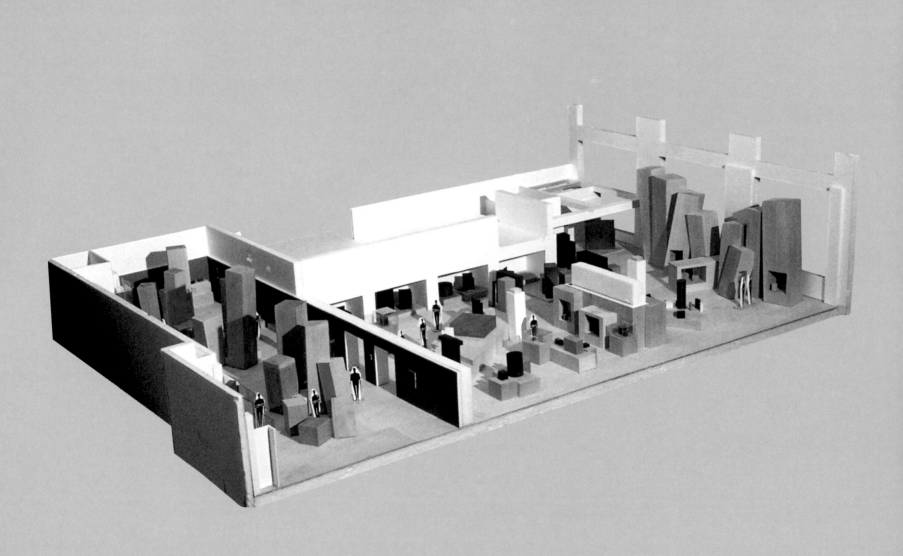

fig. 4 ▲ Frank O. Gehry and Associates, computer-generated model showing the intended internal disposition of the Montreal Museum of Decorative Arts, 1995.
figs. 5-6 ◄ ► Installation of *Designed for Delight: Alternative Aspects of Twentieth-Century Decorative Arts*, MMDA, 1997.

17

figs. 7-8 ▲ Frank O. Gehry and Associates, computer-generated studies of wire-mesh and sheet metal roofs for the street entrances to the Cultural Corridor, 1996.

vitrines impress visitors with their architectural presence, some reaching sixteen feet into the air. Most contain eye-level display spaces for objects and are fitted with lanternlike lighting at the top that is directed toward the ceiling. For the lofty cases facing Bishop Street, Gehry originally planned to include video screens which would display videotapes of the museum's collection to attract passersby.

Gehry's intent, as with his other museum designs, was to create a dialogue between the architecture and the works of art on display. He wanted the museum's new galleries to be a striking statement in their own right, but one that was conceptually complete only with the installation of the exhibits. With their huge scale and dynamic, asymmetrical planes, the vitrines—although memorable in themselves—still had to accommodate both the small and large objects on display. Objects in certain vitrines are lit beneath their glass bases and also from above, both light sources concealed from the viewer. Smaller, movable vitrines and angular modular platforms were also created to allow flexible arrangements. Gehry designed gallery seating throughout: these modular benches are upholstered with carpeting and arranged in clusters in front of the windows adjacent to the Cultural Corridor.

The heights of the walls vary drastically, from nine to twenty-three feet, but are not always finished to the ceiling. In the taller spaces, the sculptural, towerlike vitrines reach up dizzyingly, punctuating the voids. Gehry juxtaposes the quirky sculptural forms to the stark, industrial space, establishing a counterpoint between the playful and the ordinary. In opposition to the modernist concept of galleries as neutral, white volumes, Gehry planned that certain walls would be painted with colors to suit different installations.

Gehry is known for his interest in the creative use of common industrial materials and for his ability to transform them. The gallery floors are constructed of Douglas fir blocks laid on the end-grain, arranged to create a contemporary pattern. All the towers, platforms, and vitrine bases are made of Douglas fir Marine plywood panels, whose texture and hue provide a warm setting for the often colorful objects on display. The brilliance of his designs transforms these inexpensive Canadian materials with the magic of alchemy.

The museum's offices are located on a mezzanine level. All furnishings for these five offices, including file cabinets and desks, were designed by the architect—with plywood as the primary construction material, and colorful plastic laminates covering the working surfaces. A strikingly architectonic conference table is one example of the custom-designed furniture Gehry created for this area (fig. 9). Square in shape and fitted with a yellow plastic laminate top, the table rests on four massive plywood supports.

In all, the dynamic counterpoint between Gehry's gallery design and the museum's collection creates an invigorating experience which enlivens the viewer's appreciation of both the art exhibited and the architectural setting. Gehry's sympathies for the diverse objects to be displayed, yet his challenge to preconceptions of museum design, are in keeping with the point of view that formed the museum's collection: a concern for the contemporary and the classics, with a broad perspective that encompasses a variety of theoretical perspectives. This architecture joyously defies expectations—like the objects it contains.

David A. Hanks
Consulting Curator, Montreal Museum of Decorative Arts

fig. 9 ▲ Frank O. Gehry and Associates, conference table for the MMDA, 1996.

The 1950s
The Quest for Good Design

AT MIDCENTURY, THE IMPACT OF WORLD WAR II WAS STILL BEING FELT. EUROPE AND ASIA WERE STRUGGLING to rebuild, while the United States, now the world's military leader, was creating a consumer economy that would dominate international trade without interruption for the next twenty-odd years. The globe had become smaller. In 1949, a plane flew nonstop around the world, refueling in midair; and Harry Truman's inauguration as president of the United States was broadcast on television across the American continent. America's wealth was put to good purpose during these troubled times. Truman strategized to contain Soviet expansionism, as the United States entered the arms race and the Cold War with the Soviet Union and its Communist allies. This led to a war in Korea that sent Americans overseas again in 1950-53, while in the United States an extreme fear of Communism fueled investigations by Senator Joseph McCarthy in 1950-54, challenging tenets of liberalism. Nonetheless, the majority of Americans felt secure in the nation's unparalleled prosperity. The G.I. Bill sent a generation of veterans to college and underwrote first-time home-ownership. The suburbs mushroomed, doubling in size around some cities in the early 1950s. Here was the largest market for innovative design in the decade. Of necessity, consumers had been ignored during the war effort. Now the economy would benefit by responding to their pent-up demand, and with the reform of domestic industry, issues of style and theory rose to prominence.

"Good Design" was an essential concept in the 1950s, one that suited the perennial American desire to reform and improve oneself, and also the lives of other people. Advocates of Good Design believed that objects created according to universal and rational principles were imbued with an identifiable character that could be recognized, defined, and admired. The origins of these precepts were not hard to find: they descended from the teaching of the Bauhaus. The utilization of modern technology and materials, and the rejection of ornament were among these Modernist tenets. A well-designed object was to be admired for its classic, understated beauty and its fitness to purpose.

The term itself was popularized in the United States in a series of competitive *Good Design* exhibitions organized by Edgar Kaufmann, jr., of the Department of Architecture and Design at The Museum of Modern Art in New York, in collaboration with the Merchandise Mart in Chicago, the country's leading wholesale furnishings center. The objects selected by Kaufmann and his jurors reflected his own definition of Good Design: "a thorough merging of form and function revealing a practical, uncomplicated beauty."[5] For Kaufmann, Good Design had a moral dimension. It would not only enhance people's lives visually, but also uplift them spiritually. Epitomizing its uncluttered simplicity was Paul Rudolph's installation for the first *Good Design* exhibition at the Merchandise Mart, where icons of postwar design such as Charles and Ray Eames' wire-base chairs are visible (fig. 10).

Affordability was equal in importance to style, as the products of Good Design were meant to reach a broad market, including the consumers who had sacrificed during the war years and whose tastes were believed to need improving. This concern was also addressed by The Museum of Modern Art's *International Competition for Low-cost Furniture Design* in 1950. Although the *Good Design* exhibitions concluded in 1955, MoMA continued as the self-anointed arbiter of taste and quality in design throughout the 1950s and well into the following decades. It was not alone. The Walker Art Center in Minneapolis had begun devoting space to design in its Every Day Gallery starting in 1944. In 1951 and 1952, the Walker Art Center organized *Useful Gifts*, exhibitions intended to display contemporary products chosen for their adherence to the precepts of "simplicity, intelligent use of materials, straightforward design, and pleasing appearance."[6] These concerns were shared in the marketplace. Knoll Associates and the Herman Miller Furniture Company manufactured furnishings by progressive Americans such as

Harry Bertoia, Eero Saarinen, the Eameses, and George Nelson. Both companies were leaders in making contemporary design desirable in homes and offices. A handful of periodicals became sources of support for the champions of Good Design: *Everyday Art Quarterly* (later *Design Quarterly*) from the Walker Art Center; John Entenza's *California Arts & Architecture*; and the New York-based *Interiors* where Olga Gueft was managing editor.

Despite such prophets, however, the Good Design movement met resistance. The styles of American homes and mass-market furnishings in the 1950s were largely retrospective. For example, between 1947 and 1951, William and Arthur Levitt built more than 15,000 houses in the first "Levittown" on Long Island, choosing a generic Cape Cod cottage design. "Traditional" furniture, in styles optimistically labeled Chippendale, French Provincial, or Chinese Mandarin, prevailed at all price levels. Such diluted period looks predominated throughout the decade and beyond, despite Kaufmann's fulminations: "Designs made now in mimicry of past periods or remote ways of life ('authentic Chinese reproductions,' or 'Chinese modern'), cannot be considered as anything more than embarrassing indications of a lack of faith in our own values."[7] By the second half of the 1950s, Detroit designers were adding chrome trim and ever-longer tailfins to automobiles to distinguish one year's line from the next and thereby spur sales. Good Design was adopted only by a minority—albeit an influential one.

In the smaller, more culturally homogeneous countries of Scandinavia, Good Design was more successful. Of all European nations, Sweden, neutral during the conflict, returned to economic prosperity most rapidly. At the time of the armistice, Stockholm was the most prosperous capital city in Europe, and by the 1950s it had become a mecca for modern design. Significantly, Scandinavia

fig. 10 ▼ Paul Rudolph, installation of *Good Design* exhibition, Merchandise Mart, Chicago, 1952.

had developed a society with few rich or poor; luxury goods were not the focus here, but modest, quality products for a comfortable middle class. Building on indigenous craft traditions, the Scandinavian countries produced furniture and household goods that preserved the look and feel of handwork despite a reliance on industrial manufacturing methods. Furniture with smoothly contoured, tactile forms was constructed of native woods or teak and given a natural finish. Ceramics and glass were ancient crafts now updated in designs with the appeal of the fresh and new.

Professional design organizations in the Scandinavian countries that had been founded during the turn-of-the-century Arts and Crafts movement flourished anew in the 1950s. The Danish Society of Arts and Crafts and Industrial Design organized exhibitions and programs to promote cooperation between artists and industry, and these, along with its publication *Dansk Kunsthandwerk*, were significant postwar forces. *Form*, the prominent Swedish design magazine, then edited by Åke Stavenow, is still published today.

Abroad and at home, Scandinavian design was encouraged with government and industry support for survey expositions. *Scandinavian Design Cavalcades* were annual traveling exhibitions that circulated throughout the Scandinavian countries in the 1950s; from 1954 to 1957,

fig. 11 ▼ Tapio Wirkkala, installation of the Finnish section, Milan Triennale, 1954.

fig. 12 ► Charlotte Perriand, Louis Sognot, Serge Mouille, and Jean Lurçat, living area at the first Triennale of French Contemporary Art, Musée des arts décoratifs, Paris, 1956.

the ambitious exhibition *Design in Scandinavia* traveled to twenty-two museums in Canada and the United States. When postwar Italy recovered enough to revive its highly influential Triennale design exhibitions in Milan, Sweden was prominent at the first one (in 1947). And Finland was awarded twenty-five prizes at the Triennale of 1951, a triumph for Tapio Wirkkala, who designed his country's installations (fig. 11) and whose designs were awarded three of the medals. Nordic designers went on to win more prizes at the 1954, 1957, and 1960 Triennales. Through these means, Scandinavian design became widely known. Graceful yet practical, contemporary in style yet warm in texture and color, these unpretentious modern wares were accepted throughout the world by those of progressive taste.

Good Design was also sought in Britain, where wartime shortages lingered, yet the results met less universal applause. At midcentury, the furniture industry was still regulated by the Utility Furniture scheme which had insured that domestic furniture met strict standards during the war years. In 1951, the government-funded Council of Industrial Design took a leadership role in the promotion of Good Design when it staged the celebratory *Festival of Britain* trade fair. In an effort to effect a rapprochement of art and science, designers were asked to use geometric patterns based on natural crystals. In 1957, the Council initiated a Good Design award for British products, and it also continued to publish *Design*, an influential periodical that had been inaugurated in 1949. The postwar Labor government implemented a plan to provide economical, rationally designed modern housing and new towns across Britain, and to encourage the middle- and lower-class citizens who moved into them to adopt simple, functional furnishings. The council flat became synonymous with Socialist Modernism. Austere and colorless, indistinguishable from its neighbors, it represented the severest side of utilitarianism.

The need to rebuild cities, railways, and factories was equally urgent in France, yet Good Design was of less interest, reflecting the country's very different design heritage. Modernism had touched only a prosperous minority in France in the 1920s and 1930s. Art Deco had been a luxury style. Perhaps not surprisingly, it was in the luxury industries that France quickly reestablished

its traditional leadership. Women throughout the world had followed when Christian Dior launched the New Look in 1947, a striking hourglass silhouette requiring a profligate amount of fabric, and Paris was again the capital of fashion. In the field of expensive decoration and accessories, Modernist ideas were tempered with reminiscences of historical styles, and production was limited by a small market.

In 1929, the designers Jean Prouvé, Charlotte Perriand, René Herbst, and Jean Royère had founded the Union des Artistes Modernes to advance an alternative, populist form of modern functionalism. From late 1949 to early 1950, the UAM presented the exhibition *Formes Utiles,* a selection of "objects of our time" displayed as works of art. In the 1950s, the French Ministry of Commerce sponsored the *Beauté de France* award intended to support an intrinsically French model of Good Design. Not to be outdone by the Italians, the French organized their own Triennale in 1956 (fig. 12). Despite these benevolent efforts, the populace still approached modern design with suspicion, seeing it as a menace to the good life. The contrast between the easygoing, traditional mores of the *bon peuple* and the supposedly sterile, mechanistic environment inhabited by pretentious bourgeois converts was satirized memorably by Jacques Tati in his film *Mon Oncle* (fig. 13).[8]

Italy assumed a leading role in the design world after the war, but the restrained taste of Good Design did not dominate it. The keynote instead was invention. Italian designers, as well as Americans, were among the first to experiment with new materials, finding uses for substances developed in wartime, such as plastics, foam rubber, and new variants of plywood. Throughout the 1950s, Italian products represented a form of craftsmanship intrinsic to the country's tradition of small-scale, artisanal production. This tradition also fostered stylistic diversity, even idiosyncrasy. Rejecting the bombastic Neoclassical modernism of the Fascist era, Italian postwar designers delighted in creating objects with sensual contours and organic shapes. Furniture, motor scooters, and home appliances were given racy curves and an elegant sleekness. Harking back perhaps to Futurism, there was a strong movement in favor of sculptural forms as an alternative to the rectilinear rigor of functional Modernism. A sewing machine by Marcello Nizzoli and a toilet bowl by Gio Ponti could look uncannily like sculptures by Brancusi.

Functionalism, however, was not ignored. At the 1951 Triennale, intended as a celebration of Europe's economic recovery from the war, the Italian display, *The Form of the Useful,* featured new industrial product designs such as typewriters by the Olivetti firm and lighting fixtures by the Castiglioni brothers. Thanks to Olivetti's employment of progressive Italian designers, its office equipment won world recognition for its alluring styling. The Milan Triennales of 1951, 1954, and 1957 were given media coverage worldwide and were the design events of the decade.

Similar energy and exuberance were evident in the Americas, especially in Brazil, which became a supporter of modern design in the 1950s. Untouched by the war, Brazil had money and resources. Between 1956 and 1960, the government embarked upon the grandiose utopian project of building Brasilia, a completely new capital city in a remote province. A local version of the International Style had been introduced in the 1930s when Le Corbusier visited the country. Now the architect Oscar Niemeyer designed buildings that combined the geometry of the International Style with elegant curved forms. Italian architects such as Pier Luigi Nervi and Gio Ponti began major projects in Brazil in the 1950s, where they incorporated aspects of local styles, and a number of Italian firms, including Olivetti, built factories there. Inspired by the Venice Biennale, São Paulo inaugurated a regular series of vanguard art exhibitions; the first Bienal des Artes Plásticos was held in 1951 and included design as well as fine art. In 1957, the fourth Bienal received a new home in a pavilion designed by Niemeyer (fig. 14).

fig. 14 ▶ Oscar Niemeyer, exhibition space, Bienal des Artes Plásticos, Ibirapuéra Park, São Paulo, Brazil, 1957.

For Germany and Japan in the postwar period, Good Design meant saleable product design. In 1945, a defeated Germany was a rubble heap. Rebuilding cities and factories destroyed during the war was the first necessity, and that process, with the aid of the American-financed Marshall Plan, led West Germany to an unprecedented economic revival. But by 1950, partitioned and still occupied by Allied troops, the western part of the country had already begun the recovery that would be known as the "German Miracle." As part of the reconstruction, in 1950 the Hochschule für Gestaltung (Institute of Design) opened in Ulm, an institution explicitly founded on the teaching model of the Bauhaus (closed by the Nazi government in 1933). Under the directorship of Max Bill, the Ulm Hochschule became one of Europe's most prestigious design schools, attracting international students and teachers until it closed its doors in 1968. Its graduates went on to teach at architecture and design institutions around the world, disseminating an influence still felt today. A Bauhaus-trained architect, Bill upheld the principle of the rational in design, and Ulm Hochschule-inspired designs were characterized by clean-lined and simplified functionalist forms. These included the compact, unitary shapes that Dieter Rams gave to Braun appliances. At the same time, a countercurrent in Germany favored more organic forms closer to Italian models.

By 1952, when American occupation ended, Japan had already regained its position as a major manufacturing nation. Japanese designers sought to position themselves in the international community by participating in international design exhibitions and by adopting Western forms and concepts. In 1952, Isamu Kenmochi, one of the first Japanese designers to travel to the West after the war, wrote a report of his visit to the *Good Design* exhibition at The Museum of Modern Art for the *Kogei Nyusu (Industrial Art News).*[9] In 1957, the Japanese Ministry of International Trade and Industry announced a Good Design Selection System, an effort clearly modeled upon Kaufmann's initiative. "Made in Japan," a synonym for cheap, imitative goods before the war, soon stood for attractive, well-designed products, particularly in electronics. Companies such as Sony were poised to dominate world production in their fields in the next decade.

In the late 1950s, consumers in the "Affluent Society" in the West were tempted with an overwhelming diversity of goods and styles. Although often challenged in the marketplace, Good Design reigned supreme among theorists. But by the end of the decade, new directions began to appear. The Italian designer Ettore Sottsass was a seminal figure for the next generation. His interior design of 1959 (fig. 15) was influenced by artists such as Piet Mondrian and Theo van Doesburg, who had structured their work using primary colors arranged upon a grid. His brash use of geometric forms and bright colors was a foretaste of the future: in the 1960s, Pop art would turn Good Design on its ear. Indeed, when asked about the old ideal, Sottsass replied: "This is a question that supposes a Platonic view of the situation, that is, it supposes that somewhere, somehow, there is a place where GOOD DESIGN is deposited. The problem then is to come as close as possible to that 'good design.' My idea instead is that the problem is not a state of things . . . [but] the need a society has for an image of itself."[10] The need for an "image" would soon sweep away the moralistic criteria of functionalism, economy, and sobriety that had been the dogma of Good Design. In the 1960s, design would be Fun.

fig. 15 ◀ Ettore Sottsass, unidentified interior, c. 1959.

Charles and Ray **Eames**

1. **Cabinet: Model no. ESU, 421-C**

Designed 1949
Zinc-plated steel, birch-faced plywood,
plastic-coated plywood, lacquered Masonite
148.9 x 119.4 x 42.5 cm
Produced by Herman Miller Furniture Co.
(Zeeland, MI, USA), 1950-c. 1955
D83.144.I, gift of Mr. and Mrs. Robert
L. Tannenbaum, by exchange*

The continuity in design between the prewar and
postwar periods may be nowhere better illustrated
than in the ESU (Eames Storage Units) series.
Their undisguised industrial materials and method
of fabrication and their modularity respond
to the continued ideals of functionalism. Likewise,
their taut, linear composition of rectangles in primary
colors (and five other hues) epitomize dominant
currents in de Stijl-inspired American abstract art
of the 1930s and 1940s (fig. 16). The units are
lightweight, interchangeable boxes of steel plate
and plywood held on steel struts, and stiffened and
stabilized by lacquered Masonite panels and steel
cross-wires. Strong enough to sit on, the units
were available open, closed by sliding doors, or with
drawers; in one-, two-, and four-bay combinations;
in a desk system; and with different facings for
color or textural variety—possibilities illustrated
in the Herman Miller Furniture Company's publicity
(fig. 17). The buyer ordered the desired combination,
but he or she could also add units later, stacking
them or extending them laterally; thus they could
serve multiple and changing needs for storage

and delimit different living and working areas.

Marketed by Herman Miller as "modestly priced"
for both office and residence, the ESU series
responded to the lack of space in postwar offices
and homes in the United States. Charles Eames had
conceived a line of modular wooden furniture earlier,
in collaboration with fellow architect Eero Saarinen,
when they entered The Museum of Modern Art's
competition of 1940-41, *Organic Design in Home
Furnishings*. The concept of modularity was even
older, dating to the standardized elements designed
by the Deutsche Werkstätten and the Bauhaus
in the first third of the twentieth century. The German
Typenmöbel was intended to satisfy the maximum
number of needs and individual desires with the
minimum number of components. The Eameses
realized this modernist dream of service and
economy by getting their forthright design into
mass production. A critical success, the ESU series
was shown in the first *Good Design* exhibition, held
in Chicago and at The Museum of Modern Art in
New York in 1950.

There is an unmistakable resemblance between
the ESU system and the home that the Eameses
designed for themselves in Pacific Palisades, California,
in 1948-49, one of the "Case Study Houses" sponsored
by *California Arts & Architecture* magazine.[11] In both
of the Eameses' designs, the obvious steel skeleton,
factory-made parts, lively alternation of open and
closed planes, and use of primary colors show
the couple's grasp and humanization of Bauhaus
language. Against the basic metal grid of the
house, they arrayed their ever-changing collection
of objects, art, and plants. On a smaller scale,
the owner of an ESU system could do likewise.

fig. 16 ▲ Harry Holtzman, *Sculpture*, 1941-42.
New Haven, Yale University Art Gallery. Gift of the Artist
to the Collection Société Anonyme.
fig. 17 ► Charles Eames, 1949 photograph of the Eameses'
storage units, desks, and chairs for the Herman Miller
Furniture Company.

George **Nelson**

2. **Sofa: Table lounge unit 6GU**

Designed c. 1954
Painted steel, Formica, lacquered mahogany,
polyurethane foam, wool upholstery
73.7 x 246.2 x 61.5 cm
Produced by Herman Miller Furniture Co.
(Zeeland, MI, USA), c. 1955-59
D81.114.1

Hard-edged rectilinear forms, unornamented
surfaces, and an obvious display of the relation
between load and support characterize the modernism
of this sofa, which Herman Miller termed a "table
lounge unit." The last thing it suggests is comfort—
although its generous scale and broad cushions actually
make for good if decorous sitting. Here Nelson
displays his mastery of the International Style idiom
that he, as chief designer at the Herman Miller
Furniture Company, helped to establish as the image
of corporate America in many offices of the 1950s,
and which then became an international standard.
His three identical pairs of cushions sit on a continuous
slab reminiscent of Charles Eames and Eero Saarinen's
design of 1940-41 for storage units placed on
separate, multipurpose bases, and also of Nelson's
own platform supports for his Basic Cabinet Series
of storage units of 1946. Nelson animates his sofa
structure by cantilevering the slab at both ends;
cantilevering and canted, peglike supports were period
trademarks. The slab space between the cushions is
equal to a seat in width, and functions as a table. Such
easy-care, flexible-use seating became standard in
waiting rooms and other public spaces during the
decade (fig. 18). It was also adopted for domestic use,
at least in crisp, chic, architecturally modern homes.

fig. 18 ▲ Lounge, Rockleigh-Bergen County Golf Course, New Jersey, 1958,
showing the Nelson sofa and *Coconut* chairs.

Eszter **Haraszty**

3. **Presentation drawing: Living room**
Executed c. 1950-60
Fabric and mixed media on paper
46.5 x 66.7 cm
D88.178.1.3, gift of Eszter Haraszty*

A slab sofa, a *Butterfly* chair by Bonet, Kurchan, and Ferrari-Hardoy, a side table by Hans Bellmann, and a clamp-on table lamp—iconic designs popular at midcentury—furnish this interior designed by Haraszty, head of textiles and color planning at Knoll Associates from 1949 to 1955. The rendering was made by a Knoll draftsman and brightly colored by Haraszty, who glued on samples of the textiles she planned for the room. This collage, perhaps even more tellingly than a period photograph, reveals progressive American taste, Knoll's conception of interior design, and Haraszty's vivid color sense. The space seems vast, living and study areas interpenetrate, and the sharply contoured furnishings line up parallel or at right angles to the walls, strengthening the architectural lines.

At Knoll, it was Haraszty who supplied the brilliant color that enlivened the company's otherwise dry Modernism. Nonetheless, the Knolls were astute in their choice of furniture designs. The appeal and usefulness of the pieces shown in this rendering is suggested by the many cheap imitations made in the 1950s: knock-offs of such slab sofas, their cushions pushed together, serviced many sleepovers, and no college dorm was without a *Butterfly* chair, its original leather replaced by an inexpensive canvas sling.

fig. 19 ▲ Florence Knoll, showroom for Knoll, Inc., San Francisco, 1956, showing Mies van der Rohe's *Barcelona* chairs and table, the Saarinen *Womb* chair and ottoman, and other Knoll furniture.

4. Armchair: *LAR Chair*

Designed c. 1949
Fiberglass, steel, rubber
64.1 x 63.5 x 62.2 cm
Produced by Herman Miller Furniture Co.
(Zeeland, MI, USA), 1950-c. 1972
D81.111.1

Such molded fiberglass armchairs—or variants of them—were everywhere in the 1950s, especially in schools and public places. Light, durable, modestly priced, cheerfully colored, stackable in some versions, these were among the earliest mass-produced chairs in fiberglass and forecast the popularity of molded plastic furniture in the 1960s. The Eameses' aesthetic is notable for its whimsy: the wire support of this chair became known as "cat's cradle" after the child's game with string. Its spiky geometry plays off the fluid curves of the chair body in the same way that linear cages contrast with biomorphic shapes in earlier and midcentury American painting and sculpture (fig. 20).

The style of the *LAR Chair* (*Low ARmchair*) as well as its practicality and many possible variations (fig. 21) made it a classic of design, like many of the Eameses' chairs. Like those classics, it was the result of longtime experiments. The thin sculptural shell of the *LAR*, which unites back, arms, and seat in a continuous shape, was based on Charles Eames and Eero Saarinen's plywood-shell furniture which won first prize in The Museum of Modern Art's epochal competition of 1940, *Organic Design in Home Furnishings*. That furniture, in turn, was the result of Charles Eames' explorations of bent plywood in the late 1930s, triggered in part by the pioneering plywood chairs that Alvar Aalto created in the early 1930s. Whether in laminates, metal, or fiberglass, all these designs were aimed at producing a handsome but economical chair with the fewest possible parts.

fig. 20 ▲ Arshile Gorky, *Organization*, 1933-1936. Washington, D.C., National Gallery of Art, Ailsa Mellon Bruce Fund.

fig. 21 ▼ Herman Miller Furniture Company, c. 1965 publicity photograph, "Ladder of 44 Chairs," showing the range of Eames chairs in production.

fig. 22 ▼ Charles Eames, 1951 photograph of the patio of the Eames house, Pacific Palisades, California, designed 1948-49, showing an *LAR Chair* and tables with similar wire bases.

Harry **Bertoia**

5. **Armchair: Model no. 421-1,** *Diamond*
Designed 1950-52
Vinyl-coated steel, polyurethane foam,
cotton upholstery
77.5 x 85.7 x 69.7 cm
Produced by Knoll Associates, Inc.
(New York, NY, USA), c. 1953 to the present
D85.154.1

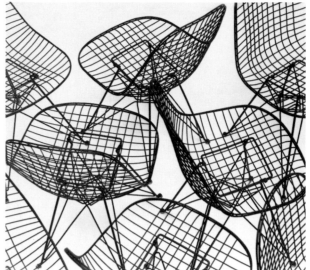

fig. 23 ▲ Herbert Matter, c. 1952-54 photograph of Harry Bertoia with examples of his metal sculptures.

fig. 24 ▲ Charles Eames, 1952 photograph of his wire chairs.

Among art collectors, Bertoia is known for his airy, geometricizing, abstract sculpture of the late 1940s and 1950s (fig. 23), which turned the all-over markings of certain Abstract Expressionist paintings into welded metal. But he may be more widely appreciated for the design of this chair, a stylish parallel and contrast to Charles and Ray Eames' wire-shell side chair of 1951-53 (fig. 24). The wit of Bertoia's seating comes from its transformation of a gridded plane into a large, three-dimensional diamond form containing smaller, curving diamonds of wire. The vinyl-coated metal is resilient; the upholstery in this model adds comfort, though at the expense of the transparency notable in other versions to which Bertoia gave only a seat cushion.

The artist saw both his sculpture and furniture as "concerned primarily with space, form, and the characteristics of metal. . . . [This and his other wire-mesh chairs] are mostly made of air, much like sculpture. Space passes right through them."[12] He designed the line for Florence Knoll, his former student at Cranbrook Academy, and her husband, Hans, principals of Knoll Associates, who in 1950 gave him a salary and studio, without obligation, near their furniture factory in Pennsylvania. Bertoia created reliefs and freestanding sculpture, and also this design in lounge and side chair models, which Knoll technicians helped him make ready for production in 1953. In 1951, however, the Eameses had presented their first wire chairs, manufactured by the Herman Miller Furniture Company. While the Eameses played the upright grid of the seat and back against the curved rim of their shell, Bertoia turned the mesh on the bias and molded it in three directions. As the result of a lawsuit between Knoll and Herman Miller, the Eameses won the copyright, even though Bertoia had probably influenced their design: he had worked in their office in 1943-46 and, as a metal sculptor, he doubtless showed them his concurrent art in wire and welding.

Isamu **Noguchi**

6. **Dining table: Model no. 311**

Designed c. 1953, redesigned c. 1957
Formica, veneered beaverboard, enameled iron,
chrome-plated steel
73.5 x 119.5 x 119.5 cm
Produced by Knoll Associates, Inc. (New York, NY,
USA), c. 1957-74
D81.102.1

Noguchi's wire-base dining table originated in a
plastic rocking stool that the artist had designed in
1951 following a trip to Japan. By 1953 the manufacturer Hans Knoll was preparing Bertoia's wire
chairs (cat. 5) for the market, and he suggested that
Noguchi design the stool "in some sort of wire, à la
Bertoia." Probably as a further complement, "they asked
me to adapt the stool to a table," Noguchi recalled.[13]

This origin seems to account for the relative
anomaly of Noguchi's chaste table in both his
furniture designs and his more celebrated sculpture:
he rarely used wire in his furniture and never in his
sensuous stone carvings of the period (although
Henry Moore, Barbara Hepworth, and other
contemporaries had set wire and strings in linear
counterpoint to the abstract, organic shapes of
their sculpture). Still, the minimalism of Noguchi's
table accords with progressive tendencies in art
and design of the 1950s, as does the contrast
between its cagelike, tapering pedestal of gleaming
rods and its enameled cast-iron foot and Formica-
covered tabletop. Such a visual separation of
functionally separate and materially different parts,
also seen in the Eameses' *LAR Chair* (cat. 4),
reflects the rationalism of much postwar design.

Isamu **Noguchi**

7. **Coffee table: Model no. IN-20**
Designed 1944
Lacquered laminated birch, aluminum
39.7 x 127 x 91 cm
Produced by Herman Miller Furniture Co.
(Zeeland, MI, USA), 1949-51
D81.117.1

fig. 25 ▼ Noguchi, Coffee table IN-50, c. 1947.

The vital form language of biomorphism survived through the war, as is witnessed by this coffee table (and a companion dining table, fig. 26), in which the sculptor Noguchi ignored the conventional composition of a table as a rectangle on four legs. Instead, he chose curvilinear shapes and set up an amusing contrast between the rounded triangle of the top and the elongated triangles of the three legs, which differ among themselves: one is a solid fin of wood, the other two are aluminum rods in hairpin forms. A hole in the top of the dining table allows the insertion of a flower holder. Such an engaging detail, and the play between open and closed shapes, and between hovering planes and looping lines, remind us that Noguchi knew the American sculptor Alexander Calder as early as 1927, when both were in Paris and beginning their artistic careers. The same year, Noguchi was Brancusi's assistant, and in his table he may also have distantly recalled Brancusi's works such as the *Fish*.

The table also relates to Noguchi's celebrated and much-reproduced glass-topped Coffee table IN-50, which he designed around 1947 (fig. 25). There too the legs have organic associations and differ from the top. These sculptural works contrast with Noguchi's wire-base table (cat. 6), and thereby demonstrate his ambidextrous skills: he could design in idioms derived from both biomorphism and Constructivism.

fig. 26 ▼ Herman Miller Furniture Company publicity photograph, c. 1949, showing a room setting with Noguchi's Dining table IN-20 and stools.

Isamu **Noguchi**

8. **Floor lamp:** *Akari*, **Model E**
Shade designed c. 1954; base 1962
Mulberry-bark paper, bamboo, iron, steel
191 x 57.7 x 57.7 cm
Shade produced by Ozeki & Co. (Gifu, Japan),
1962-c. 1966; base produced by K.K. Ohi Kojo
(Tokyo, Japan), 1962 to the present
D86.245.1

fig. 27 ▼ Noguchi, *Lunar* table lamp, c. 1945.
Montreal Museum of Decorative Arts.

Born in the United States of Japanese and American
parents, Noguchi visited Japan as a youth in 1930-
31, but when he returned there in 1950 it was
as a mature, recognized sculptor and progressive
designer. In Japan he was invited to the town of
Gifu with the hope he might revive the local lantern-
making tradition. Early on, Noguchi's interest in
light-emitting forms had led him to incorporate such
elements in sculptures he called *Lunars,* and around
1945, he designed a plastic and wood lamp for Knoll
which became one of the most popular table lamps
of midcentury (fig. 27). That design unites base
and shade in a glowing cylinder suspended on three
spindles: it evokes the ancient Japanese craft of
paper lanterns while its geometric simplicity satisfied
Western tastes of the 1950s.

In Gifu, Noguchi advanced beyond the simply
shaped and rigid table lamp to create flexible,
sculpturally shaped lamps which were easily
packaged in flat envelopes or thin boxes. His series
was based on the model of native *chochin* or
collapsible paper lanterns. He called it *Akari* with
a sense of the word's multiple meanings: "light as
illumination" and also "lightness as opposed to
weight." "The ideal of *akari*," he wrote, "is therein
exemplified with lightness (as essence) and light
(for awareness). The quality is poetic, ephemeral,
and tentative."[14]

Although Noguchi copyrighted many of his
lamp designs, they were widely copied and debased.
For the next twenty-five years, he invented continually
more complex and expensive forms both to escape
such piracies and to explore the sculptural potential
of the *Akaris.* Elegant in its double trumpet
silhouette, this model stands tall on a dark base
and has internal metal supports. Lighted, the shade
seems suspended in thin air, an example of a time-
honored Asian craft modernized for Western and
Asian audiences. Compared to the simple and popular
"bubble lamps" and other hanging light fixtures sold
in the 1950s and 1960s by Howard Miller, in which
wire cages were sprayed with a self-webbing vinyl
to make their skins, Noguchi's line has the delicacy
yet daring of a major artist's design.

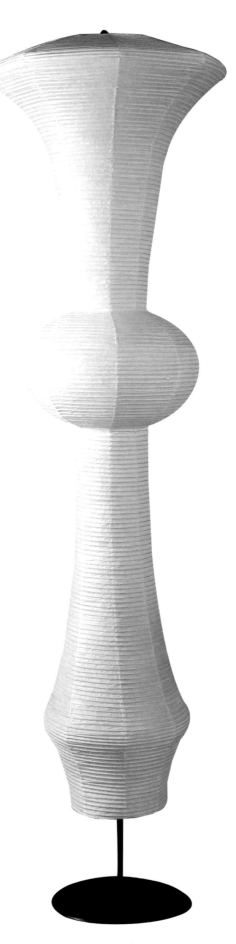

Arne **Jacobsen**

9. **Chair: Series 7, Model no. 3117**
Designed 1955
Beech-faced plywood, steel, rubber
83 x 52 x 47 cm
Produced by Fritz Hansens Eft. A/S
(Copenhagen and Allerød, Denmark),
1955 to the present
D91.329.1, gift of Norbert Schoenauer

As simple and sexy as a leotard, Jacobsen's hourglass-shaped plywood chair on a steel base is a high point of postwar design, both attractive and practical, still sold and commonly seen in public places. The concept is not entirely original: Aalto had designed all-plywood chairs as early as 1932 and the Eameses' plywood and metal chair with potato-chip-like back and seat was manufactured from 1946 onward. With each generation, the plywood was molded into more complex three-dimensional forms. Here, the back and the seat form a scooped-out receptacle for the sitter. This model was intended for office use: its height is adjustable and its swivel base on castors allows one to move it easily. Jacobsen's first version of this chair was even simpler: it was supported on four splayed metal legs, allowing the chair to be stacked. The Series 7 chairs won a Grand Prize at the 1957 Milan Triennale. They were initially manufactured with wood veneers, as seen here, and later also with painted and ebonized finishes as well as upholstered surfaces.

The modest cost, lightness of both appearance and weight, and the minimalist curvilinear elegance of these bentwood furnishings are hallmarks of midcentury Scandinavian design and were largely responsible for its quick international acceptance. It helped too that chair seats such as Jacobsen's resembled the biomorphic shapes by Jean Arp, Joan Miró, Alexander Calder, and other vanguard artists who were internationally accepted among cognoscenti by the 1950s. This upper-middle-class group of urbanites has been credited with assuring the positive reception of Good Design at midcentury, notably in Scandinavia and the United States.

Arne **Jacobsen**

10. **Armchair: Model no. 3316,** *Egg*

Designed 1957
Chromed steel, fiberglass, polyurethane foam, leather
106.2 x 87 x 78.7 cm
Produced by Fritz Hansens Eft. A/S
(Copenhagen and Allerød, Denmark),
1958 to the present
D87.131.1

fig. 28 ▲ Jacobsen, reception area of the SAS Royal Hotel
and Air Terminal, Copenhagen, 1956-60, showing *Egg* chairs.

The 1956-60 SAS (Scandinavian Airlines System)
Royal Hotel and Air Terminal in Copenhagen is
Jacobsen's best-known building and virtually a
museum of the architect's designs (fig. 28). For this
impressive structure, he produced all the fixtures and
furnishings, among them this womblike, welcoming
armchair called *Egg*, and a related model called
Swan. As curvilinear as his earlier Series 7 swivel
chair (cat. 9) and *Ant* models but now fitted with
lushly upholstered fiberglass shells, both the *Egg*
and the *Swan* chairs illustrate the luxury and comfort
he wished to suggest in the SAS building, one
intended to be identified with ultra-modern, upscale
travel. The *Egg* armchair turns a traditional wing chair
into the continuous shape of a big tilted cup. Like
the *Swan*, it required meticulous handcraftsmanship
for its leather upholstery. Neither armchair is wholly
original in form: both derive from Saarinen's late-1940s
experiments with plastic shells molded in three
dimensions and from his *Pedestal* chair of c. 1955
(cat. 22). Nevertheless, Jacobsen's designs (like
Saarinen's *Pedestal* line) are still in production—a
credit to their sculptural silhouettes, comfort, and
high quality of industrial and hand fabrication.

Poul **Henningsen**

11. **Hanging lamp: Model no. PH 5**
Designed 1956
Enameled aluminum
25 x 53 x 53 cm
Produced by Louis Poulsen & Co. A/S
(Copenhagen, Denmark), 1958 to the present
D99.146.1, gift of Lynne Verchere

The design principle of this and most of Henningsen's lamps is simple: nested bowl shapes of different diameters and depths shade a central light source. The results, however, are visually complex as well as functional. The circular shades are adroitly positioned to distribute the light evenly: no matter how the lamps are installed or what power of incandescent bulb is used, that bulb is masked, eliminating all glare. The shades are suspended with separations between them, which ventilate the bulb and also dramatize the shapes of the lamps' individual parts when the light is turned on. Here, furthermore, the topmost shade is directed upward to create ambient illumination.

Some of Henningsen's lamps have acquired names with allusions to nature, such as *Snowball* and *Artichoke*, but his conceptions originated with geometry. Such artistic preoccupations can be found as early as 1924, when his entries won the competition for illuminating the Danish pavilion at the Paris *Exposition internationale des arts décoratifs et industriels modernes* of 1925. This competition marked the beginning of his affiliation with the Louis Poulsen company, a firm that went on to dominate postwar lamp manufacture in Denmark. The PH 5 lamp made its debut at the Danish Museum of Decorative Art in Copenhagen in 1958, and the *Artichoke* was shown at the 1960 Triennale in Milan (fig. 29). Both designs were acknowledged as successes. The Poulsen company is also known for producing the creations of other progressive Scandinavian architects and designers, including Alvar Aalto, Arne Jacobsen, and Verner Panton.

fig. 29 ▲ Henningsen, installation of the Danish section, Milan Triennale, 1960, showing his *Artichoke* lamp.

Hans **Wegner**

12. **Armchair: Model no. JH 501, *Round***

Designed 1949
Teak, alum caning
75.5 x 63 x 52.7 cm
Produced by Johannes Hansen (Copenhagen,
Denmark), 1949 to the present
D85.156.1

Consumers quickly embraced Wegner's furniture
when it was first presented. The Museum of Modern
Art included his work in the influential exhibition
of 1948, *International Competition for Low-cost
Furniture Design,* although Wegner's furniture was
not cheap. And Americans also saw it in the widely
publicized exhibition *Design in Scandinavia,* which
traveled to twenty-two cities in 1954-57. A
combination of handcraftsmanship and industrial
production distinguishes the best-known seating
by this Danish architect and designer. The *Round*

chair, which the American magazine *Interiors* called
the most beautiful chair in the world in 1950, boasts
a crest rail that is not laminated or bent but carved
of three pieces of teak which are ingeniously joined.
Sensitive carving is essential for the gently curving
lines of the flaring back and armrests, and for the
fluid transition from rail to front stiles. In addition,
the cane seat is handwoven.

In the Modernist tradition, the beauty of all
Wegner's chairs derives not from any applied
ornament but from their forms, the display of their
method of construction, and the nature of their
materials: easy-care, moisture-resistant, beautifully
grained teak, and caning in appealing patterns.
In accord with the Scandinavian inflection of
Modernism, however, Wegner's forms relate not
to machined geometries (even though they required
machine production), but to time-honored, efficient
chair types, which he began exploring around 1943.
He turned to vernacular sources such as Shaker
and Windsor chairs, as well as Chinese furniture,

and those influences can be felt even in this chair.
The U-shaped crest rail, for example, is a form
ultimately derived from such sources but transformed
into a highly personal idiom. Similarly, Jens
Quistgaard's teak ice bucket for Dansk International
Designs (fig. 30) evokes Japanese vessels in the
handle that bridges its all-in-one construction, as well
as the staved hulls of Viking ships, yet Quistgaard's
final design is distinctly personal and modern.

In the 1950s, objects such as Wegner's and
Quistgaard's blended well with more traditional
furnishings, allowing owners to support progressive
design without totally renovating their homes.
In interiors incorporating Scandinavian Modern,
new and old designs could harmonize, since both
favored natural materials. Handsome woods,
with their reassuring familiarity, deep pile rugs,
and exposed brick walls appealed to the tactile
as well as visual senses of consumers who found
a modernism of plastic and chrome-plated steel
too severe.

fig. 30 ▲ Jens Quistgaard,
ice bucket, pre-1958. Montreal
Museum of Decorative Arts.

Sori **Yanagi**

13. **Stool: *Butterfly***

Designed 1954
Rosewood-faced plywood, brass
39.2 x 41.7 x 30.5 cm
Produced by Tendo Co., Ltd. (Tendo, Japan),
1954 to the present
D87.173.1, gift of Gallery 91

Two identical, inverted L-shapes of molded laminate
set opposite one another and bolted together in
two places are the sole elements of this small and
graceful stool, appropriately named *Butterfly* by its
Japanese designer. Yanagi's minimalist, organic
conception is balanced by a sensuous execution in
shallow curves of rosewood. "In industry the straight
line is used most frequently, but it gives a hard
impression," Yanagi said later about another of his
designs. "I try to avoid that as much as possible
and use molds that eliminate sharp corners from
the forms."[15] In this stool, he married modernity
and tradition, using the industrial process of molding
plywood to create a calligraphic shape evocative
of Japanese pictographs.

    Butterfly, Yanagi's best-known design, reflects
postwar efforts in Japan to reconcile Western
influence and native heritage. The stool recalls
the headrest of time-honored use in Japan, but also
the pared-down aesthetic and revelation of materials
in American and Scandinavian Good Design in
the 1950s. The stool is an attempt to transcend
the segregation practiced in Japanese prewar homes
between native and Occidental furnishings. In the
West, it was praised from the 1950s onward, and
won a gold medal at the Milan Triennale in 1957.
But since stools are not often used for seating, the
little *Butterfly*—only some fifteen inches high—was
probably admired less for its utility than for its
transcultural allusions, and for its rich graining and
pleasing abstraction of form. While rarely seen in
photographs of interiors of the 1950s, it achieved
a cultlike status by the end of the century (fig. 31).

    Yanagi's interest in bridging Eastern and Western
design traditions had been sharpened in 1942,
when he served as an assistant to Charlotte Perriand
during the brief period she was in Japan advising
the country on product design. Tendo, the manufacturer
of *Butterfly,* was established in 1940 as a cooperative
of carpenters and cabinetmakers, and it specialized
in molding plywood. With conceptions such as
Yanagi's, it pioneered in the mass-production of work
by independent designers and gave international
standing to Japanese postwar furniture-making.

fig. 31 ▲ Living area in the residence of Steven Roden,
Los Angeles, California, showing two Yanagi *Butterfly* stools
at the fireplace, c. 1998.

fig. 32 ▲ Juhl, didactic display for the *Chieftain* chair, furniture exhibition of the Copenhagen Cabinetmakers' Guild, 1949.

Finn **Juhl**

14. **Armchair: Model no. P4-107,** *Chieftain*

Designed 1949
Teak, polyurethane foam, leather upholstery
92.8 x 100.6 x 88.2 cm
Produced by Niels Vodder (Allerød, Denmark),
1949-80
D85.122.1

Among leggy Scandinavian furniture, Juhl's *Chieftain* looms rather anomalously—a broad, low, sculpturally articulated throne. Many postwar chairs emphasize a cagelike structure and often eliminate upholstery, but this design holds verticals and horizontals in muscular equipoise. The seemingly suspended, leather-covered back, seat, and armrests are visually separate from the skeleton beneath, and the chair even promises comfort. To indicate his artistic ambitions, Juhl displayed the chair with some of its inspirations in a 1949 exhibition (fig. 32), creating a photographic montage worthy of André Malraux's concept of the "Museum without Walls." The reproductions that Juhl chose, of tribal art, Cycladic carvings, and other non-Western artifacts, typify the art world's fascination with the forceful beauty of the "primitive," renewed after the war, and they underline the archaic associations of *Chieftain*, which offers shield, blade, and spearlike forms—motifs worthy of a chief. Juhl coined the name when the chair was shown at an exhibition in Copenhagen opened by King Frederick of Denmark.

Here and in all his designs, including his carved bowls, Juhl avoids right angles, relying on emphatic curves for dramatic effect. Yet he also rewards a close look by playing large planes against small details. Notice the crook, for example, above the juncture of the back support and rear stile in *Chieftain*. Best seen from the side, the chair reflects the artisanal tradition espoused by Juhl and contemporary Scandinavians. Recalling their success, Hans Wegner explained in 1983: "Technically there was nothing new in our work, and there was certainly no money to carry out major technical achievements. The philosophy behind it was . . . to show what we could do with our hands: to try to make the material come alive, to give it a sense of spirit, to make our works look so natural that one could conceive of them in that form only and in no other."[16] This Modernist ethos characterizes much Danish design of the period, but it also allowed individual creativity, as witnessed by the expressive differences between Juhl's and Wegner's furniture.

Piero **Fornasetti** and Gio **Ponti**

15. **Secretary: *Trumeau Architecture***

Designed 1950
Lithographed paper on Masonite, painted wood,
sheet metal, glass, brass, felt, neon light
218 x 80 x 40.5 cm
Produced by Piero Fornasetti (Milan, Italy),
1951–70, c. 1980; by Immaginazione s.r.l. (Milan,
Italy), 1989 to the present
D97.172.l, gift of Senator Alan A. Macnaughton, Sr.

That progressive taste in postwar Italy was not monolithic is demonstrated by this extravagantly decorated secretary. The case was designed by Gio Ponti and originally had a concave pediment and peglike legs (fig. 33). Later, it was decided to omit the pediment, and a block-footed base was added, as seen here. But far more important than the form of this piece is its embellishment by Piero Fornasetti. He adapted seventeenth- and eighteenth-century architectural prints to cover every surface. Fornasetti, although a dropout from Milan's Brera Academy of Art, rendered its classical courtyard on the drop front, the staircases of Genoa's university (formerly a palace designed by Galeazzo Alessi) on the drawers, a Bramantesque palazzo in Milan on the top doors,[17] and rusticated stonework on the sides. Behind the doors, the inside presents a palace interior (suitably enough) whose deep perspective is clearly visible through the glass shelving.

Here, as in all his designs, Fornasetti's artistry blends northern Italian traditions—Renaissance trompe-l'oeil decoration, seventeenth-century architectural drawing, eighteenth-century stage scenery and view painting—with the Surrealist wit of dislocation. In this secretary he created parallels between architecture and cabinetwork: both have tiered facades expressing their various purposes; both have doors opening upon interior spaces;

and architectural marquetry appears on eighteenth-century furniture. But more amusing are the contradictions Fornasetti presented between decoration and object: between the ornate Grand Manner of Italy's hallowed past and the plain surfaces and basic shapes of the 1950s. Like the Surrealist painters Max Ernst and René Magritte, Fornasetti scavenged old and popular graphic sources to make illusionistic but illogical artworks, and, like Giorgio de Chirico, he may be mocking Italy's cultural pretensions with his imagery of empty palaces of learning placed, significantly enough, on a writing desk.

A contemporary photograph (fig. 34) indicates how Fornasetti conceived positioning his furniture: in an interior in which every surface and object is covered with his trompe-l'oeil designs. Indeed, over his career he decorated thousands of objects, from plates, umbrella stands, and bicycles, to fabrics and screens. The *Trumeau* secretary is not an example of art furniture conceived in isolation, but an object meant to be used and enjoyed in a sophisticated residence, a stage setting itself for objects as theater.

In the 1970s, Fornasetti's eccentric creations fell somewhat from fashion, but in the joyously eclectic and historicizing spirit of 1980s Post-Modernism, his critical fortunes rose again, especially with the support of Ettore Sottsass and the Memphis design group.[18]

fig. 33 ◄ Fornasetti and Ponti, *Trumeau Architecture* secretary as first produced, c. 1951.
fig. 34 ▼ Fornasetti and Ponti, living area in the Lucano apartment, Milan, 1950.

Antonia **Campi**

16. **Table lamp:** *Conchiglia*
Designed 1954
Glazed earthenware
28.5 x 23 x 13 cm
Produced by Società Ceramica Italiana
(Laveno, Italy), 1955–c. 1965
D97.160.1

Conchiglia, Campi's name for this small table lamp, means *Seashell* in Italian, but it seems a prosaic term for the extraordinary, windblown shape of this small table lamp, resembling an aquatic plant imagined by Salvador Dalí. *Conchiglia* results from both the technical freedom possible in ceramics and the survival in postwar Italian design of eccentric currents originating in art of the 1930s. A thin sheet of clay was hand-curved to fit around the bulb housing and then glazed and fired; the shell-like, asymmetrical form serves as both the base and shade of the lamp. Campi's uninhibited design and her highly decorated tablewares of a similar organicism reveal that Italy was not dominated by Rationalism in the 1950s. The aesthetic vitality of the country's small, craft-based factories fostered individual expression, as was seen in the 1950 exhibition *Italy at Work*, organized by American museum curators and circulated with Italian government support. Campi's ceramics were represented in that show, and she also designed a large Picassoid ceramic bas-relief for the ninth Milan Triennale in 1951.

Trained in sculpture at the Brera Academy, Campi had joined the influential Società Ceramica Italiana in 1948, and was encouraged to give artistic expression to the factory's small fancy articles. She traded sculptural ideas with such Scandinavian glass and ceramic designers as Gunnar Nylund, Stig Lindberg, and Nils Landberg, and at the same time derived forms from Rococo and Surrealist paintings and Henry Moore's sculpture. By the end of the decade, however, it was evident that her ceramics, with their asymmetries, looping shapes, and ornament painted in bright colors, were inspiring coarse commercial imitations, and so in 1958 she turned from small ceramics to designing metal utensils and bathroom porcelains. The daring form of this lamp celebrates Campi's—and Italy's—defiance of a single definition of good taste.

Massimo **Vignelli**

17. **Hanging lamps: Model no. 4035L**

Designed 1954
Glass
Each lamp: 50 x 18.4 x 18.4 cm
Produced by Venini (Murano, Italy),
c. 1957–c. 1970, c. 1986
D85.151.1-3

These jewel-hued hanging lamps derive from the vividly striped glassware called *fasce* that Venini, one of Murano's time-honored glasshouses, introduced in 1950. Around 1954, the manufactory's director, Paolo Venini, was asked to fabricate a number of hanging shades designed by Studio Architetti BBPR for the Olivetti store in New York City. They employed Venini's *fasce* technique, and the result pleased him so much that he initiated his own line of lighting fixtures. Massimo Vignelli, then an architecture student at the University of Venice, was hired to work with Venini's concept of radiant color and his craft methodology: the shapes were blown in molds, allowing control over the form, but the stripes of color could vary in hue, width, and slant, allowing a degree of invention to the glass blower.

Such a combination of control and creativity was one key to the success of this and other artisanal work produced in Italy's manufacturing firms after World War II. As seen in these three examples, the conical forms are uniform in their silhouette and thus the shades can be grouped attractively. Each shade is opaque, diffusing the light, and predominantly a single color—royal blue, yellow, or aqua—while the variations in the contrasting stripes—swirling in rings of red, blue, and aqua—produce a customized look of painterly vivacity. In their energy and formal simplicity, they foretell aspects of Vignelli's later style as a graphic designer.

fig. 35 ▲ Costantino Corsini and Giuliana Grossi, living room in an apartment, Milan, showing Vignelli's hanging lamps, c. 1957.

Gio **Ponti**

18. **Chair: Model no. 699,** *Superleggera*

Designed 1955
Ash, rush
83.5 x 40.5 x 44 cm
Produced by Figli di Amedeo for Cassina S.p.A.
(Meda Milano, Italy), 1957 to the present
D83.115.1

Ponti's side chair is so light (*Superleggera* means *Superlight*) that the owner can lift it with one finger (fig. 36). Even before the war, progressives of every persuasion idealized lightness—furnishings that not only looked but were lightweight, requiring less material than traditional pieces, easier for the manufacturer to ship and for the user to move. And given postwar shortages—of gas for shipping and space for furniture—and the increased mobility of young, growing families, the aesthetic of lightness made a virtue of necessity.

Ponti's design also updates a nineteenth-century Italian peasant tradition, the simple rush-seated wood chairs made in the Ligurian countryside around Chiavari. Using vernacular as well as classical sources to create designs both modern and appealingly traditional had been one of Ponti's strategies since the 1920s. From 1928 onward, the architect, designer, and writer was editor of *Domus,* a prestigious magazine that championed Rationalist design and enjoyed renewed international influence after World War II. Here and in his buildings and furnishings, Ponti espoused Rationalism with a patriotic slant: like contemporary Scandinavian designers, he and other Italians distinguished themselves from politically discredited Germany by insisting on their humanistic interpretation of Bauhaus principles. Their sleek designs in wood—directed toward an enlightened urban middle class—became identified with liberal social ideals and progressive design.

fig. 36 ▲ Ponti studio, c.1958 publicity photograph showing Letizia Ponti lifting her father's *Superleggera* chair with one finger.

Achille and Pier Giacomo
Castiglioni

19. Stool: *Mezzadro*

Designed 1954-57
Chromed steel, painted sheet steel, beech
51.4 x 48.8 x 50.8 cm
Produced by Zanotta S.p.A. (Nova Milanese, Italy),
1970 to the present
D90.201.1

An example of the Castiglioni brothers' ability to turn mass-produced utilitarian objects into novel designs, this stool cantilevers a tractor seat on a springy strip-steel support and offers comfortable, no-maintenance seating. Indeed, their promotion of the piece attempted to show how flexibly the stool could be used for a variety of sitting positions (fig. 37). Importing a farm item (*mezzadro* means *tenant farmer*) into a dwelling might seem ironic: for some observers, the stool comments on the modern transformation from rural to urban economies, and recalls Dada provocations of the 1910s like the bicycle wheel that Marcel Duchamp designated an art work. But the Castiglionis' design is consistent with their Rationalist efforts to use industrial products and processes for a middle-class market, which was still faced with postwar privations and scarce materials in the mid-1950s. And though not original—Mies van der Rohe and Design Unit New York presented tractor-seat furniture earlier—*Mezzadro* reflects the brothers' witty humanization of Modernist principles. The thirteen-year gap between design and production suggests, however, that the brothers' wit was not immediately grasped.

fig. 37 ▲ Studio Castiglioni, c. 1957 publicity photographs showing the *Mezzadro* stool in use.

George **Nelson**

20. **Storage units:** *Comprehensive Storage System*

Designed 1959
Aluminum, walnut, steel
Pole: 246 x 3.5 x 3.5 cm
Produced by Herman Miller Furniture Co.
(Zeeland, MI, USA), 1959-73
D87.241.1, gift of Geraldine Ferend

Domestic storage space never seems to keep up with the demand, but this need, special to the modern age of mass production, was felt most keenly during the 1940s and 1950s. Housing construction had halted during the war years, but when it resumed, fueled by the baby boom, the largest number of homes erected were elemental, with no extras. For shelving and storage, the owner had to become a do-it-yourself carpenter or turn to a solution like Nelson's. Multi-purpose, modestly priced, and easy to assemble, his system was a quick success.

Nelson's *Comprehensive Storage System* involves interchangeable wooden cabinets—open, closed, with drawers, or with drop-down desk surfaces—hung between aluminum poles that are pressure-fitted with spring-loaded caps. The poles extend from floor to ceiling, leaving the wall behind untouched, while the shelves "float" on movable brackets cantilevered from the poles. The tension system assured the shelving was sturdy, even though the structural components were lightweight. The basic armature let buyers customize the storage for the proportions of their rooms and individual needs. Easily shipped and sold in knock-down form, Nelson's units could be speedily carried off when owners moved to new homes.

Nelson had begun exploring the issue of modern storage in 1944 with his *Storagewall*, a system of closets and shelving (fig. 38).[19] His solution of 1959 for Herman Miller, more daring in its engineering feats, reflects the period's taste for clean lines and suspended cubes, the ethos of Le Corbusier's often repeated definition in 1925 of the house as "a machine for living." Yet compared with the Eameses' Storage Units system (cat. 1) with its obviously factory-made skeleton and exposed tension wires, Nelson's system with its handsome wood surfaces is more suavely accommodated in the domestic interior (figs. 39-40).

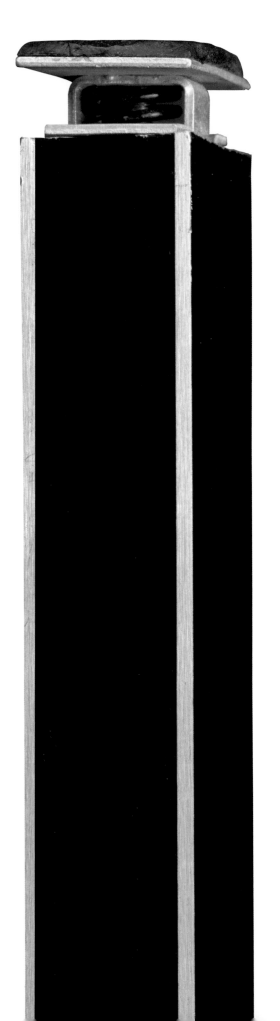

fig. 38 ▲ Herbert Gehr, c. 1944 photograph of Nelson's *Storagewall*.

fig. 39 ▲ Herman Miller Furniture Company, 1960 publicity photograph showing Nelson's *Comprehensive Storage System* and *Coconut* chair and ottoman.

fig. 40 ▲ Challen & Floyd, living room in unidentified residence, London, showing Nelson's *Comprehensive Storage System* and a Charles and Ray Eames lounge chair and ottoman.

fig. 41 ▲ Eames Office, drawing for a Herman Miller Furniture Company advertisement showing the elements of the Eameses' lounge chair and ottoman, c. 1958.

fig. 42 ▲ Richard J. Neutra, Casa Tuja, Ascona, Switzerland, c. 1961 photograph of living area showing the Eameses' lounge chair and ottoman.

Charles and Ray **Eames**

21. **Lounge chair: Model no. 670**
Ottoman: Model no. 671
Designed 1956
Rosewood-faced plywood, aluminum, rubber, polyurethane foam, leather upholstery
Chair: 84.6 x 86.5 x 82.1 cm
Ottoman: 66 x 43.6 x 55.1 cm
Produced by Herman Miller Furniture Co. (Zeeland, MI, USA), 1956 to the present
D81.127.1-2, gift of Dr. and Mrs. Robert L. Tannenbaum*

This lounge chair and matching ottoman, constructed with clearly separated plywood shells in graduated sizes, climax the Eameses' series of molded chairs. This seating can be assembled or demounted by one person with a screwdriver (fig. 41), a feat of design reflecting Charles and Ray Eames' longtime concern for the everyday owner. The lounge and ottoman are also highly responsive to the owner's needs: the seat and headrest can be tilted at will, and both the chair and stool swivel on their bases. This flexibility is announced by the seating's segmented forms: they define the different kinds of support offered, while the contrasts of materials—metal, wood, and tufted leather—distinguish support from comfort. Thus the Eameses' work is and *looks* rationalized, while it radiates an air of solid luxury through its expansive scale and opulent materials.

This is a far cry from the wooden splints that the Eameses designed during World War II—though the knowledge they gained then of the technology of three-dimensionally molded plywood bore fruit in the couple's postwar furnishings. The lounge chair was the Eameses' costliest design to date; it sold in the United States for $634 in 1957, whereas the *LAR Chair* (cat. 4) then cost only $38. The interest in such luxurious furniture mirrors something of American prosperity in the Eisenhower years.

Eero **Saarinen**

22. **Table: Model no. 175, *Pedestal***
Designed 1955
Aluminum with fused vinyl finish, fiberglass-reinforced polyester, Formica-covered plywood
75 x 242 x 132 cm
Produced by Knoll Associates, Inc.
(New York, NY, USA), 1956 to the present
D92.169.1, gift of Edgar Kaufmann, jr., by exchange*

Armchair: Model no. 150, *Pedestal*
Chair: Model no. 151, *Pedestal*
Designed 1955
Aluminum with fused vinyl finish, fiberglass-reinforced polyester, polyurethane foam,
nylon upholstery
Armchair: 82 x 67.5 x 60.2 cm
Chair: 82 x 50.5 x 56 cm
Produced by Knoll Associates, Inc.
(New York, NY, USA), 1956 to the present
D92.169.7, D92.169.2; gifts of Edgar Kaufmann, jr.,
by exchange*

Saarinen's graceful design for the *Pedestal* chair, as thrilling as a prima ballerina balanced on one point, ran ahead of the technology then available to realize it. He sought "to clear up the slum of legs" with a chair on a single support. It would be "all one thing . . . a structural total cast in one piece of one material. . . ."[20] But the fiberglass used for the shell of the chair did not meet mass-production standards for strength and durability in the base. The base thus had to be cast in aluminum, and the total was spray-painted white to conceal the juncture. Nevertheless, the wineglass-like design, also popularly known as the *Tulip*, quickly became an icon of the late 1950s.

Saarinen's *Pedestal* chairs and matching tables in various sizes, his last series of furniture designs, sum up the aesthetic he first presented, in collaboration with Charles Eames, in the molded plywood chair they submitted to the 1940 competition *Organic Design in Home Furnishings* held by The Museum of Modern Art. Even when advances in technology allowed plywood to be bent in three dimensions, the sandwich of various wood layers and glue required relatively lengthy molding under heat and pressure, and the plywood's edges revealed the layers used. Fiberglass, and the polymers that became available later, were not only stronger than plywood but solved these problems. They satisfied Saarinen's and other designers' desire for a single, moldable material. His *Pedestal* series foretells the spirit in which many designers would use plastics during the 1960s. It defies the revelation of relations between load and support present in traditional furniture and even most Bauhaus design.

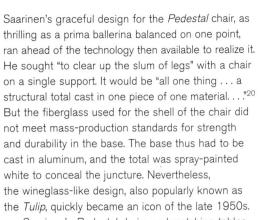

fig. 43 ◄ Herbert Matter, *Single Pedestal Furniture Designed by Eero Saarinen,* advertising flier for Knoll International, c. 1957. Montreal Museum of Decorative Arts.

Verner **Panton**

23. **Chair: Model no. K-2,** *Cone*
Designed 1958
Stainless steel, polyurethane foam, wool upholstery
80.7 x 57.2 x 60.4 cm
Produced by Plus-Linje A/S (Copenhagen,
Denmark), 1959-c. 1966
D88.187.1, gift of Mrs. Lilian Korman

This delightful and diminutive conical shape is
Panton's version of a pedestal chair: it stands less
than three feet high and is made of stainless steel
mesh on a steel cruciform base. The cone revolves
or can be locked into a fixed position. The round
seat cushion comes in colors and fabrics matching
or contrasting with the upholstery. In one model,
the mesh cone is not upholstered, allowing the
owner to choose transparency over comfort.

Like Arne Jacobsen, for whom he worked in
1950-52, Panton sought to design popular seating
with the smallest number of parts and simplest
production methods. Here, however, and in his more
famous molded plastic, cantilevered chair of 1960-
67 (cat. 36), Panton went beyond the organicism of
his mentor and created pieces that were fanciful yet
functional, with associations that linked them more
closely with vanguard art and contemporary Italian
designs than with Scandinavian Modern. In fact,
the simple geometric form of the *Cone* chair and
its brightly hued upholstery associate it with
contemporary hard-edged abstraction, especially the
work of Victor Vasarely, which Panton admired and
later imitated in fabric and carpet designs (fig. 44).
Whereas Jacobsen's *Egg* and *Swan* chairs evoke
Henry Moore's biomorphic sculptures with their
archetypal allusions, Panton's *Cone* is fun furniture,
prophetic of the light-hearted, youth-oriented spirit
of 1960s art and design. Panton's career flourished
in that decade, when he explained, "By experimenting
with lighting, colors, textiles, and furniture, and
utilizing the latest technologies, I try to show new
ways to encourage people to use their fantasy and
make their surroundings more exciting."[21]

fig. 44 ▲ Panton, exhibition in Zurich, 1961, showing the *Cone* chair among his other furniture and his *Geometry I* carpet and curtain designs.

fig. 45 ▲ Nelson, living room in the designer's country home, showing his prototype for the *Marshmallow* sofa, c. 1958.

George Nelson
Associates

24. **Sofa: Model no. 5670,** *Marshmallow*
Designed 1954-55
Painted steel, polyresin latex foam,
vinyl upholstery
87 x 133 x 85.9 cm
Produced by Herman Miller Furniture Co.
(Zeeland, MI, USA), 1956-c. 1965
D81.138.1, gift of George Nelson*

With a brash humor and bold graphic sense that anticipate American Pop art, this sofa is made out of eighteen bar-stool cushions attached to a grid of painted steel. The cushions' resemblance to marshmallows and their commercial source forecast the American Pop artists' embrace of popular tastes (especially in foodstuffs) and love of mass-produced objects in the early 1960s, and they parallel the same interests in London's Independent Group in the early 1950s. Despite the sofa's artistic associations, however, it is still a 1950s object in its lightness, low silhouette, and slablike composition, an aesthetic Nelson presented more severely in his table lounge unit (cat. 2). His preference for unornamented geometric shapes and spindly supports was shared at the time by many progressive designers.

This sofa is the prototype developed for Herman Miller, and was designed by Irving Harper, an associate of Nelson's. Unlike the white painted frame here, in production the steel was either painted black or given a satin chrome finish. Also, it was manufactured in different lengths (in some examples, with up to ten cushions in a row) and the cushions could be covered in vinyl or cloth. Such choices were made possible through the additive fabrication of the piece: the standard mass-produced seats were set on rods attached individually to the metal skeleton. Herman Miller could thus offer buyers ways of customizing their purchase.

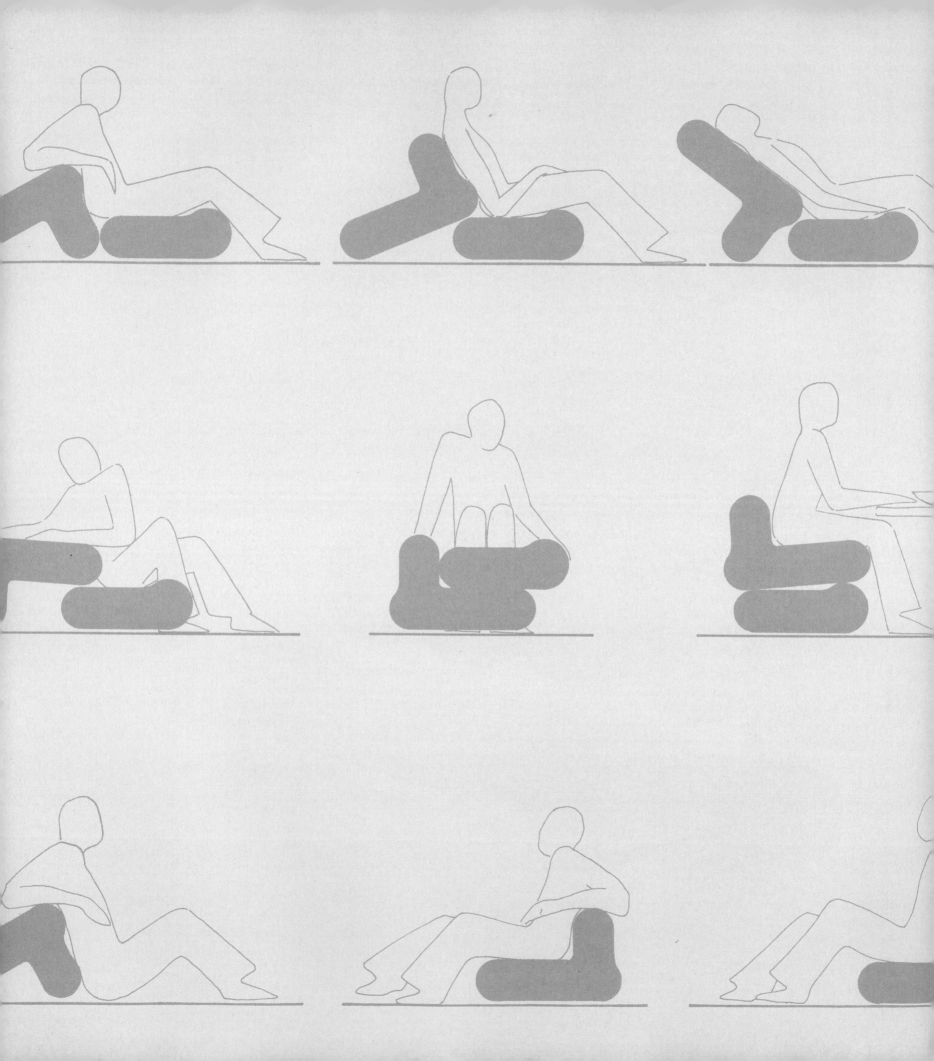

The 1960s
Design Revolutions

THE COLD WAR CONTINUED IN THE 1960S AND THE ISOLATION OF EAST FROM WEST WAS REINFORCED BY the construction of the Berlin Wall in 1961, the year that the United States broke diplomatic relations with Cuba over the control of nuclear missiles in their hemisphere. Nonetheless, John F. Kennedy's election as president a year before had set the tone for the United States in the new decade: youth, energy, and glamour replaced the sobriety and conservativism of the Eisenhower 1950s. The country could afford change. The Gross National Product had risen 250 percent between 1945 and 1960, and consumer credit had exploded 800 percent in the ten years after the end of World War II. Americans applauded Kennedy's 1961 launch of the space race to beat the U.S.S.R. to the moon, and hailed the promises of President Lyndon Johnson's "Great Society" to extend opportunities in education, employment, and housing to African-Americans and the poor. Spirits lifted—both with the standard of living and NASA's successful rockets.

The United States was not alone in reveling in prosperity. Italy, which would dominate design in the 1960s, traced the beginning of its economic miracle to 1958, when it joined the newly formed European Common Market. The United Kingdom, with the Conservatives in power, had finally overcome postwar shortages and, like France, Germany, and Japan, it began to harvest the fruits of investments in reconstruction made in the 1950s, as new and revitalized older industries produced for domestic and export markets. Everywhere in the West, consumers seemed to rule, with mass communications and market research helping manufacturers take their pulse—and raise it.

"Gropius wrote a book on grain silos, Le Corbusier one on aeroplanes, and Charlotte Perriand brought a new object to the office every morning; but today we collect ads," the English architect-theorists Alison and Peter Smithson asserted in 1956.[22] In such observations as well as in collages, paintings, and mixed-media exhibitions, vanguard Britons forecast Pop art, the American-centered movement that most influenced design in the 1960s.[23] Such artists as Andy Warhol, James Rosenquist, Roy Lichtenstein, and Claes Oldenburg embraced mass-marketed products, from Coca-Cola and Campbell's soups—the fast foods of a plentiful and pleasure-seeking society—and also the languages of advertising and packaging used to sell them. Pop art's blatant graphics, high-voltage colors, oversized forms, synthetic materials, and simplified but instantly recognizable images were translated into design, fashion, and even architecture and city-planning schemes. When Pop artists represented the United States at the 1964 Venice Biennale and Robert Rauschenberg won the grand prize, European designers of the same generation were quick to seize this alternative to the aesthetics of Good Design surviving from the 1950s.

In 1960s design, curvilinear patterns, sensuous organic metaphors, and anthropomorphic references supplanted the steel-skeleton skyscraper as a model. Some 1960s furnishings were humorous and openly imitative—not of high art by de Stijl or Surrealist painters as in the 1950s, but of real-life objects, from space-age inventions and children's toys, to food cartons and natural objects.[24] "I am for an art that is political-erotical-mystical, that does something other than sit on its ass in a museum," proclaimed Claes Oldenburg in 1967.[25] Artists designed one-of-a-kind or limited-edition furniture, with a delight in mixing media and crossing art and cultural categories typical of Pop. And handicrafts flourished, as fields such as weaving, ceramics, and glass-blowing allowed young artists to explore individual creativity—a value opposed to what they saw as the conformity of their parents' lives, circumscribed by offices and suburbia.

While designers of the 1950s sought to create definitive objects that would solve problems defined as timeless and universal, their 1960s counterparts denied such design goals and ignored functionalist problem-solving almost entirely. Consumption mattered more than production; and markets were viewed not as monolithic but as multifaceted and fluid, divided more by age than class. Baby boomers emerged as consumers in the 1960s; they were upwardly mobile and liberal in their mores and politics, and they stimulated manufacturers to create high-volume, moderately priced items in a plurality of styles. Practicality and durability mattered less than eye-appeal. Form followed fun.

Plastic, in its protean nature, accommodated this pluralism. It was the teak of the 1960s, thanks primarily to the creative alliances between Italian designers and manufacturers such as Kartell and Artemide. These alliances, which had been initiated in the previous decade, helped restore plastic to its prewar identification with avant-garde style and futuristic technology. In the 1960s, Italian designers set milestones in molded plastic furniture that were both best-selling objects and engineering feats: for example, the first all-fiberglass armchair—Joe Colombo's *Elda* (cat. 30); the first all-plastic, single-mold chair—Marco Zanuso and Richard Sapper's children's chair (fig. 64). In 1967, Colombo teamed with Gae Aulenti to create an exhibition of design at Gimbel's department store in New York spotlighting Italian plastics (fig. 46). Their furniture was installed on the left and right, respectively, of a long gallery, allowing viewers to compare their different uses of sleek surfaces and bold colors. Italian preeminence in plastic manufacture was obvious at the 1968 Milan Triennale, where Colombo's lounge area offered padded plastic seats complete with earphones, plastic ashtrays, and plastic glass-holders (fig. 47).

A petroleum derivative, plastic was cheap in those days of oil glut, but the high cost of making molds required mass sales to recoup the investment. This encouraged design for instant

fig. 46 ► Joe Colombo, 1968 photograph of his and Gae Aulenti's installation of their exhibition at Gimbel's, New York.

fig. 47 ► Joe Colombo, photograph of his lounge area at the exhibition *Italian Expression and Production*, Milan Triennale, 1968.

attraction, wide consumption, and rapid obsolescence. The different kinds of available plastics (PVC, ABS, vinyl, acrylic, polyurethane foam, etc.) themselves supported this direction: they could be molded in a vast range of forms, with different degrees of thickness and hardness, opacity and transparency, and intrinsic color, applied patterns, or decoration added later. The Rationalist dictum of "truth to materials" did not apply. Rather, plastics in their very lack of limitations could easily serve symbolic socio-cultural needs as well as practical functions. The new shapes they so promiscuously assumed—comic, startling, futuristic—and their bright hues identified their owners as young and mod.

In the mid-1960s, progressive design in all forms was global, youthful, and cheerful. The groovy chick might sport a geometric Sassoon haircut, a Pucci-style top, a Mary Quant miniskirt, and knockoffs of Courrèges vinyl boots, while the hip guy might flaunt a Carnaby-Street ruffled shirt and bell-bottom pants (fig. 48). They would drive a Volkswagen Beetle with psychedelic decals, dig the Beatles on their Sony portable tapedeck, and flip for Sean Connery (as James Bond) and Ursula Andress in *Dr. No*. Their pad might have inflatable or disposable furniture, modular and much of it in plastic; big Marimekko patterned pillows; and a reflective, Mylar-covered wall, like those in Andy Warhol's Factory or the Italian Pavilion at the 1964 Milan Triennale. As at that Triennale, the rock music might be deafening.

This youth culture and the fracturing of markets and tastes in the 1960s created news that was swiftly and delightedly covered in the burgeoning mass media, particularly television, and then dissected in academe. The architect-partners Robert Venturi and Denise Scott Brown taught at the University of Pennsylvania in the 1960s and wrote with seminal effect about such phenomena and the wider culture. Their *Complexity and Contradiction in Architecture* (1966) and *Learning from Las Vegas* (1972) proved to offer effective answers to the doctrines of traditional Modernism. In celebrating the diverse communication systems of mass culture such as advertising, and the logic and charm of vernacular building, they pointed out democratic alternatives for design to follow. Venturi and Scott Brown blessed variety in aesthetics created by local needs and tastes. To Mies van der Rohe's often-repeated prescription "less is more," they replied, "less is a bore."[26]

Venturi and Mies represented the poles of advanced design at large in the 1960s, which can be seen as a decade of oppositions as well as revolutions. Although it is easy to concentrate on the shock of the new, it should be remembered that the values of Bauhaus Modernism continued and perhaps even dominated. Mies' last project, the National Gallery in Berlin, opened its glass doors in 1968, the year before his death. The world-famous director of the Bauhaus had lived to see his style of building—the classically proportioned, exquisitely detailed steel box with glazed curtain walls—appropriated by the corporate world, and similar skyscrapers reflected each other in business districts from New York and Toronto to Paris and London, from Sydney to Hong Kong.

Inside these glass monoliths, power offices were designed and furnished by Knoll Associates. In 1969, the firm was renamed Knoll International, reflecting its increased penetration of global markets. Knoll stood for unified interiors based on Modernist precepts, and its furnishings combined prewar designs by Mies, Marcel Breuer, and others with new lines by Eero Saarinen and Harry Bertoia, among American designers. In the 1960s, Knoll specialized in creating corporate identities, notably through the graphic design of Massimo Vignelli. A second American firm, the Herman Miller Furniture Company, also expanded its international prominence in the 1960s. While it commissioned new designs by Scandinavians such as Verner Panton and Poul Kjaerholm, it sold designs of the 1950s and 1960s by Charles and Ray Eames, George Nelson, and Isamu Noguchi outside the United States, helping to make the market for progressive design global and the company more international in scope.

In the 1960s, the Swiss-based firm Vitra began to produce Verner Panton's one-piece, molded-plastic chair, and under license from Herman Miller it manufactured designs by the Eameses and George Nelson. Together, Knoll, Herman Miller, and Vitra shared a philosophy and integrity distinct from the average furniture manufacturer. These firms upheld a set of design values that permeated their product lines and led to new contemporary work.

In Japan, consumer product development continued in the 1960s. Although not a leading contender in the market of furniture and lighting, Japan produced original designs that allied native craft traditions with Modernist aesthetics. Between 1955 and 1966, government-subsidized designers and architects studied abroad, while corporate energies at home were focused on developing the powerful industries of electronics, household appliances, photography, and automobiles. With the transistor, an American invention, in attractively designed and priced Japanese radios or televisions, and high-powered lenses, based on German models, in user-friendly Japanese cameras and camcorders, Japanese firms gained world dominance and aggressively marketed their electronic goods. The wealth and international exposure they earned for Japan would spur native creativity in furniture design in later years.

These developments did not all proceed smoothly, however. By the second half of the 1960s, social fissures were widening. The Vietnam War had escalated, dividing generations from each other, aggravating differences between hawks and doves, spurring draft-card burnings, bombings of draft centers, and marches of millions on Washington, D.C., as well as demonstrations in cities and universities around the world. At the 1968 Democratic Convention in Chicago, policemen attacked war protesters, who warned, "The world is watching"—and they were right. The war had become a world concern. The same year, the pacifist black leader Dr. Martin Luther King, Jr., was assassinated, touching off race riots in cities across the United States. In Czechoslovakia, when Socialism was attempted in place of Communism, the "Prague Spring" of 1968 ended with the violent Soviet occupation of its satellite country. That same year in France, Charles de Gaulle's government nearly toppled during weeks of general strikes in Paris. Laborers and students seeking to overthrow France's capitalist government brought the country to a halt.

The socio-cultural fault lines dramatized by these events had already given rise to questioning by many designers about their potential role in altering the complacent, materialistic society that had emerged the decade before. Positive solutions to overcrowded, anonymous, and costly city dwelling were offered at the 1967 Montreal World Exposition (Expo 67), in which seventy countries responded to the design theme "Man and His World." Moshe Safdie's modular dwelling system called Habitat (figs. 49-50) was most discussed, for it was a landmark experiment in construction: capsulelike apartment units were mass-produced and then hoisted by crane into place. Constructed off-site, each rectangular housing unit was cast in concrete and contained built-in appliances and plastic bathroom and kitchen equipment. The units faced in different directions, allowing unobstructed views, and they varied from one- to four-bedroom apartments, each with a private roof garden and separate access. Though downscaled from a thousand to 354 apartments, owing to technical problems and cost increases, Habitat nonetheless showed one way that housing design could allow for individuality and privacy within a communal complex.

figs. 49-50 ▲ ▶ Moshe Safdie, interior and exterior views, Habitat Dwelling System, 1967 Montreal World Exposition.

Such goals were explored earlier in the decade by the British group Archigram, which envisioned a "Plug-In City" (1964) with a core of long-term services connected to add-on, temporary domestic and commercial units. This visionary group of six young architects (led by Peter Cook, with encouragement from the architectural historian Reyner Banham) emphasized systems of use over Modernist structure and style, thus opening fevered debate over the goals of city planning and design in general. The idea of multi-purpose components filling varied and changing needs would evolve by the end of the decade into environments conceived by Joe Colombo (fig. 61), Olivier Mourgue, and others, fleshed out with actual products, and exhibited by forward-looking manufacturers as models for international application.

Archigram's experimental and somewhat playful ideas were hardened into confrontational positions when they were appropriated by the radical groups formed in Florence in 1966, Archizoom and Superstudio. They and like-minded collaboratives such as UFO and Gruppo 65 described themselves as "Anti-Design"—meaning that they opposed the design of discrete objects of Modernist style because that represented complicity with a hated authoritarian production system. Instead, they adopted Pop art's populist idiom and purposely added kitsch styling to irritate purveyors of good taste. Demonstrating against the design establishment, members of these groups, including Andrea Branzi, occupied the Milan Triennale building in 1968, delaying the exposition opening for over a month and thus calling world attention to their alternative values (fig. 51). They challenged the entire structure of design in Italy (and by extension the West) from education to manufacture and distribution, and dramatized its latent paradoxes. The Triennale purported to display design solutions of broad application, yet its pavilions promoted national rivalries. Italian design was internationally recognized, yet the Anti-Design groups claimed that manufacturers were not always able to produce what was exhibited, so that the prototypes or limited-edition runs unavoidably became costly and elitist *objets d'art.* Designers were forced further and further from their intended markets, and the chasm between rich and poor in Italy was exacerbated by those who sought to bridge it.[27] Furthermore, it was claimed, there was no efficient connection between furniture design, architecture, and city planning, given antiquated construction methods and labor relations in that country.

fig. 51 ▶ Demonstrators at the Milan Triennale, 1968.

All this alarmed the Japanese architect Arata Isozaki, an eyewitness who later wrote, "I consider the course of modern architecture pioneered by the avant-garde to have been changed definitively and qualitatively by the confrontation resulting from the occupation . . . which was in turn part of a cultural revolution whose origins were in Paris. I later came to regard the year of the Triennale as a cultural watershed, comparable to 1527 when the Sack of Rome helped to stimulate Renaissance architecture."[28]

Whether or not the occupation stimulated a new renaissance of architecture and design, it proved how profound were the differences between approaches at the end of the 1960s. When the designer and architect Emilio Ambasz organized the exhibition *Italy: The New Domestic Landscape* for The Museum of Modern Art in 1972, he noted that "three prevalent attitudes toward design" ruled Italy: "The first is conformist, the second is reformist, and the third is, rather, one of contestation, attempting both inquiry and action." These ideas were becoming applicable not just to Italy but to design worldwide. The first category, Ambasz wrote, "continue[s] to refine already established forms and functions . . . exploring the aesthetic quality of single objects—a chair, a table, a bookcase—that answer the traditional needs of domestic life." He included works by Joe Colombo, Marco Zanuso and Richard Sapper, Leonardi-Stagi, and others in this group. The second category, according to Ambasz, believes that design cannot be renovated without structural change in society, but designers refuse to undertake it themselves, and thus they focus on "redesigning conventional objects with new, ironic, and sometimes self-deprecatory sociocultural and aesthetic references."[29] Here he included pieces by Gaetano Pesce, the Castiglioni brothers, Ettore Sottsass, Hans von Klier, and Gae Aulenti, and he acknowledged the meanings signaled by their Pop or historicizing styles. In the third category are those concerned with the uses of their designs in a changing society. Their objects are conceived, he wrote, as "environmental ensembles [that] permit different modes of social interaction . . . [and] allow the user to make his own statement about both privacy and communality."[30] Works by Matta, Colombo, and Cini Boeri were included. Thus *The New Domestic Landscape* linked objects to environments, and linked environments to the less visible systems of behavior and exchange. When preserving the natural environment from man and the manmade became an issue in the 1970s, theorists built on the understanding of the designed object that arose in the 1960s. They defined design as inseparable from the socio-political matrix, and viewed it as either part of the problem or part of the solution.

Eero **Aarnio**

25. **Chair: *Ball* or *Globe***

Designed 1963-65
Fiberglass, aluminum, polyurethane foam,
wool upholstery
119.5 x 103.5 x 85 cm
Produced by Asko Oy (Lahti, Finland), 1966-80,
c. 1983-87; by Adelta (Dinslaken, Germany),
1990 to the present; by Artekno Oy
(Kangasala, Finland), 1992 to the present
D87.245.1, gift of Nannette and Eric Brill*

Half space helmet, half womb, this large fiberglass
sphere on a swiveling aluminum pedestal became
an emblem of 1960s design. Inside, the shell is fully
upholstered and comes with an optional telephone
and stereo speakers to complete its self-contained
world. The cushioning allows users to sit or curl up,
with the informality typical of 1960s manners—
manners permitted even in an office reception area
(fig. 53). Customers could buy the chair in white, red,
black, or orange, with a matching or contrasting color
for the base and the upholstery.

Aarnio's elemental geometric form reflects his
longtime quest for simplified design, as well as the
reductivism in structure and form that functionalist
designers first sought in the 1930s. Nevertheless,
the *Ball*'s futuristic metaphor of Captain Video gear
or even an orbiting Sputnik places it among popular
fascinations of the 1960s. The space race between
the United States and the Soviet Union, announced
by President John F. Kennedy in 1961 and achieved
in 1969, when Americans first landed on the moon,
gripped most imaginations worldwide, even entering
textile designs (fig. 52). The *Ball* chair, in production
three years before the moon walk, evokes what was
then the magic of technology in a more optimistic
age, the most expensive and elaborate technology
ever marshalled and for a most ambitious goal.

Fashion more than function made the *Ball*
successful. This locates it in the culture of instant
gratification, conspicuous consumption, and built-in
obsolescence that emerged, most visibly in the United
States, in the late 1950s. Designers no longer had
to seek the single perfect solution to needs defined
as eternal and universal. Aarnio's form follows a new
function: to capture the fickle consumer's fancy.

fig. 52 ▼ Eddie Squires, *Lunar Rocket* textile, 1969.
Montreal Museum of Decorative Arts.
fig. 53 ► Stanley Felderman, waiting area in the executive
offices of Fabergé, New York, 1970-71, showing Aarnio's
Ball chair.

Gae (Gaetana) **Aulenti**

26. **Table lamp:** *Ruspa*

Designed 1967
Lacquered steel, iron
47 x 32.5 x 29 cm
Produced by Martinelli Luce S.p.A (Lucca, Italy),
1967 to the present
D90.206.1

The allusions of this lamp to robots, hair dryers, the stylizations of human forms in Constructivist sculpture around World War I, and other sources, all reflect Aulenti's wide, democratic visual culture. One of Italy's few female architects, she had already distinguished herself as an interior designer, notably of showrooms for Knoll and Olivetti, as a professor of architecture, and as an editor (of the influential magazine *Casabella*) when she designed this lamp. The *Ruspa* (*Bulldozer*) is related to Eero Aarnio's ball-shaped chair (cat. 25) and to Vico Magistretti's *Eclipse* lamp of 1965-66 (fig. 54), but Aulenti's lamp outweighs them in functional and formal complexity. The bifurcated, spherical shade, each half containing a bulb, tilts on its "neck," which also tilts for further freedom in directing the light. The play of shapes, open and closed, halved and quartered, makes this a piece of impressive abstract sculpture; in Aulenti's arrangement of its parts, the lamp also resembles a studious humanoid.

Magistretti's charmingly small lamp, by contrast to Aulenti's, is strictly an engaging space-age sphere and a half. *Eclipse*, winner of the 1967 Compasso d'Oro award, earns its name when its inner white hemisphere is rotated through 180 degrees to cover some or all of the bulb. The movable parts of *Ruspa*, on the other hand, allow more than control of the direction and amount of light: adjusting them can emphasize either the abstract or figural qualities of this large-scale work. The abstract dominated, for example, when Aulenti grouped it as a foursome in a studio in Genoa which she codesigned (fig. 55).

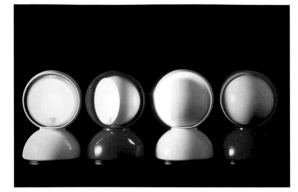

fig. 54 ▲ Artemide, c. 1967 publicity photograph of the Magistretti *Eclipse* table lamp in different positions.

fig. 55 ► Aulenti with Takashi Shimura and Federico Zürcher, living area in unidentified residence, San Michele di Pagana, Genoa, 1970-73, showing four *Ruspa* lamps.

Achille and Pier Giacomo
Castiglioni

27. **Floor lamp:** *Arco*

Designed 1962
Marble, stainless steel, aluminum
243.8 x 188 x 30.6 cm
Produced by Flos (Brescia, Italy), 1962 to the present
D82.104.1, gift of Barbara Jakobson*

The Castiglioni brothers' masterly blend of efficient function and stylish form is displayed by this floor lamp, a buoyant eight-foot-tall "drawing in space" (to use a phrase applied to Calder's mobiles). A popular and critical success in the 1960s, *Arco* solves the problem of illuminating a dining table or living area without installing a hanging fixture or obstructing the residents' movements (fig. 57). It thereby allows maximum flexibility in furniture arrangement, one of the key values of postwar interior design.

As in their *Mezzadro* tractor-seat stool (cat. 19) and equally elemental *Luminator* floor lamp (fig. 56),

the Castiglionis used a minimal number of parts for *Arco*: a rectangular marble base, a stainless steel shaft with three telescoping arcs, and an aluminum shade in a helmet shape. The contrast of traditional marble, especially honored in Italy, with the obviously modern materials of steel and aluminum lends additional wit to this bold design, as well as a sense of luxury. Indeed, the deluxe marble and the amplitude of the arc distinguish the lamp from the modest, stick-figure *Luminator*, whose aesthetics reflect the 1950s. One hole in the base of *Arco* allows insertion of the shaft; another allows you to grasp the heavy stone block or thrust a broom handle through it to move the lamp. The three pieces of the arc are adjustable, permitting alteration of the height and angle of the lamp. More than these functional features, however, the lamp is memorable for its silhouette: distantly related to the gauche gooseneck lamps of the past, it turns the goose into a swan and gives it grand, simple, gravity-defying flight.

fig. 56 ▼ Castiglioni brothers, *Luminator* floor lamp, 1959. Montreal Museum of Decorative Arts.

fig. 57 ▼ Stendig USA, c. 1976-82 publicity photograph showing the Castiglioni *Arco* lamp, the Colombo *Elda* chair, the Aarnio *Ball* chair, a Vignelli sofa, and a Mascheroni coffee table.

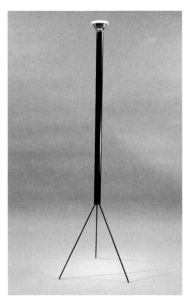

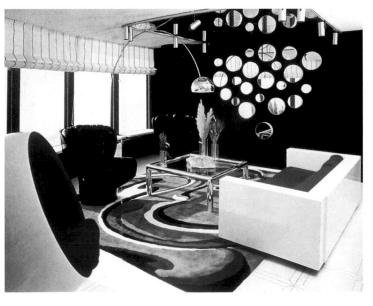

Eero **Aarnio**

28. **Chairs: *Pastille* or *Gyro***

Designed 1968
Fiberglass-reinforced polyester
53.3 x 92.7 x 92.7 cm
Produced by Asko Oy (Lahti, Finland), 1968–c. 1985;
by Adelta (Dinslaken, Germany), 1990 to the
present; by Artekno Oy (Kangasala, Finland),
1992 to the present
D94.333.1-2, gift of Eleanore and Charles Stendig
in memory of Eve Brustein and Rose Stendig*

In its elemental form, Aarnio's *Pastille* or *Gyro*
chair goes beyond the simplification of seating
represented by his *Ball* chair (cat. 25) and works
by fellow Scandinavian designers: this legless chair
is all fiberglass-reinforced polyester, molded in only
two parts. *Pastille* is Pop-art-flavored, humorously
recalling candy or bubblegum shapes; furthermore, it
is manufactured in vivid confectionary colors including
lemon and lime, as seen here. Italian and British
designers produced insubstantial imitations, but this
chair is solid and thick-walled, hardy enough for

outdoor use. The Scandinavians disdained the flippant
ethic of disposability seen in some circles in the
1960s; their designs were realized with the same high-
quality production they had applied in previous years.

That furniture might happily resemble foods and
toys, rendered in outscale size and synthetic materials,
was Pop art's gift to 1960s design. Some chairs,
notably the *Sacco* (by Gatti, Paolini, and Teodoro)
and *Joe* (by De Pas, D'Urbino, and Lomazzi; cat. 48),
pay direct homage to Claes Oldenburg's soft sculpture
made in this decade, first in cloth and then vinyl. The
American dethroned and humanized sculpture by
challenging the rigid materials and the noble subjects
traditional to the art. Designers who were equally
anti-establishment did the same with traditional
seating and lighting. *Sacco* is a big leather beanbag
of polystyrene chips that shape themselves to the
sitter; and *Joe* is a giant baseball mitt named for the
legendary Joe DiMaggio. *Pastille* is less literal in its
metaphor than *Sacco* and, lacking upholstery, it may
be less comfortable than *Joe*. Nonetheless, Aarnio's
low-slung pillow shape has the plump forms of
children's playthings; it memorably illustrates the
regressive emotional appeal of much 1960s design.

fig. 58 ▼ Clyde Rich, apartment on Central Park West,
New York, c. 1970, showing the Aarnio *Pastille* and
Colombo *Universal* chairs.

Gruppo **Architetti Urbanisti Città Nuova**

29. **Table lamp: *Nesso***

Designed 1962
ABS plastic, cellulose acetate
34.3 x 53.6 x 53.6 cm
Produced by Artemide S.p.A. (Pregnana Milanese, Italy), 1965-87; 1999 to the present
D94.123.1, gift of Louise Lalonde

Nesso (*Nexus* or *Connection*) may be a pun on the double allusions of this lamp and its function as an electrical connection. Monochromatic, simple, and continuous in form, it relates to the fiberglass spheres of Eero Aarnio with their space-age associations (cat. 25). It also resembles a giant mushroom, a form that inspired Aarnio's *Kantarelli* (*Chanterelle*) low table of 1965 where a simple disc flows into a pedestal support. *Nesso* is more organic in silhouette, but its smooth, regular shape in molded plastic announces its industrial method of production. Indeed, it suggests a mushroom engineered by science, an updating of the analogy made by Art Nouveau designers between lighting and plant forms. Available in different sizes, *Nesso* sheds a diffuse light from four small bulbs, and this, as well as its lack of adjustable parts, commends it for area illumination rather than reading, as can be seen by a contemporary interior where it is placed near a circular "conversation pit" (fig. 59). The lamp realizes functionalism's ideal of reductivist simplicity, but with the organic associations still beloved in the 1960s.

Nesso was designed by Architetti Urbanisti Città Nuova a year after the group was formed in Bologna; the lamp was subsequently shown in The Museum of Modern Art's influential exhibition of 1972, *Italy: The New Domestic Landscape*. Although the group's six architect-members devoted themselves primarily to city planning and interior and industrial design, they are best known for this mass-produced lamp.

fig. 59 ► Shoei Yoh, living area in the architect's home, Fukuoka, Japan, c. 1972, showing the *Nesso* lamp above a "conversation pit."

Cesare (Joe) **Colombo**

30. **Armchair:** *Elda*

Designed 1963
Molded fiberglass, polyurethane, leather upholstery
92 x 92 x 92 cm
Produced by Comfort (Milan, Italy), 1963 to the present
D90.147.1, gift of Paul Leblanc

Before "the Age of Resin," as one wag called the 1960s, expressing the nature of wood and metal was a moral imperative of Rationalist design. But plastics and polyurethane foam have no inherent structure: these materials let design take flight in the 1960s. For this imposing work, the first large-scale armchair in fiberglass, Colombo used two pieces of the malleable material: the front half of the swiveling

base extends up and forward to form the seat, the back half swells up and outward to form the barrel-like back. Inside, he stuffed seven doughy polyurethane cushions covered in dark leather: the total looks like a command post for a *Star Trek* villain. In his home, Colombo used *Elda* (named for his wife) like a giant set of earphones. He exploited both its shape and padding for reading and lounging (fig. 60).

To the critic Peter Dormer, Colombo was "the James Dean of Italian design, inventive and daring and dying young."[31] In 1962, he began his career in interior and industrial design, opening a studio in Milan. Trained as an architect and a painter, he used popular culture as well as advanced art as formal sources; his free use of allusions to both and his invention with new materials distinguish Colombo's brief nine years of innovative and probing work.

fig. 60 ▲ Photograph of Colombo at home in Milan, sitting in his *Elda* chair, c. 1965.

Cesare (Joe) **Colombo**

31. **Chair: *Multi-Chair***

Designed 1969
Polyurethane foam, synthetic knit upholstery,
steel, leather
41 x 59 x 129 cm
Produced by Sormani (Milan, Italy), 1970-c. 1973
D96.147.1

The *Multi-Chair,* as its name suggests, can assume
multiple positions and shapes, from upright sitting to
horizontal reclining, with many intermediate positions
to suit varied needs and personal physical styles.
The user merely moves the metal hooks and leather
fastenings on both sides of the two stuffed cushions
to connect them in any of the eight arrangements
illustrated by the designer's diagram (fig. 62).
The work is low, legless, and fully upholstered,
a comfortable, sculptural, high-tech version of
all-purpose floor-seating. Thanks to its compact form
and limited number of parts, it can be shipped fairly
conveniently. Such benefits concerned Colombo,
who recognized the accelerated mobility of families
in the 1960s and their need and willingness to
move to new homes.

The space limitations of middle-class residences
challenged Colombo throughout his short career,
and his work includes discrete furniture like the *Elda*
armchair (cat. 30), multi-use pieces, and complete
living systems. Whereas the *Multi-Chair* addresses
the problem of seating, his mini-kitchen on wheels,
designed in 1963, tackles efficient food preparation:
it provides a refrigerator, cupboard, drawers, chopping
block, stove, and a stove cover that doubles as a
serving tray, all in a cubic trolley. Colombo synthesized
these ideas in the environments he designed in 1969,
the *Visiona Habitat* for the Bayer plastics company
and the *Roto-Living* unit for Sormani (fig. 61), in which
he placed the *Multi-Chair*. Sleeping, cooking, eating,
leisure, and hygienic functions could occur in a small
space because he replaced discrete furniture pieces
with space- and labor-saving systems of multi-use
design. The *Roto-Living* dining table rotates away
when not needed, and the hood over the bed descends
for privacy. Whereas Colombo's habitat concept draws
on Japanese domestic traditions and prewar utopian
ideas of functionalism, his execution evokes the
period's most romantic metaphor, the space station,
which he imagined as the eventual dwelling of
many of us, a place where humanity and technology
would live in harmony.

fig. 61 ▲ Colombo, *Roto-Living* unit at his home in Milan, 1969.

fig. 62 ▲ Colombo, diagram illustrating possible arrangements of his *Multi-Chair*, 1970.

fig. 63 ▲ Milan apartment with Cini Boeri's *Serpentone* seating and Gae Aulenti's *Pipistrello* lamp, 1970-71.

Eleanore **Peduzzi Riva**, Heinz **Ulrich**, Klaus **Vogt**, and Veli **Berger**

32. **Sofa: Model no. DS-600,** *Nonstop*
Designed 1968
Plywood, steel, polyurethane foam, Dacron, nylon carpeting, leather upholstery
73.7 x 304.8 x 100.3 cm (total for 10 units)
Produced by de Sede (Klingnau, Switzerland) for Intrex, Inc. (Harrison, NJ, USA), 1968 to the present
D94.156.1a-j, gift of Eleanore and Charles Stendig in memory of Eve Brustein and Rose Stendig*

The *Nonstop* seating system realizes the functional and economic goals of all modular furniture designers: to create one or two units capable of multiple arrangements, thus pleasing a maximum number of consumers with a minimal product. The ingredients of *Nonstop* consist of modules with arm elements at right or left, and armless sections. Two of the armless modules combined with two sections with arms create an armchair. For a sofa, as many seating pieces as desired can be hinged and zipped together—leather strips between them covering any small gaps of space—and the owner can add arm elements to complete the ensemble at each end. This concept by the Italian designer Peduzzi Riva, assisted by three Swiss designers, adds a new flexibility to modular seating. Unlike the modular furniture of the late 1940s and 1950s, which was intended to fit the rectilinear grid of most interiors of that time, the *Nonstop* buyer can add an infinite number of sections to circle into a "conversation pit" or snake off around architectural features. The seating also speaks of 1960s taste in its simple contours and overscaled leather upholstery. Like Joe Colombo's *Elda* armchair, it summons up images of space capsule cockpits and other high-tech power places.

In those years many Europeans, including Marco Zanuso, Pierre Paulin, and Jørn Utzon, created similar serpentine modular seating. A further simplification of the *Nonstop* concept was made by Cini Boeri in her *Serpentone (Jumbo Snake)* seating, designed in 1970-71 (fig. 63). Composed of injection-molded, self-skinned polyurethane slices glued together, it could dispense with both internal structure and upholstery since the exterior hardened into a protective surface. What mattered most to Boeri was the clean line of *Serpentone*, unobscured by fabric. However, *Nonstop* has survived best in use, even in public spaces, because it is preserved by its leather upholstery, and its wooden base is covered with easy-care nylon carpeting.

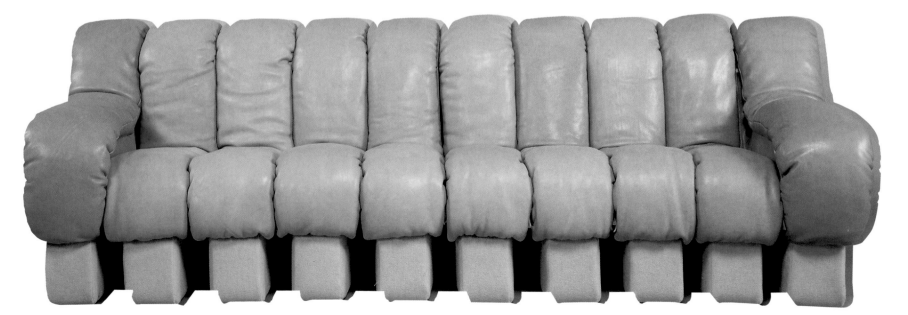

Cesare (Joe) **Colombo**

33. **Chairs: Model no. 4860,** *Universal*

Designed 1965
ABS plastic
71.4 x 42.1 x 48.5 cm
Produced by Kartell S.p.A. (Milan, Italy),
1966 to the present
D87.164.1-2; D87.141.1

A full-sized chair molded in plastic in one piece was the quest of designers and manufacturers from the moment that synthetics were introduced for peacetime use. No costly assembly would be needed; only one mold would be required. Colombo's design for injection-molding by Kartell is considered the first (even though the chair feet are molded separately and inserted). His *Universal* chair beat out designs by Vico Magistretti, who was pursuing a similar idea with Artemide, and Marco Zanuso and Richard Sapper, who had produced a child's stacking chair for Kartell in 1964, which was toylike enough to spark a child's fantasy but too heavy for that child to throw (fig. 64). Strong and substantial, Colombo's *Universal* chair not only stacks but can be linked with ones beside it to allow continuous seating. It takes legs of regular height; also longer or shorter legs can be inserted to turn the seating into a bar stool or a child's chair (fig. 65).

Kartell, established outside Milan in 1949, helped pioneer the manufacture of quality household objects in plastic. Its first products, by its in-house designer Gino Colombini, were limited by the then-available technology to small utensils such as buckets, brushes, and dustpans. The appealing and functional shapes of his objects distinguished them from the cheap and garish trinkets made by other plastic manufacturers. Thus, when the manufacturing technology for synthetics advanced sufficiently to allow large-scale furniture production, Kartell and other Italian companies were already identified internationally with attractive, low-cost designs in plastic.

fig. 64 ▲ Kartell, 1964 publicity photograph of Marco Zanuso and Richard Sapper's stacking chairs for children.

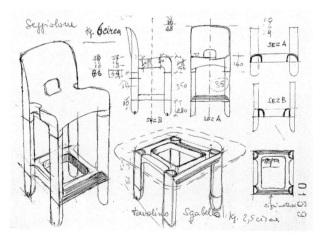

fig. 65 ▲ Colombo, drawing for the *Universal* chair, bar stool, and small table, c. 1965-66.

Cesare (Joe) and Gianni
Colombo

34. Table lamp: *Acrylica*
Designed 1962
Perspex acrylic, lacquered steel
23 x 23.7 x 24.7 cm
Produced by O-Luce (Milan, Italy), 1962 to the present
D91.322.1, gift of Guy Alexandre Miller

One of Joe Colombo's first product designs, this was a collaboration with his brother Gianni, a painter and sculptor. The ingenious but formally simple, C-shaped table lamp won a gold medal at the Milan Triennale in 1964, and identified Joe Colombo with the vanguard in Italian design. The light originates in the fluorescent unit in the steel base, then travels around the curves of the clear acrylic, and radiates magically from its end. The work as a whole shows Colombo's grasp of the optical properties and tensile strength of acrylic, which is molded under pressure and high heat, and here acts as a light convector.

Although Joe Colombo may have acquired his feeling for lighting in his family's electrical equipment manufacturing business, his understanding of plastic and command of memorable shapes extended into his many designs for products, furniture, and interiors. All of them were motivated by his conviction that items in everyday life should be inexpensive, well made, and easy to use. As practical as he was idealistic, he also believed that household objects should present a saleable image, a feature that technology and design had already given to objects in other fields. In all this, *Acrylica* satisfies Colombo's demands.

Superstudio

35. Table lamp: *Gherpe*
Designed 1967
Perspex acrylic, chromium-plated steel
Closed: 20 x 42.9 x 20.3 cm
Produced by Poltronova (Montale Pistoia, Italy),
1967-72
D94.139.1, gift of Eleanore and Charles Stendig
in memory of Eve Brustein and Rose Stendig*

Superstudio was a radical Italian design group founded in Florence in 1966 (like Archizoom Associati) and was mobilized by that period's political unrest and European critiques of capitalism. Its young members—Cristiano Toraldo di Francia, Alessandro and Roberto Magris, Piero Frassinelli, and Adolfo Natalini—sought nothing less than to redefine consumer products, housing, and urban planning for their generation, considering Modernism out of touch with new social realities.

An early sketch for this lamp, possibly by Natalini, was inscribed "if you don't behave, the *gherpe* [a big bird of prey] will get you" (fig. 66). Despite the nursery-like threat, this Pop-styled lamp was intended to radiate a political message. Its very lack of a pedestal, its shocking pink plastic material, and its adjustability—the plastic bands open and close, cabriolet-fashion, to alter the amount of light emitted—imply a different, younger, and more adventurous audience than the buyers of Good Design. For the Italian "Anti-Design" groups emergent in the late 1960s, such Pop art allusions meant they embraced mass consumers and mass communication systems. Popular culture was seen as intrinsically democratic and potentially subversive, for it was believed capable of decentering cultural power and fostering plurality.

These oppositional attitudes and philosophic questionings typified Superstudio and other such groups in Italy, and turned their offices into think tanks, producing many polemics and works on paper. For them, the designer-architect was no longer just an engineer of the practical, but now also a political critic and a shaman ministering to society's cultural and spiritual needs.

fig. 66 ▲ Superstudio, drawing for the *Gherpe* lamp, 1967.

Verner **Panton**

36. **Chairs: Model no. PA 100**
Designed 1960-67
Luran-S Thermoplastic
83.7 x 49.5 x 56.6 cm
Produced by Vitra GmbH (Basel, Switzerland) for
Herman Miller International (Zeeland, MI, USA),
1968 to the present
D83.136.1, gift of Herman Miller Inc.; D87.200.1,
gift of Luc d'Iberville-Moreau

An icon of 1960s design, this luscious dollop of
plastic was the first single-form chair to reach mass
production. Molded like the fiberglass crash helmets
and buckets that impressed Panton in the 1950s,
his chair needed no assembly. Cantilevered like
Gerrit Rietveld's *Zig-Zag* chair of 1934, it trumps this
source by melding legs and base into a single curved
form. This shape allows leg room, and the smooth
undulations of the overall S shape promise comfort.
The chair is also stackable, a feature that required
the most work from Panton and his engineers at
Vitra. They had to reduce the thickness of the chair's
walls without compromising its strength. Finding
the right plastic, a high-resistance, injection-molded,
fiberglass-reinforced polyester, and shaping it
properly with twenty-two supporting ribs under the
seat took eight years between Panton's prototype
and its commercial production.

In its sleek curvaceous form, Panton's chair
relates both to the streamlining of the 1930s and to
Eero Saarinen's *Pedestal* chairs and table of about
1955 (cat. 22). Technically, Panton's achievement
was built on pre- and postwar Scandinavian
experiments in molded plywood. Indeed, in 1950-52
he worked in Arne Jacobsen's architectural office
in Copenhagen, where bent plywood was a hallmark.
His design also retains a prewar interest in
cantilevering and in the possibilities of restructuring
form through engineering. Nonetheless, in this chair
and many designs in general, technical innovation
followed, rather than preceded, the will to form.
Panton (like Eames and Saarinen before him) found
his syrupy shape before the fiberglass-reinforced
plastic that made it possible to fabricate structurally
sound seating. That plastic, in turn, inspired later
extravagances of form in other furnishings.

fig. 67 ▲ Panton, interior of the designer's home with his stacking side chairs,
Basel, c. 1975.

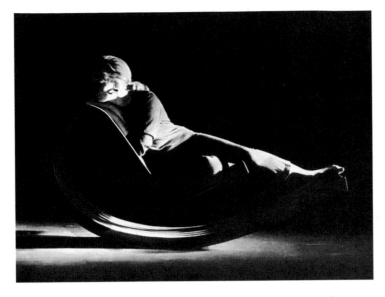

fig. 68 ▲ Elco, c. 1969 publicity photograph showing a woman sitting on the *Dondolo* chair.

Leonardi-Stagi, Architetti

37. Rocking chair: *Dondolo*
Designed 1967
Fiberglass
75.5 x 174.9 x 40 cm
Produced by Elco (Venice, Italy), 1967-70
D87.154.1, gift of Geoffrey N. Bradfield*

In the daringly cantilevered design of this rocking chair, the architect-designers Cesare Leonardi and Franca Stagi flaunt the tensile strength of fiberglass. Like Panton's cantilevered stacking chair, *Dondolo* (Italian for *Swing*) has a ribbonlike simplicity and elegantly curving silhouette. It seems to condense the rocker, seat, and back of earlier Thonet rocking chairs and the 1929 chaise longue by Charlotte Perriand, Pierre Jeanneret, and Le Corbusier into a linear gesture that telegraphs the rocking movement. Here no arms or legs are necessary. This reductivism is apparently made possible by the molded fiberglass but, in fact, the chair had to be strengthened with the addition of longitudinal fiberglass ribs, which are carefully integrated with the design to avoid marring the hairpinlike contour or its thinness. In its aesthetic of lightness, *Dondolo* reflects the postwar period's taste for furnishings that appeared to be and *were* easily movable. In its distant recollection of prewar designs, it bears witness to their current revival by manufacturers, such as Cassina, which returned the classic chaise longue by Perriand, Jeanneret, and Le Corbusier to production in 1965.

Archizoom Associati

38. Sofa: *Superonda*

Designed 1966
Polyurethane foam, PVC upholstery
89 x 237.5 x 72 cm
Produced by Poltronova (Montale Pistoia, Italy)
for Archizoom Associati (Florence, Italy),
1970 to the present
D90.221.1, gift of Jay Spectre*

Superonda (or *Superwave*) represents a lighthearted side of the "Anti-Design" movement among Italian practitioners of the late 1960s. Its double wave form of slick, vinyl-covered polyurethane foam invites one not to sit, but to loll (fig. 69). The two waves, cut from one slab of foam and placed at right angles to each other, can serve as a couch; placed side by side, they serve as a platform bed. Strengthened by its gleaming vinyl skin, the work needed no internal structure or expensive tooling, and so it was relatively cheap to manufacture. It was clearly intended for mass consumers—and for their amusement.

Expressing an aspect of Pop taste, the sofa alludes to hip advertising graphics of the 1960s. Such undulating curves were leitmotifs of psychedelic art, that updating with Day-Glo colors and rock-music themes of Alphonse Mucha and Victor Horta's whiplash Art Nouveau calligraphy of 1900. These and other fin-de-siècle graphic and architectural designers were rediscovered by collectors in the mid-1960s, who sought alternatives to the Rationalist traditions of the 1930s and Good Design. The decorative, organic styling of Art Nouveau appealed to younger Italians like those in the Archizoom group, in part because of its distance from the crisp, dry International Style.

Archizoom, like Superstudio, was founded in 1966 by rebellious architecture graduates of the University of Florence. Archizoom took its name from the radical English architecture group called Archigram and from an issue of *Zoom*, that group's magazine. All three associations attacked Bauhaus-based styles and, instead, elevated irrational and poetic design, design that would nevertheless be produced for a broad public using industrial means. Led by Andrea Branzi, Archizoom also included Gilberto Corretti, Dario and Lucia Bartolini, Massimo Morozzi, and Paolo Deganello.

fig. 69 ▲ Lounging on *Superonda* sofas in the home of Massimo and Cristina Morozzi, Milan, 1966.

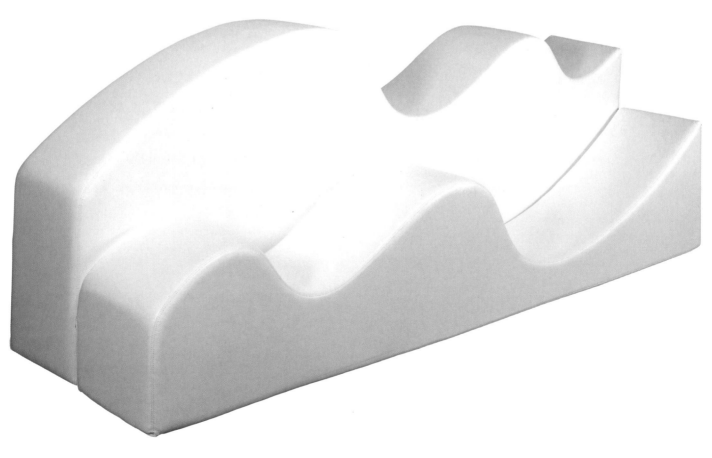

fig. 70 ▲ Scene from *2001: A Space Odyssey*, 1968, showing the Space Hilton lounge with Mourgue's *Djinn* chairs and sofas. Art direction by John Hoesli.

Olivier **Mourgue**

39. **Lounge chair: *Bouloum***

Designed 1968
Fiberglass, steel, polyurethane foam, nylon jersey upholstery
66.1 x 76.2 x 142.9 cm
Produced by Airborne (Montreuil, France), 1968-74; by Arconas Corporation (Mississauga, Ontario, Canada), 1975 to the present
D93.257.1, gift of William Prévost

The elasticity of stretch fabrics such as nylon jersey meant that complex curved volumes could be upholstered for a modest cost. No tucks were necessary, and the smooth undulant surfaces of designs such as Mourgue's remain wrinkle-free. For this chaise longue, the jersey and a layer of polyurethane foam cover a plastic shell molded amusingly like a reclining figure. (It was based on the silhouette of one of Mourgue's childhood friends and given his nickname.) Without upholstery, the shells can be used outdoors—as they were at the 1970 World's Fair in Osaka, Japan, where they stood vertically like attendants and held signs. In upholstered variants, the *Bouloum* offered seating in the fair's French pavilion.

Lightweight and stackable, the *Bouloum* evolved from the softly flowing lines of Mourgue's *Djinn* series, designed in 1963, but it replaced the latter's tubular metal frame with a fiberglass shell. Such shells could be molded at high speed (in fact, the 1966 *Bofinger* chair, a single-mold fiberglass piece by Helmut Bätzner, came off the production line at the rate of one every four minutes). However, with their charm and air of upholstered comfort, Mourgue's designs do not look cheap. Their futuristic flavor appealed to the filmmaker Stanley Kubrick, who used the *Djinn* series to furnish the Space Hilton in his *2001: A Space Odyssey* (fig. 70).[32]

Gaetano **Pesce**

40. **Armchair and ottoman: UP5 and UP6,** *La Mamma*

Designed 1969
Polyurethane foam, viscose/nylon/Lycra upholstery
Chair: 100 x 113.7 x 125.1 cm
Ottoman: 59.1 x 59.1 x 59.1 cm
Produced by C & B Italia S.p.A. (Novedrate, Italy), 1970-72; by B & B Italia (Novedrate, Italy), 1973-81, 1984, 1994 to the present
D84.179.1-2, gift of B & B Italia

Pesce's comically ballooning chair, one of six designs in his UP line, is radical in both its metaphor and production method. Anthropomorphic, like much of the innovative furniture by this designer, artist, and architect, it was also politically topical in relation to the nascent movement for women's rights. Pesce intended it to resemble a prehistoric female fertility symbol, like the *"Venus" of Willendorf*, but he gave it a ball and chain, because, as he said, "a woman is always confined, a prisoner of herself against her will."[33] That we can enjoy her condition, and that the home doubles for the womb through its most comfortable furnishings, appear to be Pesce's subtexts here.

Equally astonishing was Pesce's exploitation of the properties of polyurethane foam to shortcut the conventional construction and shipping of chairs. Of high density, the foam needs no rigid internal structure to support a sitter. Once the chair was formed and upholstered in a synthetic stretch jersey, it was placed in a vacuum chamber and, as the air in the foam was withdrawn, it was pressed flat between vinyl sheets. Then the sheets were heat-sealed, producing a conveniently small, economical shipping package. After the buyer opened this package, the chair immediately inflated as air entered and filled each of its polyurethane cells (fig. 71), a process that was not reversible.

Pesce, who collaborated with artists across Europe in the early 1960s, was fluent in the languages of Pop, Serial, and Kinetic art. *La Mamma* shares Pop's laughing recognition of the sex appeal encoded in consumer product designs; opening its box gave each owner the fun of participating in his or her own Happening.

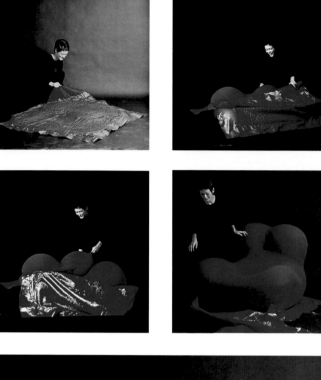

fig. 71 ▲ B & B Italia, 1969 publicity photographs showing five phases of the inflation of the UP5 *La Mamma* armchair.

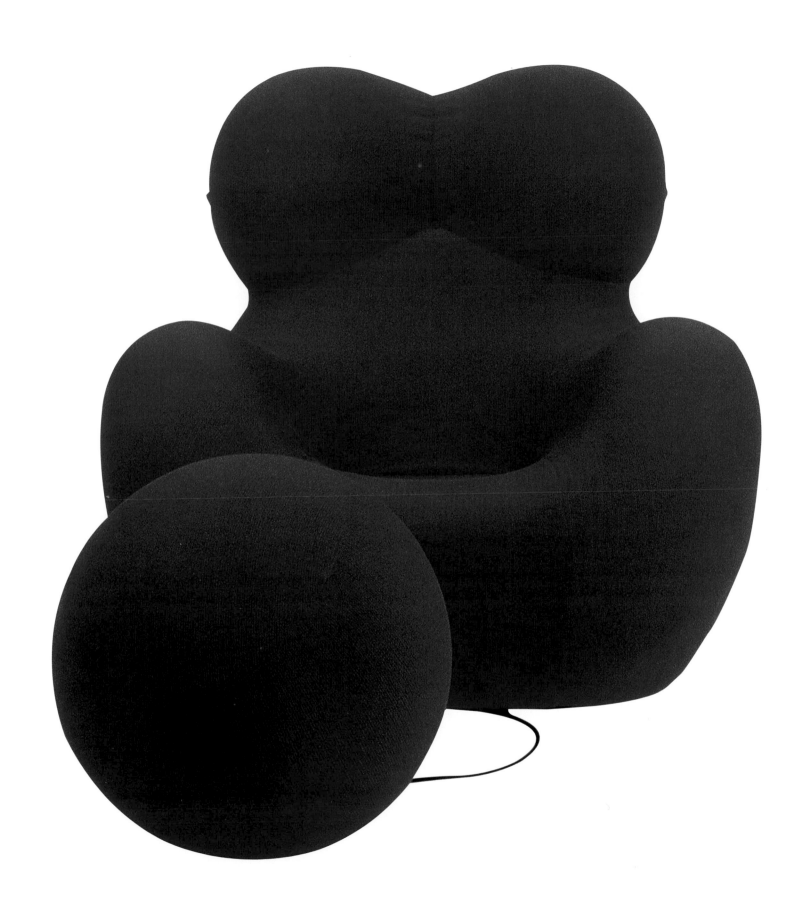

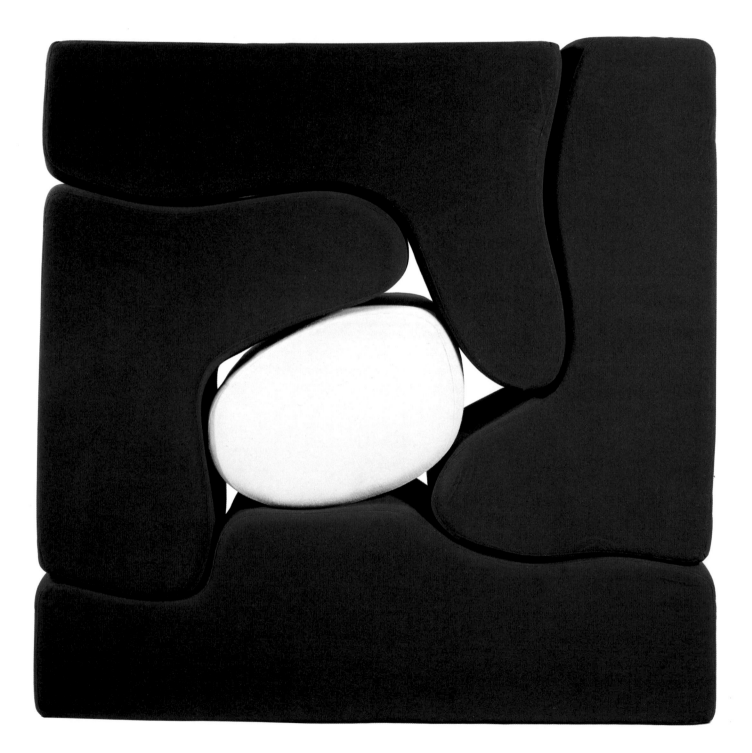

Matta

(Roberto Sebastian Antonio Matta Echaurren)

41. Lounge chairs and ottoman: *Malitte*

Designed 1966
Polyurethane foam, stretch wool upholstery
Assembled: 160 x 160 x 63 cm
Produced by Gavina (Foligno, Italy), 1966-68;
by Knoll International (New York, NY, USA), 1968-74
D89.137.1

That polyurethane foam lends itself to a curvilinear aesthetic is evident in Matta's *Malitte* seating and in Archizoom's *Superonda* sofa (cat. 38), both designed in 1966. Defying rectilinear geometry, the five freeform sections of *Malitte* were cut from a single slab of foam and transformed into four lounge chairs and an ottoman. The owner can arrange them at will (fig. 73). For transport, saving space, or as a sculpture, they stack back into a square, with the ovoid ottoman of contrasting color in the middle. Like *Superonda*, the total relates to earlier and contemporary art rather than to architecture, which had been the model of much 1950s design.

Malitte's designer is best known as a Surrealist painter. Matta named the seating after one of his wives, and created it at the request of a friend, the vanguard furniture designer Dino Gavina. Gavina evidently challenged him to work with polyurethane foam, then a relatively new material, and Matta set himself the task of using all of the block.[34] The result resembles not his own paintings—which were outer-space fantasies with translucent robot populations—but the plywood reliefs of clouds and egg shapes made by the Dada-turned-Surrealist Jean Arp, beginning around 1920 (fig. 72). Matta's humor lies in his transformation of Surrealist biomorphism into practical forms: the ova of Salvador Dalí and Yves Tanguy now give birth to four seats. The painter also designed two more chair-homages to fellow artists— one shaped like a huge bowler hat with a green apple pillow in honor of René Magritte, and another based on Marcel Duchamp's *Chocolate Grinder*—but *Malitte* is Matta's most successful and versatile seating.

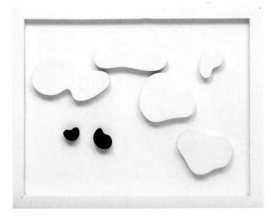

fig. 72 ▲ Jean Arp, *Constellation with Five White and Two Black Forms: Variation 2*, 1932. The Museum of Modern Art, New York. The Sidney and Harriet Janis Collection.

fig. 73 ▲ Matta, *Malitte* lounge chair and ottoman, disassembled.

Pierre **Paulin**

42. **Armchair: Model no. F582,** *Ribbon*

Designed 1966
Steel, lacquered wood, rubber, latex foam,
stretch jersey upholstery
69.8 x 102.4 x 78.7 cm
Produced by Artifort (Maastricht, the Netherlands),
1966 to the present
D91.372.1, anonymous gift

As simple in conception yet as complex in visual
form as a Möbius strip, Paulin's *Ribbon* chair
suggests his past, both as a sculpture student
and as a designer of Citroën car interiors and
seating for Thonet. Tubular steel provides the frame
of Paulin's elegant low-slung chair, in which seat,
arms, and back form a continuous curve and defy
distinctions between inside and out. The upholstery
marks its modernity and comfort: rubber sheeting
was stretched over the steel frame and covered
with latex foam; then the form was slipped into
a presewn stretch fabric cover. Traditional springs
and slipcover tucks were unnecessary, lowering
production costs. And the seat, like a sports car's
bucket seat, fits the sitter.

Double-knit fabrics became available in the
late 1950s, measurably affecting fashion design,
including lingerie and hosiery. Together with latex
and polyurethane foams, they enabled designers
to create freeform furnishings with easy-to-make
upholstery and minimal structural reinforcement.
The dramatic, sculptural shapes that stretch fabrics
could assume are visible in the installation of *Textiles
USA*, a 1956 exhibition at The Museum of Modern
Art (fig. 74). Whether humorously anthropomorphic,
as in Pesce's *La Mamma* and Mourgue's *Bouloum*,
or purely abstract, as in Paulin's *Ribbon*, such
chairs exploit the symbiosis of these inexpensive,
industrially produced materials in inventive ways.

fig. 74 ▲ Bernard Rudofsky, installation of the exhibition *Textiles USA*, The Museum of Modern Art, New York, 1956.

Jonathan **De Pas**, Donato **D'Urbino**, Paolo **Lomazzi**, and Carla **Scolari**

43. **Armchair: *Blow***

Designed 1967
PVC plastic
83 x 103.5 x 97.5 cm
Produced by Zanotta S.p.A. (Nova Milanese, Italy),
1968-69, 1988-92
D99.134.1

fig. 75 ▲ Zanotta, 1967 publicity photograph for the *Blow* armchair.

Blow, the first furniture design by these four architects, was also the first inflatable chair mass-produced for domestic use. Comically bulbous and wholly transparent, it denied the distinction between indoor and outdoor seating, and it could be used for both purposes. It may evoke beach rafts and pool toys, and their associations with childhood and play, but its conception derives from inflatable boats. Still, *Blow* was technically innovative, since its cylinders are not rubber but PVC (polyvinyl chloride) plastic and they are not glued together but rely on high-frequency welding to assure strength. The squat shape was inspired by the Michelin tire company's Bibendum man—an instance of advertising's comic effect on design in the 1960s. And the complete transparency of the chair fully reveals its sitter to onlookers (perhaps to the delight of both in that exhibitionist decade). The chair is as quickly deflated as it is inflated, responding to the desire for furnishings that could be easily moved, shipped, and stored. It was inexpensive, almost as light as air, and a famous fad of the 1960s. However, consumers eventually noticed that the PVC was hot and sticky for prolonged sitting, and that the chair could lose air. Nonetheless, in one blow, it pricked the bourgeois definition of furniture as solid, heavy, and permanent.

Gae (Gaetana) **Aulenti**

44. **Rocking chair: *Sgarsul***

Designed 1962
Lacquered beech, leather
86.5 x 73 x 106.5 cm
Produced by Poltronova (Montale Pistoia, Italy),
1962 to the present
D87.155.1, gift of Dr. and Mrs. Sidney Lerman*

This red-lacquered bentwood rocker with its inviting leather sling seat seems far from revolutionary today. A single teardrop shape of bentwood forms the armrests and the rocker, while a piece shaped like the number 6 loops from under the arms to form the back of the chair. This is an updating of the Thonet classic bentwood rocking chair No. 1 of about 1862, and it also recalls Charlotte Perriand, Pierre Jeanneret, and Le Corbusier's tubular steel chaise longue of 1929, but it offers sharp corners and a taut profile instead of tendril-like terminations and an elongated silhouette.

The historicism of *Sgarsul* (*Street Urchin* in Neapolitan slang) was startling in advanced design circles at the beginning of the 1960s, and it illustrates Aulenti's place in the controversial Neo-Liberty group. Rejecting Modernism, which

in Italy had Fascist associations, as well as native versions of Good Design, the group revived Art Nouveau (the *stile Liberty* in Italy) with its curvilinear grace and zoomorphic metaphors, as well as other styles. Aulenti's allusions implicitly critiqued the antihistorical approach of Rationalism, as well as its supporters' indifference to popular taste (inexpensive versions of the Thonet rocker were widely sold in the 1960s). In these years, her learned criticality was also displayed in her architectural teaching and editorial positions. Since then, her gift in using historic styles to address current philosophic issues in design has flourished, notably in her renovations of such public buildings as the *belle époque* Gare d'Orsay in Paris, the *moderne* Milan Triennale galleries, and the Neoclassical San Francisco Museum of Asian Art.

fig. 76 ▲ Aulenti, the designer's bedroom, Milan, 1974, showing her *Pipistrello* table lamp.

Gae (Gaetana) **Aulenti**

45. **Table lamp:** *Pipistrello*
Designed 1965
Lacquered aluminum, stainless steel, perspex acrylic
70 x 53 x 53 cm
Produced by Martinelli Luce S.p.A. (Lucca, Italy),
1966 to the present
D88.122.1, gift of Martinelli Luce S.p.A.

Aulenti's table lamp, like her bentwood rocker, gives historical sources a suave, contemporary look. In this case, the delicate lines of the *Pipistrello* (or *Bat*) lamp call to mind the elegant designs of Josef Hoffmann and other Vienna Secessionists active in the first decade of the twentieth century. Their restrained, geometricized version of Art Nouveau, with smooth surfaces and elongated silhouettes, was rediscovered by sophisticates in the 1960s. Aulenti updated the Austrian antecedents for this lamp by expanding its scale—in this way relating it to the enlargements adopted from Pop by Italian groups like Superstudio—and by using stainless steel for the shaft and perspex acrylic for the shade. The shaft telescopes to variable heights, thus enhancing its functionalism.

Also in the 1960s, Aulenti designed lamps in plastics for Artemide, Kartell, Poltronova, and other adventurous manufacturers, using outscale spheres more typical of Pop morphology, and she gave traditional materials and types like marble-topped tables an ironic twist. Such ease in using historic and contemporary styles to engage sophisticated consumers forecast Aulenti's later work as an architect of interiors, as well as the approach of Italian Post-Modernists emergent in the late 1970s. Noting that her work is guided by analysis, synthesis, and a "prophetic capacity," she recently explained her relation to history: "If cultural tradition is not something that one passively inherits but something that one builds day by day, then this third ability [the prophetic] must be an aspiration to create an effect of cultural continuity, to construct its forms and its figures with personal, contemporary content."[35] Older cultures, which the Neo-Liberty group used oppositionally in the 1960s, evolved into a source of "continuity" for Aulenti.

46. **Wardrobe**
Designed 1966
Plywood, plastic laminate, chrome-plated steel
215.3 x 83.8 x 83.8 cm
Produced by Renzo Brugola (Lissone, Italy), 1988
D90.207.1, gift of Paul Leblanc

This wardrobe sends intriguing mixed signals.
A simple plywood box with a pole inside for hanging
clothes, veneered on the outside with plastic
laminates in yellow and white, and set on a black-
and-white-striped base, it resembles some sort of
traffic barrier crossed with a Color-field painting or
a piece of Minimal sculpture, like the contemporary
cubic forms by Tony Smith, Donald Judd, and Robert
Morris, American artists whom Sottsass admired.

Sottsass designed this and other highly
influential furnishings with the recognition that
consumer products are value-laden symbols, as well
as objects of everyday use. The designer and curator
Emilio Ambasz included the prototype of this work
in the seminal 1972 exhibition at The Museum
of Modern Art, *Italy: The New Domestic Landscape*
(fig. 77), and he described its type as "conceived
as an altarpiece for the domestic liturgy."[36] Perhaps
not surprisingly, the cabinet was never put into
production. This example was specially executed at
the request of the Montreal Museum of Decorative
Arts. With its basic form and slick contemporary
finishing, Sottsass' wardrobe is a totem of a
consumption-oriented society, and destined to
contain items briefly consecrated as high fashion.
It typifies Sottsass' understanding of the symbolism
of objects in society and his canny use of diverse
communication systems—including advertising,
contemporary art, and historic design—to give his
work wide significance. He often draws attention
to these systems through startling dislocations—here
of graphics reminiscent of traffic signs transported
into the home, of Color-field painting motifs applied
to a wardrobe.

fig. 77 ▲ Sottsass, prototypes of wardrobes
designed for Poltronova, 1971.

fig. 78 ▲ Aldo Ballo, 1969 photograph of a woman holding a von Klier *Gli Animali* miniature cabinet.

Hans **von Klier**

47. **Cabinet:** *Gli Animali* **series**

Designed 1969
Lacquered wood, steel
67.8 x 35.7 x 36.2 cm
Produced by Planula S.p.A. (Montale, Italy),
1969-86
D97.163.1

This delightful, many-footed little cabinet in von Klier's *Gli Animali* (*The Animals*) series is his counterpart to Sottsass' menhir-like wardrobes, all of which were included in The Museum of Modern Art's exhibition *Italy: The New Domestic Landscape*. Sottsass' pieces were depicted in the catalogue as somewhat mysterious monoliths in empty bedrooms—"forcing a crack in the optimistic view of bourgeois progress," according to Andrea Branzi.[37] Von Klier, by contrast, used small scale and repetition to turn a neutral container into an endearing toy (fig. 78). In fact, von Klier designed educational toys in the early 1960s. He worked in Sottsass' studio from 1960 to 1968 (on the design of Olivetti office machines and furniture), and there doubtlessly recognized the formal impact of the Italian's use of simple cubic forms finished in brilliant colors, their rounded feet set off by different bright shades. Among other things, these expanses of saturated color—whether in von Klier's lacquers or Sottsass' plastic laminates— separate their work of 1966-69 from later, chunky geometric furnishings by Post-Modernists. The latter are self-consciously "decorated" with patterns warring with each other and with perception of structure; these early containers, on the other hand, are dramatized in their elementary shapes and hollowness by their closed surfaces with a limited number of hues. Nevertheless, the Italians' cabinets prophesy the slick-skinned, symbol-laden, disconcerting yet appealing designs of the Memphis group in the 1980s.

The 1970s
Conservation and Pluralism

THE REBELLIOUS SPIRIT OF THE 1960S LIVED ON INTO THE 1970S. EXPERIMENTAL, YOUTH-ORIENTED, PLEASURE-loving, liberal if not radical in their ideologies, the designers who came of age in the 1960s continued to conceive furnishings and settings, from simple interiors to futuristic cities. But they and their elders were faced with more demands, as special-interest groups proliferated, and the general mood was tempered by sobering world events. In 1973, American forces withdrew from Vietnam, signaling a humiliating failure for the world's greatest military force. The same year, Arab nations moved to embargo shipments of oil to the United States, Western Europe, and Japan in retaliation for their support of Israel in the Israeli-Egyptian strife. In 1974, global inflation began a spiral upward that ultimately reached over eighteen percent annually in the United States and close to twenty percent in Italy. The costs of food, production materials, and goods skyrocketed alongside the costs of filling the gas tank and heating the home and office. Italians called this decade "the years of lead." For a time the economic growth of most industrialized countries dipped dangerously near zero.

Meanwhile, the result of decades of exploitation of nature for short-term gain was becoming obvious. The faith of the 1950s and 1960s in an ever-abundant supply of natural resources was shaken. The accumulation of toxic wastes—found in smoggy city air and fouled country streams—demanded drastic reform. Concern about the destruction of both natural and man-made environments drove many developed countries to action. In 1970, the United States Environmental Protection Agency was formed, and massive demonstrations were held in the United States on what was named "Earth Day" to protest the pollution of the planet. The multi-national Conference on the Human Environment took place in Stockholm in 1972 and led to the development of programs to address environmental issues on an international level. Affecting individuals directly, environmental protection laws were passed across Europe and in North America which banned certain pesticides, required returnable bottles, legislated acceptable fuel emissions, and the like. By the mid-1970s, the Green Party, devoted to ecological issues, had become a meaningful voice in German politics. As the numerous articles in professional periodicals of the time attest, designers were urged to participate in the movement to take responsibility for the environment. Radical designers of the late 1960s had already demanded more attention to socio-economic problems and the cultural meanings of their products; many designers of the 1970s focused less on Good Design than on socially responsible design.

The approach to plastics was symptomatic. Because they are derived from oil, natural gas, and coal, they became a less appropriate material in the 1970s. Once affordable, plastics now became expensive to produce. Furthermore, they are virtually indestructible, thus making their disposal difficult. This cheerful emblem of the 1960s—often used for avant-garde furniture and lighting—was now employed with great deliberation, in pared-down designs using less of the plastic or in cheaper grades, and in furnishings of maximum efficiency and multi-use.

Some designers of the 1970s continued to conceive objects in isolation and for the luxury market, responding in part to a new conservative spirit created by the ambiguous results of 1960s radicalism. Other designers were heirs of that radicalism, however, and saw themselves as responsible for the built environment and the consequences of the wasteful overproduction of virtually identical objects. Many were affected by the ardent polemic of the theorist Victor Papanek, whose *Design for the Real World: Human Ecology and Social Change* (1971) demanded that design for mass production respond to the environment, the elderly, the handicapped, and Third World societies. "Design for Need" was the theme of a 1976 conference in London of the International Council of Societies of Industrial Design (ICSID), and the phrase became widely current as a synonym for design with idealistic social concerns.

Designers of this reforming bent reacted to the energy crisis in various ways. Rejecting entrepreneurial schemes of planned obsolescence, they sought to create longer-lasting designs that would demand less of manufacturers and consume less energy. Alternatively, by creating objects made of recycled materials, they demonstrated their commitment to conserving natural resources. In the United States, for example, Frank Gehry conceived highly original furniture made from corrugated cardboard, a cheap packing material that in turn could be made from recycled paper (cat. 54-56). In 1978, the German Blue Angel label was introduced to designate German products meeting specific environmental criteria, and companies in Great Britain, Canada, and Japan soon followed this trend.

On a larger scale, the decade saw passionate theorizing and visionary proposals for environmental solutions. It was posited that if humans were to survive into the next century, drastic changes in individual and communal living must occur. Unplanned suburban growth was seen as an enemy of nature. The way in which modern cities are linked to mushrooming suburbs by fuel-devouring highways was proclaimed a dangerous anachronism. Of the various ecological design schemes explored in the 1970s, "Arcosanti" by the Italian-born architect Paolo Soleri then seemed one of the most compelling.[38] Soleri applied his concepts of "arcology" (architecture and ecology) to the development of sixty acres near Phoenix, Arizona (fig. 79). Here, in linked, multistoried, mostly saucer-shaped megastructures, he confronted the problem of congestion by condensing the human habitat even further, thus preserving the land for agriculture and recreation. Arcosanti conserved energy by relying on solar power; greenhouses doubled as sources for food and heat for the community. The goal was to eliminate the suburban sprawl of commercial services and community facilities, as well as the need for the automobile, a primary polluter. This community survived the 1970s and today continues to function with approximately sixty inhabitants.

Although the preservation of the earth's natural resources was a primary issue, designers also recognized that the built environment was at risk. Noteworthy buildings were being threatened with destruction by unregulated development. The razing of the Van Horne house in Montreal stimulated a militant preservation effort in Quebec province. After having lost such Paris landmarks as Les Halles and the Gare Montparnasse to the wrecking ball, and nearly losing the Marché Saint-Germain, the French government claimed protection for important monuments and offered

fig. 79 ▼ Paolo Soleri, Arcosanti viewed from the South Mesa, Mayer, Arizona, 1970.

guidelines and financial aid for the historic preservation of buildings. The 1966 demolition of Pennsylvania Station in New York City and of Frank Lloyd Wright's Imperial Hotel in Tokyo in 1967 galvanized the preservation movement in the United States and Japan, and inspired a variety of creative ideas for adaptations and reuse from architects and designers. Privately funded organizations devoted to historic preservation grew more sizable and vocal in the 1970s.

Many architects endeavored to integrate new schemes with older buildings. Aldo Rossi, for example, designed his 1979 floating Teatro del Mondo as a series of towers to harmonize in its historical allusions with Venice and the adjacent church of Santa Maria della Salute (fig. 81). These historically sensitive architects also designed new furnishings to accompany older pieces in their interiors. The British architectural critic and historian Charles Jencks, the first to define Post-Modernism in architecture, lent significant credence to the preservation movement by championing pluralistic, historic styles and the revival rather than the erasure of past tastes.[39] In Jencks' words, Post-Modernists "claim positively that their buildings are rooted in place and history, unlike the abstract buildings of their immediate predecessors and competitors, and that they bring back the full repertoire of architectural expression: ornament, symbolism, humor, and urban context, to mention a few of their restorations."[40] Preserving the architectural resources of the past became socially, ecologically, and aesthetically desirable.

Looking to the future in its 1972 exhibition, *Italy: The New Domestic Landscape*, The Museum of Modern Art commissioned selected designers under age thirty-five and design groups to conceive model environments for living. "Neither the experiences of today nor the vision of tomorrow can be emphasized at the expense of one another," wrote the exhibition curator Emilio Ambasz. "The search for quality in daily existence cannot afford to ignore the concomitant problems of pollution, the deterioration of our cities and institutions, and poverty."[41] The competition was meant

fig. 80 ► Mario Bellini, *Kar-a-Sutra*, c. 1971.

fig. 81 ▶ Aldo Rossi, Teatro del Mondo alongside Santa Maria della Salute, Venice, 1979.

to appeal to designers of two opposing attitudes toward environmental design: those believing in the potential of design as a positive, problem-solving activity, and those of the "counter-design" persuasion who wanted to initiate philosophical discourse and political and social involvement to bring about societal and environmental change. Mario Bellini, for one, undertook to "initiate the redemption of this fascinating mechanical monster" known as the automobile.[42] He devised the *Kar-a-Sutra*, a sixteen-foot-long automobile that could carry twelve people (fig. 80). The interior furnishings consisted entirely of uniformly shaped cushions that could be rearranged for group seating and bedding as desired. Bellini's name for the car is a playful pun on the *Kama-Sutra,* the Hindu sexual treatise (which also concerns multiple positions), but his effort to rethink mass transit was serious and far from isolated. While stringent automobile emission standards were set by new laws, certain North American and European cities expanded subsidies for rail and subway systems to try to wean commuters away from their cars.

Related to this line of thought were the visionary conceptions of Archizoom and Superstudio, the two major Italian radical "Anti-Design" groups formed in 1966. In Archizoom's provocative exhibition of 1970, *No-Stop City*, for instance, communal living structures were

modeled on the continuous spatial organizations of the factory and supermarket (fig. 82).[43] Here Paolo Soleri's Arcosanti met Pop art: communal life would take place in open interior spaces where, for example, a stove and motorcycle, placed at will, would replace the discrete structures of kitchen and garage. Mirrored walls were used to demonstrate how interior space could be infinitely divided, not into apartments but open "residential lots" to be rented much like parking spaces for cars.[44] More involved in arousing thought than conceiving products, all the Anti-Design groups rejected design that catered to excessive consumption. Thus, Anti-Design was able to establish a rapport with the ecological and preservation movements, which also attempted to counter excessive consumption and planned obsolescence.

Socially responsible design also took small-scale forms. In Sweden, designers responded with an aesthetic sensibility still grounded in their practices of the 1950s and 1960s, and focused on communal concerns, especially ergonomic design to ease the discomforts of the physically disabled. For example, the Swedish designers Peter Opsvik and Hans Christian Mengshoel introduced their *Balans* series of chairs based on extensive study of human posture. A simple, economical design born from a genuine concern for the functional and beneficial, the *Balans* chair supports body weight on the knees rather than the pelvis, in order to relieve pressure on the spine (fig. 84).[45] This idea, though ancillary to Scandinavian design as a whole in the 1970s, foretold the interest that would soon arise in "universal design," products meant to account for the physical capabilities of everyone, particularly aging Western populations.

The demand for efficient designs was high in the 1970s, but there was no dominant style. The notions of beauty as inherent in Good Design and of uniform, universal criteria had been exploded in the 1960s. The result was a plurality of styles whose numbers increased in the 1970s, reflecting the bewildering fragmentation of markets.

Functionalism itself became a look, one distinguished from others primarily by its past high reputation. Among corporations and upscale families worldwide, Knoll International found a ready market for its continued production of 1920s Bauhaus designs, and its success was marked by its opening of additional showrooms in capitals internationally. The esteem of this style in Japan is represented by the designs of the architect Shoei Yoh, who combined Knoll's

fig. 84 ▲ Peter Opsvik and Hans Christian Mengshoel, *Balans Variable* chair, 1979.

fig. 85 ► Studio Alchimia, poster for first *Bau.Haus* exhibition, 1979.

chairs by Le Corbusier and Mies van der Rohe from the interwar period with the Castiglionis' *Arco* lamp in his "House with a Cantilevered Roof" (fig. 83). Nevertheless, in the 1970s Japanese design was heterogeneous. Internationally-oriented designers such as Arata Isozaki and Shiro Kuramata conceived idiosyncratic, expressive furnishings that challenged mainstream modernism and even conventional furniture types (cat. 59). Their work was representative of a new subjectivity. Indeed, in 1973, the ICSID met in Japan and tackled "The Soul and Material Things," a topic indicating the issues in current design of meaning and culture amid the proliferation of products. (Given the world dominance of certain Japanese consumer-products companies, the concern was well located.)

In Japan, the United States, and Europe, functionalism received a new inflection in designs dubbed "High-Tech" in 1978 by the *New York Times* editors Joan Kron and Suzanne Slesin.[46] From desk lamps by Masayuki Kurokawa and Richard Sapper to new museum buildings, notably the Georges Pompidou Center in Paris by Renzo Piano and Richard Rogers, designs openly displayed their mechanical systems and factory-made ingredients. Metal and glass fixtures and furnishings in aggressive industrial shapes proclaimed the efficiency of homes and offices. This styling was far from the sleek streamlining of prewar designs or the anonymous "black box" industrial designs by Dieter Rams for Braun, which dominated the appearance of postwar German manufactures. The Castiglionis' *Boalum* lamp (cat. 50) frankly reveals it is an illuminated vacuum hose, while Gijs Bakker's *Paraplulamp* (cat. 58) combines an undisguised floodlamp with a shade based on a photographer's reflector. The leitmotif of all these works is honesty, superseding aesthetic appeal.

At the same time, pure geometry was presented in 1970s design not as a scientific or technological metaphor but as a personal, sculptural expression. The Platonic shapes of cone, cylinder, and hemisphere in Vico Magistretti's *Atollo* lamp (cat. 63) reflect no ideal reductivism, but the designer's skillful play with perception and conception. Similarly, Minimalist sculptors since the mid-1960s had taken modernist abstraction and reductivism to ever-more remote and

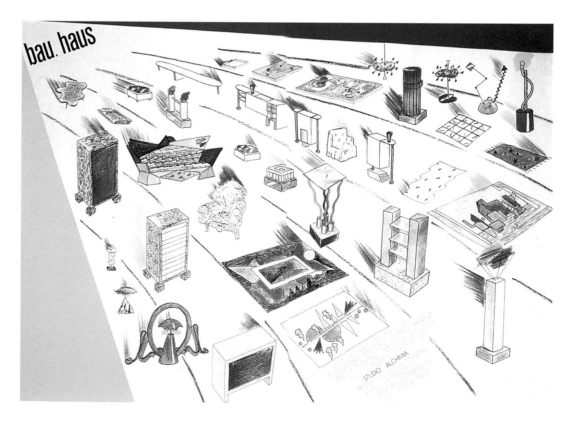

evanescent extremes. Yet as the differences between their cubes and grids became more refined, and their pursuit of theory to a logical end threatened to dematerialize the art object, they refocused attention—paradoxically—on themselves and the physical properties of their work. The exhaustion in art of the modernist quest for purification and the rebellion against art's commodification thus led to such wildly disparate movements as Earthworks (alterations of the landscape documented in photographs and videotapes) and Conceptual art (displays of words and objects intended to underline art's communication systems). Earthworks reflected the environmental interests emergent in the late 1960s, while Conceptual art drew on semiotics, the study of linguistic structures pioneered in the 1960s by French philosophers including Jacques Derrida, Roland Barthes, and Ferdinand de Saussure. In design as in art, the tools of semiotics and the shift of emphasis from unity to diversity of style, from function to meaning, served to make Post-Modernism a positive international movement by the early 1980s.

The defiance of tradition of the design group Studio Alchimia helped lay the groundwork for Post-Modernism in Italy. Founded in 1976 in Milan by Alessandro and Adriana Guerriero, the group included Alessandro Mendini as its chief theorist, as well as Andrea Branzi and Ettore Sottsass, all three of whom would become design celebrities in the 1980s. Alchemy (*alchimia* in Italian) is the age-old quest to turn base metals into gold: accordingly, the young radicals transformed common consumer objects by "redesigning them" (such as adding little flags to vacuum cleaners to stress their shape). And with similar mockery, the group staged an exhibition in 1979 that it called *Bau.Haus.* The hodgepodge of styles in its furnishings, as illustrated in one of its posters (fig. 85), tells all: the old hegemony of the chaste Bauhaus high style has ceded to polka-dotted bourgeois armchairs, Cubist sofas, and amoeboid coffee tables. Going further than designers had in the 1960s in adopting Pop idioms, Alchimia and other Anti-Design radicals not only attempted to ally high culture and mass culture but also to rehabilitate discredited or ignored older styles. Designers sought their audience directly, not through industry but through their own lively exhibitions and press coverage.

In 1979, the sixteenth Milan Triennale had a special section devoted to the theme "The Decorated House," the results of an international competition on "the home, after the functional." The same year, The Museum of Modern Art was half a century old. If modernism could be called middle-aged, its critic and successor, Post-Modernism, was about to be born.

Jonathan **De Pas**,
Donato **D'Urbino**,
Paolo **Lomazzi**,
and Carla **Scolari**

48. **Chair: *Joe***

Designed 1970
Polyurethane foam, leather upholstery
94 x 191 x 120 cm
Produced by Poltronova S.p.A (Montale Pistoia, Italy),
1970 to the present
D95.163.1, gift of Eleanore and Charles Stendig
in memory of Eve Brustein and Rose Stendig*

Named in honor of the famed home-run hitter Joe
DiMaggio, this giant baseball glove offers luxuriously
ample and soft seating with an insouciant sports
motif. A real baseball glove in a living room would
have been considered tasteless in the 1950s, but
in the 1960s and early 1970s it appealed to youth-
conscious consumers for that very reason and for
the humor of its transformation into a gigantic seat,
wide enough for two. The leather chair faithfully
reproduces a baseball glove, including the label,
but instead of presenting DiMaggio's signature,
it bears that of the designers.

Like many progressive Italians, De Pas, D'Urbino,
Lomazzi, and Scolari were fascinated by American

popular culture and by responses to it among
contemporary American artists. *Joe* evokes both a
sport identified with the United States and the soft,
sewn sculptures of common objects conceived by
Claes Oldenburg beginning in 1962 (fig. 86). Young
European designers were delighted by the work of
Oldenburg and fellow Pop artists, introduced to Europe
at the Venice Biennale in 1964, and also by American
theorists of mass culture such as Robert Venturi,
whose *Complexity and Contradiction in Architecture*
(1966) trumpeted the efficacy and appeal of vernacular
signs and artifacts. In the late 1960s, many were
passionately contesting traditions of all kinds, and
they found the defiance of the Americans liberating.

Joe is the best-known design by De Pas,
D'Urbino, Lomazzi, and Scolari, and reflects their
concern for socio-cultural symbolism in furnishings
and architecture. They had also designed the
transparent *Blow* of 1967 (cat. 43), the first fully
inflatable chair to reach commercial production,
but such works became less typical of them in the
1970s than their modular designs such as folding
furniture in wood and canvas, and the *Jointed* drawer
system. The evolution of their design from comic
seating to more practical, space-saving devices
reflects the new spirit of social responsibility
widespread by the mid-1970s. Thus *Joe*, despite
its date of 1970, could be seen as the end of an
era rather than the beginning of a new decade.

fig. 86 ▲ William Kessler & Associates, living room in the Walter O. Briggs III house, L'Arbre Croche, Michigan, 1973, showing
a boy sitting in the *Joe* chair, and the Aarnio *Pastille* chairs.

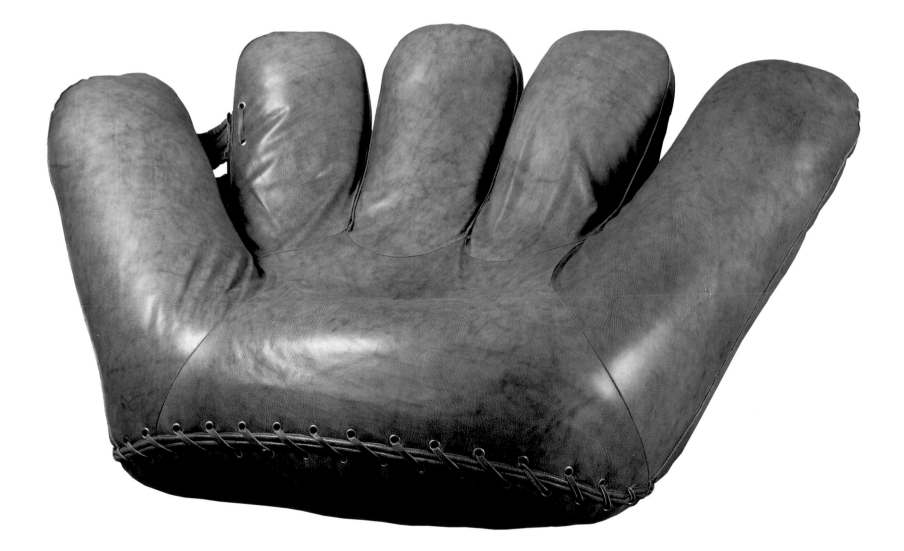

Guido **Drocco** and Franco **Mello**

49. **Coat/hat stand:** *Cactus*
Designed 1972
Painted polyurethane foam, steel
168.4 x 71.8 x 63.2 cm
Produced by Gufram s.r.l. (Balangero, Italy),
1972 to the present
D91.371.1, anonymous gift

Cactus is a Dadalike object, but one that functions. Man Ray's nail-covered flatiron, for example, is not for pressing shirts, but clothes might hang on this stand since its "barbs" are rounded. *Cactus* is also recognizable as the kitschy symbol of the American Southwest, a cowboy world coopted in "spaghetti Westerns" made by Italian filmmakers beginning in the 1960s. In proposing a cactus for a home or office, Drocco and Mello thus had their tongues in both cheeks: the imitativeness of their coat/hat stand was transgressive compared to earlier standards of Good Design, and doubly so in its populist sources. "The attitude toward design during this period," Drocco recalled, "was closely linked to the Italian cultural experience of 1968 [the year of widespread youth rebellions], which was contesting rule-based attitudes. So it was that free rein was given to imagination, to transposing functions, to the 'idea' idea."[47] This stand can support coats and hats thanks to its steel frame, but more important than its function is its easily readable form. Indebted to the ironies of Pop art, such a furnishing reveals the interest in cultural communication codes that evolved in the 1960s and that obviously did not die with that decade. It is no surprise to find *Cactus* among plastic lamps shaped like geese and cartoon characters in sophisticated interiors even in the early 1980s (fig. 87).

The manufacturer Gufram made its debut in the early 1970s with such novel products as *Cactus*— half furniture, half artwork—and marketed many of them as limited editions. In this way, it responded to the wider, younger audience for contemporary art that Pop had helped to create. These buyers, who wanted to defy what they saw as the bourgeois good taste of their parents, sought out the most challenging and the most amusing art and design.

fig. 87 ▲ Heller Designs, Inc., office of Alan J. Heller, New York, 1983.

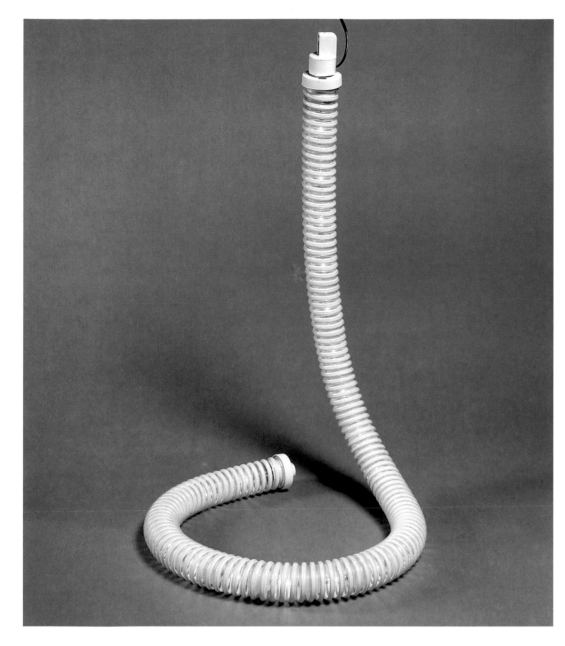

Livio **Castiglioni**
and Gianfranco **Frattini**

50. **Lamp: *Boalum***
Designed 1969-70
PVC plastic
190 x 7 x 7 cm
Produced by Artemide S.p.A. (Pregnana Milanese,
Italy), 1970-84; 1999 to the present
D97.161.1

The aesthetic born in the late 1960s of flexible,
unstructured, arrange-as-you-like designs climaxes
in these lamps. Each tubular module, containing
twenty bulbs, measures over six feet in length;
the system can comprise a maximum of seven
modules, and the lamp can be hung, draped, coiled,
fit into hard-to-light spaces, etc.[48] Few household
objects are more amusingly responsive to individual
tastes and needs.

    The idea for this snakelike light came from an
outdoor vacuum cleaner that Castiglioni and Frattini
saw used in a pool area and garden. The hose
fascinated them and, working with the technical staff
at Artemide, they devised a lighting system that had
the flexibility and simplicity of such a hose while also
providing light. Inside *Boalum*'s translucent plastic
tube is a double-spiral structure. The engineering
and material are industrial but, in use, *Boalum* softly
glows; as its name implies, it is a *boa* of *luminous*
charm for the owner to arrange.

    Although Livio Castiglioni generally worked
independently of his younger brothers, Achille and
Pier Giacomo, and specialized in electrical equipment
design, his lighting can be associated with theirs.
Like Achille and Pier Giacomo's *Arco* floor lamp
(cat. 27), *Boalum* solves a practical lighting problem
in a satisfyingly simple form.

fig. 88 ▲ Artemide, c. 1999 publicity photograph
showing *Boalum* lamps in a coiled arrangement.

Gaetano **Pesce**

51. **Armchair and ottoman: *Sit-Down***

Designed 1975
Polyurethane foam, plywood, Dacron upholstery
Armchair: 73 x 114 x 88 cm
Ottoman: 52 x 73 x 73 cm
Produced by Cassina S.p.A. (Meda Milano, Italy),
1975-80
D89.187.1-2, gift of Paul Pelletier

Large, low, amiably droopy, Pesce's armchair and
ottoman exaggerate the appearance of softness
and solace promised by conventional overstuffed
furniture. The inner plywood bases are invisible;
the foam itself is the support. To form the chair,
polyurethane foam was injected into a quilted polyester
upholstery sack that was hung over a simple plywood
frame roughly outlining the chair upside-down.
The foam expanded, filled the folds until they met
the walls of the back and seat, and then hardened.
Afterwards, the frame was unlocked, opened, and
removed. The foam body was then placed on a
plywood base. With this low-tech manufacturing
method, no two chairs, sofas, or ottomans in the
series are identical, although they are similar in
overall look and dimensions. The series was mass-
produced, but each buyer received a unique object.

Sit-Down thus represents Pesce's rebellion
against the most common results of functionalism—
what he saw as the alienating uniformity of products.
At the same time, the seating represents the realization
of certain functionalist ideals: it exploits the potential
of new materials; it is economical to make (compared
to expensive thermoset plastics); and it went into
large-scale commercial production. But Sit-Down
counters the stiff Platonic forms of functionalist
design with its pudginess and faintly Victorian
associations. As homey and comforting as a tea cosy,
the chair challenges the neutrality of Modernist
design and the flippancy of much Pop expression
with a deeper emotional appeal. Here Pesce shows
his kinship with Oldenburg, whose work he admired;
he does not imitate the American's copying of common
objects but, instead, evokes the humanoid, baggy
softness of his anti-monumental sculptures (fig. 89).

Today Pesce maintains an interrogatory position
in the design profession: he sees himself as an artist
and provocateur, and he designs objects not for
their relation to architecture and utility, but for their
potential for self-expression and their "aptitude for
meaning."[49] Thus Sit-Down's fabric pattern, designed
by Pesce, may conjure up clouds, camouflage, or
aerial maps, and its scattered irregularity suits
the individualized forms of each chair.

fig. 89 ▲ Claes Oldenburg, *Ice Bag Scale A*, 1970, displayed at the Art and Technology Pavilion,
World's Fair, Osaka, Japan, 1970.

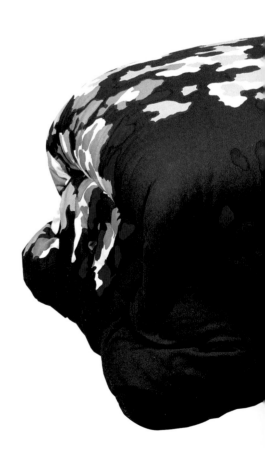

52. **Lounge chair and ottoman:** *Soriana*

Designed 1970
Plywood, chrome-plated steel, polyurethane foam,
Dacron fiberfill, synthetic velour upholstery
Lounge chair: 72.5 x 90 x 130 cm
Ottoman: 40.5 x 88.5 x 80 cm
Produced by Cassina S.p.A. (Meda Milano, Italy),
1970 to the present
D99.131.1-2

The innovation of this seating lies not in its form but in its radically simple upholstery system. Traditional upholstered chairs are wood frames with wire seats, laboriously layered with padding and then covered with hand-sewn, wrinkle-free fabric. For the *Soriana*, however, polyurethane foam is set on a plywood base and topped with Dacron fiberfill and then a loosely shaped cover of cloth or leather. The seating takes its final form from an external steel wire frame, which pinches its plump shapes at the front and back. The device is scarcely more complex than the clips used by hippies to shape their flowing garments. Indeed, the *Soriana* furniture (Italian for *tabby cat*) has some of the appeal of that casual lifestyle, which survived well into the 1970s: the soft, low-slung chaise longue and ottoman are as unpretentious in form as they are in assembly. The armchair in the line won the Compasso d'Oro in 1970, with a citation commending the "notable simplicity and consistency of its construction."

The Scarpas, a husband and wife team who designed for Cassina from 1963 onward, responded to the informality of culture in the 1960s and 1970s. Nevertheless, such works indicate no radicalism on their part. All their furnishings show their preference for simple, low, bulky forms and their taste for velours and leather, which associates them with the luxurious side of Italian design.

fig. 90 ▲ Living area in an unidentified Italian residence, c. 1970-73, showing the *Soriana* sofa in leather.

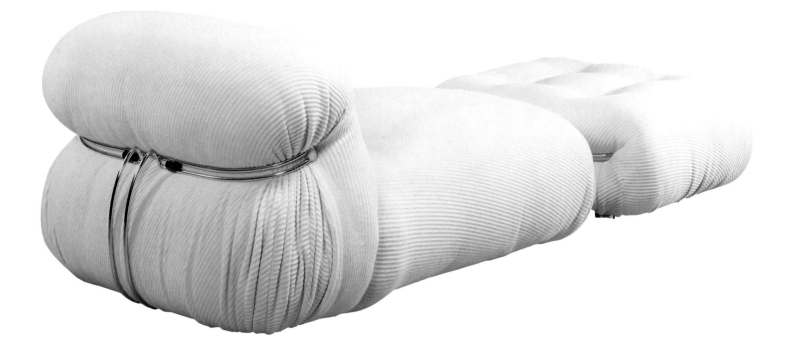

Oscar and Ana Maria **Niemeyer**

53. **Lounge chair and ottoman**

Designed 1972
Stainless steel, aluminum, polyurethane foam,
wool upholstery
Lounge chair: 67 x 77.5 x 104.1 cm
Ottoman: 27.9 x 76.8 x 76.8 cm
Produced by Mobilier International (Paris, France),
1972-78
D97.105.1-2

The architect Oscar Niemeyer, best known as the architect of Brasilia, the new capital city of his native Brazil, designed furniture for manufacture late in his career and in collaboration with his daughter Ana Maria. This chair and ottoman are close in date to their first chair design, around 1972 when they were in Paris; and like all his furnishings and much of his building, the work pushes the limits of its materials. A single wide band of stainless steel connects the bulky tufted cushions of the chair back and seat, and acts as the chair's support, a combination suggesting

resilience and comfort. The ottoman rests on a low curve of the same kind of band, one inspired by Scandinavian experiments with molded plywood. The gleaming metal lifts the squarish cushions slightly off the floor and they seem to float, despite their large size and apparent weight. "What attracts me is not the right angle. Nor the hard and inflexible straight line created by man," Niemeyer wrote. "What attracts me is the free, sensual curve. The curve that I find in the mountains of my country, in the sinuous course of its rivers, in the clouds of the sky and in the body of the woman I love."[50] Likewise, when he described his *Memorial to Latin America* in São Paulo, he could have been referring to this furniture: "This is architecture reduced to two or three elements. Clear, simple, and different. There is a search for beauty in these curving, sensual surfaces, in the thicknesses of the slabs and supports. . . ."[51] The contrasts within this elemental seating are aspects of Niemeyer's architecture, for the plays of concave and convex, solid and void, light-reflecting sculptural forms and shadows characterize his close to sixty-year career.

fig. 91 ▲ Niemeyer, sitting area in the Monument for Juscelino Kubitschek, Brasilia, Brazil, 1980, showing the lounge chairs.

Frank O. **Gehry**

54. **Chair:** *Easy Edges*

Designed 1972
Corrugated cardboard
83 x 38 x 61 cm
Produced by Stitch Pack Co., Inc. (Toronto, Ontario,
Canada), 1972; by Vitra GmbH (Basel, Switzerland),
1986 to the present
D92.213.1, gift of Luc d'Iberville-Moreau

The humor of transforming a chair or stool into a
ribbon and the daring of constructing it solely of
undisguised cardboard give the *Easy Edges* series
an impudent charm. This furniture made Gehry
a design celebrity across the United States earlier
than his architecture did. Introduced in 1972, the
seventeen pieces in the *Easy Edges* line present
open, graphic silhouettes, some of which refer
playfully to conventional furniture types. The pieces
were affordable, costing only $35 to $100, thanks
to their inexpensive material and simple, assembly-
line fabrication. Layers stamped out of single-ply
sheets were stacked together and glued with their
corrugations running at right angles to each other,
the method of plywood manufacture. The resulting
material is so strong that several *Easy Edges* chairs

could support a Volkswagen, as was advertised in
the manufacturer's brochure (fig. 92).

Cardboard furniture had been designed in
the 1960s as a cheap, lightweight, and disposable
alternative to standard forms. But plastics, stronger
and equally light, then proved more popular than
the paper product. In the 1970s, however, the energy
crisis and resultant limits to mass-market plastics
manufacture made social conscience a major keynote
of design. Gehry's line satisfied this concern,
while being affordable and attractive. Cardboard
seems even more low-end than plywood, and its
ridged brown surfaces resemble corduroy.
Furthermore, this decade realized the limits of
natural resources such as old-growth forests and,
accordingly, cardboard won high points as a furniture
material since it can be made from recycled paper.

The environment was not Gehry's inspiration
for this line, however. Rather, it grew out of both
his need to design cheap, disposable furniture
for a store display and his response to the ideas
for cardboard chairs of his friend, the light artist
Robert Irwin. Having evolved the line with these
practical and personal considerations, Gehry then
saw its broader benefits to consumers. But he
discontinued it when he felt it was stealing time
and identity from his architectural practice.

fig. 92 ▲ Frank O. Gehry and Associates, c. 1972 publicity
photograph showing a Volkswagen supported
by test versions of *Easy Edges* chairs.
fig. 93 ▶ Frank O. Gehry and Associates, living room in
the architect's house, Santa Monica, California, c. 1977-78,
showing *Easy Edges* coffee tables and stool.

Frank O. **Gehry**

55. Lounge chair: *Experimental Edges: Bubbles*
Designed 1979
Laminated corrugated cardboard, wood
91.5 x 70.6 x 198 cm
Produced by New City Editions (Venice, CA, USA),
1979-86
D93.271.1, gift of Caroline Moreau

Experimental Edges, Gehry's second series of corrugated cardboard furniture, has little in common with its predecessor, his *Easy Edges*, beyond its material of corrugated cardboard. These new, shaggy, sprawling sculptural forms are unlike the taut, linear earlier pieces and, moreover, the *Experimental Edges* series was a limited production, sold not through department store chains but in a few art galleries. Thus the two series can be seen to reflect the alternating currents in Gehry's architecture and design, as he has sometimes sought his audience in a circle of art collectors and vanguard artist-friends, and at other times pursued his liberal concern for the broad public. Nevertheless, both these lines have a high art component—the challenge of the material— and it dominates *Experimental Edges*, a title that announces Gehry's motivation for the series.

After putting aside the *Easy Edges* line to concentrate on architectural projects and interiors, Gehry did not return to furniture design until he saw a new artistic challenge: how to handle the type of large-fluted cardboard used in hollow-core doors, and how best to stack chunks or sheets of the material upon each other. The examples presented here suggest the range of expression possible with the knife-cut cardboard: the lounge chair amplifies the ribboning of *Easy Edges*, whereas the armchair and ottoman parody the ballooning forms of overstuffed chairs.

In these furniture series as in his architecture, Gehry takes a common industrial material (cardboard, plywood, chainlink fencing) and reconfigures it, working rather like the sculptors Richard Serra and Eva Hesse, who evolved their forms in the 1960s through the process of exploring new materials. Whatever Gehry's choice of substance, it retains its original, somewhat abrasive identity yet gains new life in his spirited designs. In general, his materials add a funky, downscale air to his work, which is intellectually provocative and anti-elitist.

Frank O. **Gehry**

56. Armchair and ottoman:
Experimental Edges: Little Beaver
Designed 1979
Corrugated cardboard
Armchair: 86.3 x 85.6 x 104.1 cm
Ottoman: 43.2 x 49.5 x 55.9 cm
Produced by New City Editions (Venice, CA, USA),
1986-88; by Vitra GmbH (Basel, Switzerland),
1987 to the present
D92.132.1-2

Peter **Danko**

57. **Armchair**
Designed 1976
Oak-faced poplar plywood, polyurethane foam,
wool upholstery
79.4 x 55.1 x 61.5 cm
Produced by Peter Danko (Alexandria, VA, USA),
1976-80, 1982; by Thonet Industries, Inc.
(York, PA, USA), 1980-81
D82.115.1, gift of Peter Danko

This is the first American mass-produced chair to be constructed from a single piece of laminated bentwood. In its simple construction and overt display of it, and its use of almost all of the original plywood sheet, the chair satisfies basic tenets of the Modernist movement, as well as the ecological consciousness of the 1970s. Even the portion of wood cut away from the front legs was put to use, as the foundation for the upholstered seat. The core plywood is poplar, which is light and economical yet strong; the face veneer here is oak, while choices of walnut or cherry were also available. The chair was made without joints, in a single gluing and bending process that Danko patented in 1980, the same year that the American branch of Thonet began manufacturing it. Except for attaching the seat, no screws or other joining elements were used.

The sturdiness of Danko's chair, as well as its open, ribbony silhouette, recall the achievements of Aalto and the Eameses in laminated-wood chairs from the 1930s through the 1950s. And its single-piece construction recalls the work of the British Modernist, Gerald Summers, in the 1930s. Danko's concern for the everyday client is also similar. For example, his seating does not require a chair rail to protect the wall from scrapes because of the extension of the back legs.

Gijs **Bakker**

58. **Table lamp:** *Paraplulamp*
Designed 1973
Chrome-plated steel, rayon
72.4 x 22.9 x 22.9 cm
Produced by Artimeta (Heerlen, the Netherlands),
1973-89
D93.207.1, gift of Helen Williams Drutt English
in honor of the Emmy Van Leersum retrospective

The shade of this lamp resembles an umbrella
(*paraplu* in Dutch), and it opens on the same
principle, but Bakker has actually adapted studio
photography equipment and put it to domestic
lighting purposes. Photographers use such reflector
shades to reduce harsh shadows and create even
ambient lighting, but whereas they attach the
adjustable devices and their floodlights to poles with
clunky metal clips, Bakker has designed an elegant
wire cage for the *Paraplulamp* to support the

floodlight bulb. Its glistening openwork contrasts
with the swelling shape of the five-ribbed reflector,
and the beauty of these elements contrasts with
the readymade nature of the undisguised bulb.
Thus, the lamp might seem both at home and slightly
incongruous in a residence or office.

Bakker began his career as a jeweler (and he
continues to design jewelry), which accounts in part
for the refinement of *Paraplulamp*'s chromed base;
and he created the lamp while he was teaching design
in metal and plastics at the Art Academy in Arnhem,
the Netherlands. At the beginning of the 1990s, he
helped found the Dutch collaborative called Droog
Design, which specializes in finding new uses for
familiar, often readymade objects—an interest this
lamp and Bakker's witty and surprising jewelry
foretell. In some of his necklaces of the 1980s,
for example, he laminated photographs under plastic
and added gold or precious stones, a juxtaposition
of "low" and "high" materials that provoked thought
about the nature of preciousness in jewelry.

Shiro **Kuramata**

59. **Chests of drawers: *Side I, Side 2* (*Furniture in Irregular Forms*)**

Designed 1970
Ebonized and lacquered ash, brushed steel
Side 1: 170 x 44.7 x 60.5 cm
Side 2: 170 x 63 x 49.7 cm
Produced by Fujiko (Tokyo, Japan), c. 1970-75;
by Cappellini International Interiors (Arosio, Italy),
1986 to the present
D91.414.1-2

With the fastidious craftsmanship for which Japanese design is famous, this pair of curvilinear chests is fashioned of ebonized and lacquered ash, joining tradition with a contemporary reconception of storage furniture. The two pieces are as dizzying as objects seen in a fun-house mirror. Tall and narrow, they barely seem to stand securely. Do they fit together? Not conventionally. The swelling bombé front of

Side 2 fits only into the side of *Side 1*, thus defying traditional construction based on efficient use of materials and space, and making it impossible to open one set of drawers. The casters confirm that the owner is free to invent changing configurations for the pair.

Furniture as art objects, reflecting the designer's fantasy and unconscious, had been explored by Surrealist artists in the 1930s. Furthermore, furniture by artists reappeared in the 1960s, as functionalism came under fire and vanguard art mixed previously "low" and "high" genres, leaping the barriers between media. Kuramata, who opened his own office in Tokyo in 1965, was aware of contemporary experiments, especially in Italy and the United States, and that spirit —if not its forms—inspired him to invent the designs he put into limited production. Here he indulges his childhood fascination with drawers as containers for hidden treasures (this pair offers thirty-six), and in earlier works he stacked drawers in pyramidal chests or used them to occupy the empty spaces under chair seats.

fig. 94 ▲ Cappellini, c. 1990 publicity photograph showing the *Side 1, Side 2* chest of drawers in a nightclub setting.

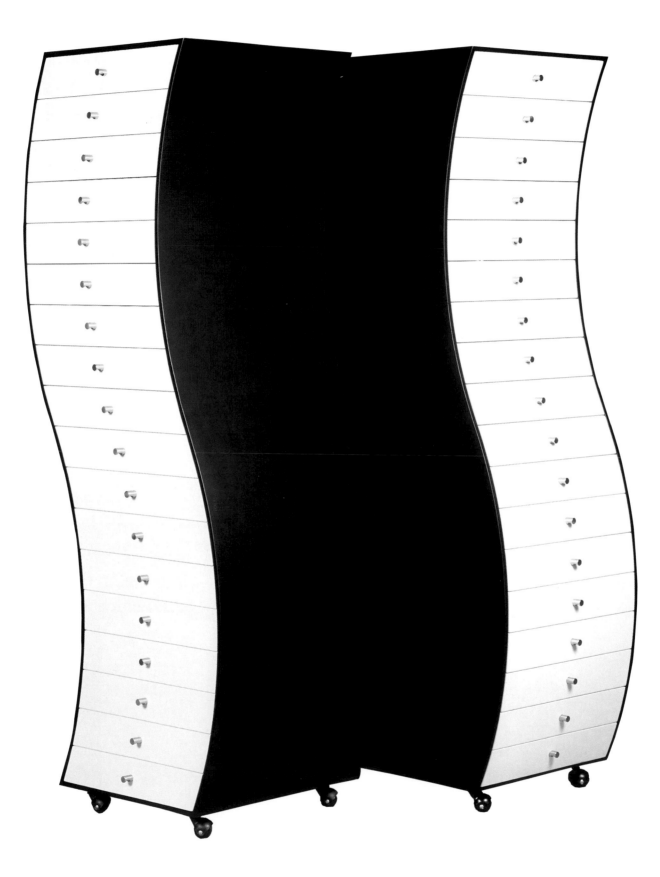

Vico **Magistretti**

60. **Armchair:** *Vicario*

Designed 1970
Fiberglass-reinforced polyester
68.4 x 72 x 65.5 cm
Produced by Artemide S.p.A. (Pregnana Milanese,
Italy), 1971-93
D91.379.1, gift of Artemide Ltée

The Italians' preeminence in furniture design in plastics continued into the 1970s, as seen in *Vicario* (*Vicar*). The armchair typifies Magistretti's style in its assertive, low-slung silhouette, rounded edges, and fluid shapes. The vertical indentations in the legs, S-shaped in section, were first introduced by Magistretti in his *Stadio 80* table of 1967 (fig. 95) as a way of strengthening the form. Then he employed them in his *Selene* stacking chair of 1968, the *Vicario*'s predecessor. Both of these chairs are innovative as stackable forms made of fiberglass-reinforced polyester stamped out of a single mold. Although more conservative in structure than Panton's cantilevered plastic chair (cat. 36), Magistretti's chairs and table provided mix-and-match versatility to a chic international clientele.

The competition to design and produce the first single-mold stackable chair in plastic had been won by Verner Panton with his chair of 1960-67. But the economies enjoyed by the Scandinavians and Italians in using a single mold were limited by the energy crisis that began in 1973. With oil prices skyrocketing, plastics (which are petroleum-based) became too expensive for the mass market that had originally enriched Artemide and other manufacturers. Some designs were taken out of production or were adjusted to use less material. Some manufacturers substituted lighter grades of plastics. In cases such as *Vicario*, the increased cost was passed on to consumers.

fig. 95 ▲ John Guest, living area of the architect's home, Kensington, London, showing Magistretti's *Vicario* armchairs and a *Stadio 80* coffee table.

fig. 96 ▲ Piretti, 1970 publicity photograph showing *Plia* folding chairs.

Giancarlo **Piretti**

61. **Chair:** *Plona*

Designed 1970
Aluminum, methacrylate
71.7 x 68 x 56 cm
Produced by Anonima Castelli (Milan, Italy), 1970-86
D87.183.1

Plona is more unusual in form than its older sibling, Piretti's famed *Plia* chair, 1968 (fig. 96), but the two designs should be judged together because of their shared ingredients. Both parade the transparency and pliancy of the plastic methacrylate, and its contrast with the chair's shining aluminum frame. Both fold and stack, relying on an ingenious, round hinge linking their seats and U-shaped legs. Both are elegant, dematerialized, silver-edged minimalist settings to show off sitters from back and front, reflecting the enduring Pop taste for alluring see-through fashions. Intended to replace folding card-table chairs as additional seating, these chairs epitomize the stylishness and technical invention that made Italian design famous from the 1960s through the 1970s.

Plona never saw the mass production of *Plia* (over six million by 1999), but it reveals that Piretti had not exhausted his geometric vocabulary. Indeed, *Plona* offers an all-in-one form for seat and back, reducing the chair elements from four to three, and reveals the moldable nature of methacrylate in its deep, round indentation. The name is Piretti's combination of *pliante* (French for *folding*) and *poltrona* (Italian for *easy chair*).[52] Piretti's next variant on the form, using the same hinge, was a folding desk he called *Platone* (1971), where a flat writing surface replaced the hollowed-out seat. All three designs are lightweight and strong enough for both indoor and outdoor use.

Cesare (Joe) **Colombo**

62. **Bar stool:** *Birillo*

Designed 1970
Chrome-plated steel, fiberglass, rubber,
polyurethane foam, vinyl upholstery
96.5 x 43.2 x 49.2 cm
Produced by Zanotta S.p.A. (Nova Milanese, Italy),
1970 to the present
D92.159.1, gift of Muriel Kallis Newman*

Colombo's design of this bar stool typically combines
visual wit and functionalism. *Birillo* (*Bowling Pin* in
Italian) looks like a cartoon version of one: the stool
back is a tiny disc, juxtaposed to the big, rounded
squares of the seat and the rubber-ringed base.
The X-shaped housing on this base conceals fully
rotating wheels, allowing the chair to be moved
easily. Once the user sits down, however, the rubber
of the base grips the floor and the stool becomes
stationary. The seat rotates with automatic return,
acknowledging that ease in getting on and off is
as important as back support. At the same time,
the svelte design, with its contrast of leather-like vinyl
and chromed steel, redolent of automobile styling,
is attractive enough to enhance the aura of a public
space like a bar or café.

In the same series, Colombo designed small
armchairs, a low table, and a low stool. He intended
them for offices as well as bars, assuming that the
look of smooth, rounded geometries and polished
industrial materials would equally suit work and play.
In this multi-use conception, Colombo remains part
of the Italian design generation of the late 1950s
and 1960s, whereas the Italian designers who
emerged later, like those of the Memphis group,
virtually ignored office furnishings.

fig. 97 ▲ Colombo's *Birillo* stools
in an unidentified Milanese bar.

Vico **Magistretti**

63. **Table lamp:** *Atollo*
Designed 1977
Lacquered aluminum
68 x 49.5 x 49.5 cm
Produced by O-Luce (Milan, Italy),
1977 to the present
D99.157.1

Like a drafting exercise, this lamp consists of three Euclidian solids: its base is a cylinder topped with a cone; its shade is a perfect hemisphere. Seen head on, the cone tip precisely abuts the hemisphere in an apparent balancing act. Like the American Minimalist sculptors Donald Judd, Dan Flavin, and Larry Bell of the 1960s, Magistretti plays in *Atollo* with the differences between what we know about geometry and what we see of it in a manufactured object. We assume cones, cylinders, and spheres are simple, solid, and invariable, but here they look mysterious and airborne: the lampshade, unless viewed from below, appears to hover unsupported above its pointed base (though it is actually held on an aluminum rod). Like other high-tech designers of the 1970s, Magistretti demonstrates that geometries are not absolute (as they seemed to be for earlier, functionalist designers) but are as idiosyncratic as any other form language. The loss of faith in such earlier certainties was a by-product of the cultural revolutions of the 1960s; their positive legacy in the 1970s was a pluralism of values and tastes. In Richard Sapper's *Tantalo* clock (fig. 98), for example, the cylindrical base is sliced at an angle for the clock's round face: this unitary geometric form seems humorously heliotropic, as if facing the sun.

Magistretti is well known thanks to the beige, sandy-surfaced *Atollo* (*Atoll* in Italian), which won the Compasso d'Oro in 1979. Its elemental, precisely poised forms can be found in his architecture, which he has pursued since the 1950s in the idiom of the International Style.

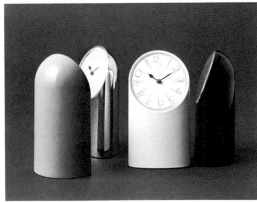

fig. 98 ▲ Artemide, c. 1971 publicity photograph showing Richard Sapper's *Tantalo* clocks.

Cesare (Joe) **Colombo**

64. **Cabinet: *Boby***

Designed 1970
ABS plastic, steel
73.5 x 43.4 x 42.7 cm
Produced by Bieffeplast (Caselle di Selvazzano, Italy),
1970 to the present
D99.136.1

Colombo's storage cabinets on castors became a must for trendy offices in the 1970s, particularly those of art directors and architects, and have remained so until the present. These modular, multi-use storage units were designed to be stacked to various heights, and they combined attractive styling and a variety of bright colors, all of which proved irresistible (fig. 100). In this example, three shallow, traylike drawers on one side swivel out for easy access, while shelves below them allow for open storage of larger items. On another side are middle-sized shelves; on the third side there is vertical storage of adjustable height; and the top has shallow divisions for the placement of frequently used implements. The neat cubic silhouettes of the closed cabinets convey efficiency, while the play of rectangles and curves, as well as pierced and closed surfaces, delights the eye.

Colombo's design was inspired by an all-metal draftsman's taboret, and it has been modified in molds and features over its years in production. (The European and American versions differ in drawer size, for example, to allow for different sizes of stationery.) The kinship of the cabinet with earlier and contemporary Italian designs in plastic is obvious: stackable housewares, such as Massimo Vignelli's table service of 1964 in Melamine (fig. 99), and stackable storage cabinets, like Anna Castelli Ferrieri's cylindrical units of 1970 (fig. 101), are also space savers, with rounded forms, squat proportions, and smooth, easy-care surfaces. The *Boby* cart transcends them, however, in its versatility. Colombo, who aspired to satisfy the maximum number of needs and consumers with all his designs, created a system used in homes and offices, laboratories, and hospitals. The name *Boby* came from the dog star of a French series of children's books: like man's best friend, the cart will follow you anywhere.

fig. 99 ▲ Massimo Vignelli, *Heller Designs* stacking dinnerware, 1964-72. Montreal Museum of Decorative Arts.

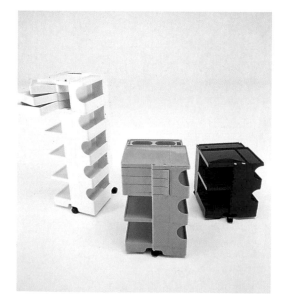

fig. 100 ▲ Bieffeplast, c. 1970 publicity photograph showing three versions of the *Boby* cabinet.

fig. 101 ▲ Anna Castelli Ferrieri, stacking storage units, 1970.

Mario **Bellini**

65. **Chair: Model no. 412, *Cab***

Designed 1976
Enameled steel, polyurethane foam, leather covering
80 x 47 x 42 cm
Produced by Cassina S.p.A. (Meda Milano, Italy),
1976 to the present
D93.254.1

This chair's leather envelope zippers over its legs like
a motorcyclist's pants—an innovation since zippers
had previously been used in furniture only for
slipcovers. The sleek saddle leather fully clothes
the chair's simple, welded-steel frame and slightly
softens its straight lines and right angles. (*Cab* is
short for *cabriolet*, an elegant, one-horse carriage
with a folding hood.) Neither conventionally
upholstered nor skeletally revealed, *Cab* is reductivist
in composition and conception, yet it does not look
stark. Earlier tubular steel furniture revealed its
structure as a point of principle and exploited the
contrast between metal and cover. But *Cab*'s frame

remains seductively concealed, while it displays
the beauty of its skin and the delicacy of its stitching
—evidence of Italy's traditional excellence in
leatherworking. Here and in other designs for
furniture, Bellini has been especially inventive.
In fact, in his 1965 design for the *932* armchair
he dispensed with structural support altogether:
the leather cushions of the legless chair were
held together by belts.

   Bellini's use of leather indicates that the high-end
client was still buying in the financially troubled
1970s. (Indeed, Armani leather coats and jackets,
as well as Gucci handbags and luggage, seemed
economy-proof.) This side chair, and a more
voluptuous armchair version, enjoy restrained
proportions; they do not look ostentatious, and their
simple lines recommend them for both home and
office use. Bellini employed what he called the
"stretched membrane" to cover both his furniture
and the business machines he designed. Under
this skin, products of complex function and myriad
miniature parts gained a similar sleek surface
and appealingly unitary form.

fig. 102 ▲ The *Cab* chair's steel frame and leather covering.

Mario **Bellini**

66. **Table lamp:** *Area 50*
Designed 1974
Iron, Makrolon plastic, fiberglass
50 x 44.5 x 44.5 cm
Produced by Artemide S.p.A.
(Pregnana Milanese, Italy), 1974-90
D91.369.1, gift of Artemide S.p.A.

67. **Wall or ceiling lamp:** *Area 50*
Designed 1974
Iron, Makrolon plastic, fiberglass
20 x 44.5 x 44.5 cm
Produced by Artemide S.p.A.
(Pregnana Milanese, Italy), 1974-90
D93.252.1, gift of Bernard François Marcil

68. **Floor lamp:** *Area 50*
Designed 1974
Iron, Makrolon plastic, fiberglass
210 x 50 x 50 cm
Produced by Artemide S.p.A.
(Pregnana Milanese, Italy), 1974-92
D91.368.1, gift of Artemide S.p.A.

Resembling folded paper or stiffened handkerchiefs, the squarish white shades of these lamps have the casual, throw-away charm that purposely unpretentious consumers came to prize by the early 1970s. The aesthetic of disposability had emerged in the previous decade, but these lamps are in fact sturdy and sensible. The head of the floor lamp tilts to direct the light, and the synthetic material used in all the shades is fire-resistant. The table lamp comes in three heights, and if all the models are used together, they create a harmonious and functional ensemble.

Multifaceted in his creativity, Bellini gives his lighting, furniture, and industrial products a low-key charm. He is best known as an industrial designer: from 1963 he was chief design consultant to Olivetti, the manufacturer of office machines, and from 1978 he worked with Renault on the company's automobiles. Underlying these activities, however, was his interest in the built environment as a whole, encompassing discrete objects. This social concern is a stance typical of the 1970s. Significantly, in 1981 he launched *Album*, an annual design magazine devoted to human activities rather than particular products (because products are necessarily "part of a wider system of objects, structures, and spaces").[53] This said, however, Bellini's designs—whether for lighting, office machines, furniture, or architecture—have a sensuous yet minimalist appeal in their own right, and are often innovative in their unexpected handling of materials, as can be seen in these lamps.

David **Rowland**

69. **Chair:** *Sof-Tech*

Designed 1979
Chrome-plated steel, PVC-covered steel
75.6 x 44.2 x 45.2 cm
Produced by Thonet Industries, Inc. (York, PA, USA),
1979-98
D86.124.1, gift of Thonet Industries, Inc.

Rowland tackled two interrelated problems in this lacy yet high-tech design for public seating: maximizing comfort and minimizing storage space. Conventional stacking chairs for mass use are thin but hard and uncomfortable, while padded chairs are thick and waste space. To assure resilient seating, Rowland invented and patented a new material for this chair's back and seat, a network of plastic-coated metal springs he called "Soflex," which move as the sitter changes position. The network is purposely open to allow air to circulate, eliminating the heat buildup that occurs with long sitting. For additional comfort, zippered seat and back sleeves with inner foam pads can be added. Because the seat and back are thinner than their frame, fifteen chairs when stacked on each other measure about three feet high. Another model has steel connectors on its back legs to allow ganging rows of chairs, and yet another variant has a finish strong enough for outdoor use.

In 1950-51, while a student at the Cranbrook Academy of Art, Rowland first experimented with webbed-wire seating: at that time he used the flat zigzag wire forms that are standard supports for upholstered furniture. The breakthrough came later when he dipped the wire in PVC, which added elasticity and thickness, and he then employed this material in conjunction with a lightweight steel frame. Another important precedent for the *Sof-Tech* chair is Rowland's *40 in 4* chair of 1963—a wire rod chair engineered with such precision that forty of them form a stack only four feet tall. Although both chairs are feats of functionalist design, they are also austerely elegant linear compositions in the spirit of Constructivist wire sculpture. Thonet adopted Rowland's design for the *Sof-Tech* chair: it was a logical extension of the firm's identification with mass-produced furniture in bent wood and metal, famed for its light weight and springiness.

fig. 103 ▲ *Sof-Tech* chairs in the restaurant of an unidentified office building, c. 1979.

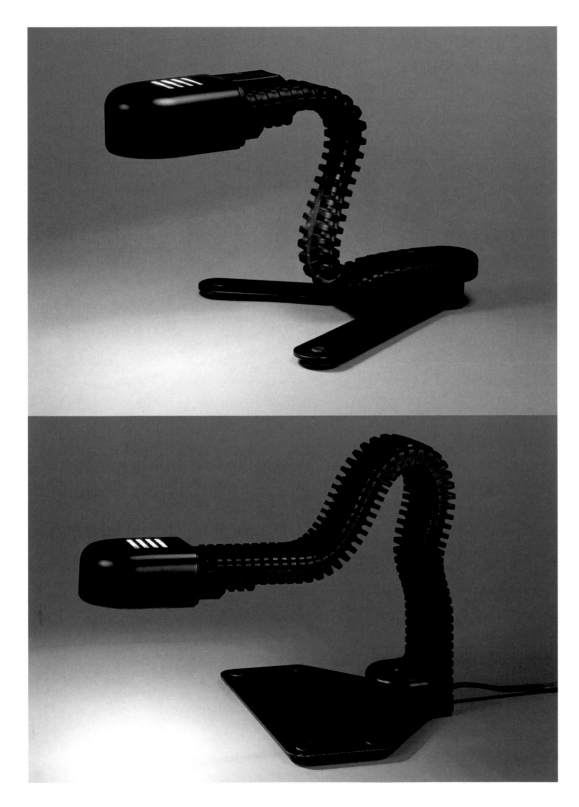

Masayuki **Kurokawa**

70. **Table lamp:** *Cobra*
Designed 1973
Neoprene, steel
Extended: 24 x 31 x 21 cm
Produced by Yamagiwa Corporation (Tokyo, Japan)
and Fuso Gomu Industry Company (Tokyo, Japan),
1973
D93.198.1, gift of Paul Leblanc

71. **Table lamp:** *Cobra*
Designed 1973
Neoprene, steel
Extended: 28 x 42 x 21 cm
Produced by Yamagiwa Corporation (Tokyo, Japan)
and Fuso Gomu Industry Company (Tokyo, Japan),
1973
D93.198.2, gift of Paul Leblanc

Flexibility is the keynote of these table lamps, as it
is of Castiglioni and Frattini's *Boalum* (cat. 50). But
the *Cobras'* adjustable, arching spines allow precise
control of the direction of the light, encouraging
a work station destination. The curving, snakelike
neck, which inspired the series' name, contrasts
with the hard geometric forms of the shade and the
rectangular and Y-shaped bases. Both lamps are
completely black, a somewhat ominous color choice
that became modish in 1970s high-tech design,
from business machines to household appliances.

In general, appliances designed by Kurokawa,
who trained as an architect, offer simple compact
shapes that convey an object's function. His quiet
pleasure in materials shows here in the contrast
between the mat Neoprene of the neck and
the shining metal shade and base. Reflecting his
primary interest in the sculptural aspect of lamps,
he remarked: "When a lighting fixture is turned on,
the fixture itself cannot be seen. The viewer just
sees the light. When the light is extinguished, only
the form is seen. It would be good if this dual aspect
could be shown more dramatically. . . . In my case,
I first think of a shape that I would like."[54]

Richard **Sapper**

72. **Table lamp:** *Tizio*

Designed 1972
Enameled aluminum, ABS plastic, Durethan plastic
Extended: 119 x 11 x 11 cm
Produced by Artemide S.p.A. (Pregnana Milanese,
Italy), 1972 to the present
D93.232.1

Weighted so that it rests in any position, Sapper's
Tizio is cantilevered over a small, swiveling, cylindrical
base. Thus this desk lamp offers easily adjustable
light and requires little space. Sapper balanced the
arms so adroitly at their two pivots that they require
no springs, and he used halogen lighting and a
transformer in the base to help reduce the bulk
of the structure. The small, high-intensity halogen
bulb requires such low voltage that the arms
themselves carry the current, eliminating the need
for wiring there. Halogen bulbs first appeared in
consumer lighting in the early 1970s. As a source
of longer-lasting, more intense, and purer white light
than incandescent bulbs, they were promoted for
their efficiency in that energy-conscious decade.
Their small size relative to conventional bulbs
of the same wattage allowed for smaller housings,
a feature that *Tizio* exploits. The lamp's thin skeleton
is enameled mat black with red accents at the pivots
and switch, thus resembling a cross between a
de Stijl sculpture and an oil-well pump. The lamp's
ultra-efficient appearance and easy functioning
made it an icon of its era—a status confirmed
by the Compasso d'Oro prize awarded to it in 1979.
Tizio means *Fellow* in Italian—suggesting its
friendliness in both the workplace and at home.

Giotto **Stoppino**

73. **Magazine rack**
Designed 1971
ABS plastic
44.5 x 40 x 27 cm
Produced by Kartell S.p.A. (Milan, Italy), 1971
to the present
D91.373.1, anonymous gift

Stoppino, like Gino Colombini, has gained international recognition for his household items through their fabrication and export by Kartell, Italy's foremost manufacturer in plastics. He designed for the company between 1968 and 1974. Sleek styling, utility, and affordable prices are at the core of Stoppino's designs. Indeed, the symmetry and streamlining of this magazine rack resulted in part from a desire for economy: to reduce the cost of its mold, it was originally made of two identical elements, held together inside at the top by a ring which also acts as a handle for lifting the rack. In 1987, the design was refined further to reduce costs, and the storage units are now made from a single mold.

The stairstep silhouette of the magazine rack is both functional and retrospective, recalling the setbacks of certain Art Deco skyscrapers. The reference was easy for Stoppino, who was already known in the 1950s for his Rationalist yet historicizing architecture and furniture design (produced in association with the architectural firm he founded with Vittorio Gregotti and Ludovico Meneghetti). Stoppino's design for this magazine rack is also prophetic of the architectural allusions of much design, especially in Italy, during the 1980s.

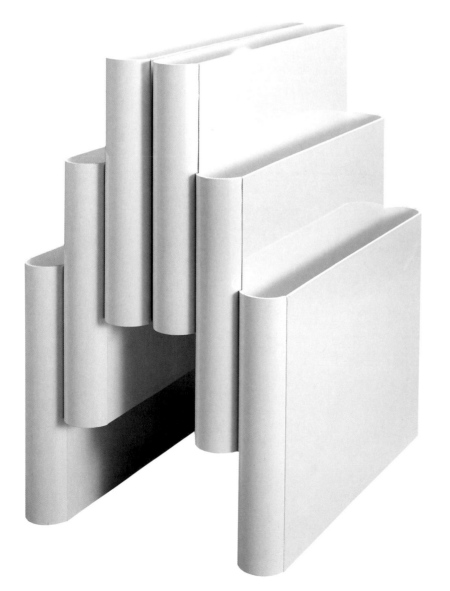

Studio 65

74. Chair: *Attica*

Designed 1972
Polyurethane, polyurethane foam, cotton upholstery
64.4 x 70.8 x 70.8 cm
Produced by Gufram s.r.l. (Balangero, Italy), 1986
D94.144.1, gift of Eleanore and Charles Stendig
in memory of Eve Brustein and Rose Stendig*

Attica is one of many imaginative designs resulting
from the partnership of manufacturers and designers
in Italy. It is also part of the international drive to
invent single-mold seating, and its fluted shape
shows the detail possible in plastic, detail that would
be more difficult to achieve in other furniture
materials. The reference of its name, *Attica,* is to the
mainland of Greece, where the Doric style originated.
However, the reference to a column is more parodic
than archaeological. In fact, the mold for this design
came from an earlier chair, the *Capitello* of 1971,
which featured an overscale, scrolled Ionic capitol
on the same fluted shaft. For a design exhibition
of 1972 organized on the theme of the home, a giant
Ionic column base served as a walk-in display house
and contained a sofa of gargantuan volutes in
polyurethane (fig. 104).[55]

Studio 65, founded by five architecture and art
students in Turin in 1965, was an Anti-Design
collaborative like Superstudio and Archizoom, and its
adaptation of classical elements was ironic in 1972,
in light of that generation's general attacks on Italian
monuments in the late 1960s. The angled cut
of *Attica*, necessary to provide a shallow back for
the chair, may also suggest it is a broken column
—a funerary symbol in Romantic art. Such styling
forecasts the tongue-in-cheek revival of classical
and other high-art idioms made by Post-Modern
designers in the 1980s. In fact, Gufram's decision
in 1986 to produce the 1972 design in a limited
edition doubtless reflects *Attica*'s renewed topicality.

fig. 104 ▲ Studio 65, *Babilonia 72* display at the fourth Eurodomus exhibition, Turin, 1972, showing an Ionic-style sofa.

The 1980s
Post-Modernism

THE EXTRAORDINARY EXUBERANCE OF THE STOCK MARKET DURING THE 1980S AFFECTED DESIGN WORLD-wide. As in the gay nineties of the nineteenth century, consumption was extraordinarily conspicuous. Just as the "robber barons" of the Gilded Age monopolized industries and bought up European culture by the box-carload, now the junk-bond traders of Wall Street and the yuppies of Margaret Thatcher's deregulated United Kingdom agreed that "greed is good" and that owning eye-catching vanguard design and art (among other luxury items) was a badge of success.

Despite the oil embargo that made 1980 a year of global recession, and despite the widening gap between rich and poor in the United States exacerbated by Ronald Reagan's laissez-faire economic policies, the overall market for design and its abundance of diverse styles during the decade seemed unaffected. The AIDS virus (identified in 1981) took an epidemic death toll among designers, artists, and architects, but design creativity itself seemed unlimited. The fall of the Berlin Wall in 1989 symbolized the triumph of capitalism over Communism. Even in Russia, materialism was embraced as the new religion.

The designers who had come of age in the Swinging Sixties and joined Anti-Design movements in the 1970s were now mature. Younger colleagues from different countries gathered around them, and they formed groups and firms of international influence, some with offices in far-flung capitals. Borders between media were also fluid: architects designed objects, artists contributed to design projects and exhibitions, and also designed art furniture, and designers of one-of-a-kind pieces prospered. Gloria Vanderbilt had already designed jeans; now the architect Michael Graves designed the best-selling *Bird* tea kettle (1985), and couturiers splashed their initials on handbags, scarves, and perfume bottles, and widely licensed their names for ready-to-wear lines, appealing to spendthrift status-seekers.

The plurality of styles and groups loosely gathered under the label of Post-Modernism created the tenor of the 1980s. Practitioners saw design and architecture as free of any necessary responsibilities to functionalism and social utility. They looked outward rather than up to some ideal; their model was not the engineer, the technician, or the utopian city planner, but the social critic, the anthropologist, the psychologist, the artist—as well as the fashion consultant, media observer, and pollster, some observers sniffed. Post-Modern attitudes were ironic, sometimes critical toward their audiences and their artistic sources but, most often, witty, learned, and playful. It is no wonder that they made design a popular commodity and a subject for wide debate. Although the affiliations and exhibitions of Post-Modernism were often international, their scavenging took directions that suggest national tendencies. Named and given a history by Charles Jencks in his books of 1975 and 1977, and ratified by the 1980 Venice Biennale with its exhibitions of Post-Modern architecture and "Banal Objects," Post-Modernism dominated most art media of the 1980s, although it began to fracture into other tendencies by the end of the decade.

Emblematic of Post-Modernism was Philip Johnson and John Burgee's AT&T building in New York City, begun in 1978 and completed in 1982 (fig. 105). Johnson, who with Henry-Russell Hitchcock had defined the International Style in 1932, here embraced Post-Modernism with the icon of a skyscraper with a Chippendale pediment and a porticoed Renaissance entrance. Johnson had deserted the cause, and this caused great consternation to the followers of the traditional Modernist canon. This building and others established that overt historical references and decoration, previously anathema to functionalists, were now permitted. Post-Modernism was elected the new style of choice for corporate structures throughout the world, and for their interior design and furnishings. Even Knoll International hedged its longtime bet on the International Style, and its new owners commissioned the Post-Modern firm of Venturi, Rauch & Scott Brown to design its new showroom in New York. In the 1980s, Knoll introduced furniture lines by Robert Venturi and Denise Scott Brown, Ettore Sottsass, and Frank Gehry to

fig. 105 ▶ Philip Johnson and John Burgee, AT&T building, New York, 1978-82.

revitalize the company (while it continued to produce many modernist classics by Mies van der Rohe, Marcel Breuer, Eero Saarinen, and Harry Bertoia, which have remained in production right up to the present).

Post-Modern styles inspired immediate interest, for many Americans had always hungered for exuberant decoration. In an acerbic tract of 1981 on modern building, Tom Wolfe caught the paradox in corporate America's acceptance of Rationalist architecture, observing that "every great law firm in New York moves without a sputter of protest into a glass-box office building with concrete slab floors and seven-foot-ten-inch-high concrete slab ceilings and plasterboard walls and pygmy corridors—and then hires a decorator and gives him a budget of hundreds of thousands of dollars to turn these mean cubes and grids into a horizontal fantasy of a Restoration townhouse."[56] In the 1980s, innovative architecture and design celebrated historical fantasy and also appealed to a broad public. Visual references drawn from popular culture, daily life, and art and architectural history gave context and multiple layers of meaning to Post-Modern objects. Functionalism became a secondary issue, at best.

Some of Post-Modernism's origins lay in the 1960s, in Pop art's assimilation of styles and motifs from contemporary commercial culture, but past high art styles as well as kitsch expressions were also welcomed. The targeted consumer was not liberal youth but the well-heeled yet avant-garde Establishment. In the United States, the movement is most associated with the buildings and furnishings of Venturi and Graves. Venturi and Scott Brown's chair designs for Knoll (cat. 83-84) summed up East Coast Post-Modernism in their sophisticated allusions to older high styles. Similarly knowing and elegant in their styles, Charles Moore, Robert A. M. Stern, Richard Meier, and Peter Eisenman were other American architects—termed Late Modernists by Charles Jencks—associated with the smoothly eclectic approach. On the West Coast, by contrast,

Gehry continued to mix Pop and factory references in his raffish work, inspiring younger designers (notably in Japan) to employ industrial materials in unexpected ways.

In Italy, the Memphis group began exhibiting in 1981 and flourished triumphantly by utilizing all the strengths of postwar design in that country: its creative atelier-manufacturer relations and heritage of craftsmanship, its openness to Pop art and other international aesthetic currents, and its tradition of radical experiment and theoretical debate from the 1960s and 1970s (staged at the Milan Triennales and in the pages of leading design magazines). Memphis adopted the oppositional attitudes of Studio Alchimia and made the products embodying them commercial, with financial backing from the Milanese lighting firm Artemide and other Italian companies. In 1981, Andrea Branzi, who showed with Memphis in its debut that year, described the aims of this new design in *Modo*, the magazine he edited. "1) Putting behind [us] the myth of the 'unity' of a project and concentrating on a free discontinuity of parts. . . . 2) The search for a new linguistic 'expressive' quality as a possible solution to the enigma of design. . . . 3) Recycling all possible idioms now in circulation. . . . 4) Recuperating decoration and color as signs of freedom and nobility of creative invention. 5) Going beyond ergonomic limits and concentrating on an affective relation between man and his things."[57] Sottsass, who also migrated from Studio Alchimia and became the elder statesman for Memphis, articulated the group's differences with Bauhaus values. "Memphis, which allows the surface to send more sensorial information and tries to separate the object from its schematic idea of functionalism, is an ironic approach to the modern notion of philosophical pureness. In other words, a table may need four legs to function, but no one can tell me that the four legs have to look the same."[58]

Steadfast in its opposition to the reductivism of the International Style, Memphis stood for happy eclecticism through its very name. It came from Bob Dylan's recording of "Stuck Inside of Mobile with the Memphis Blues Again," playing at Sottsass' house where the group gathered one night in December 1980. The name covered millennia as well as high and low culture: "Blues, Tennessee, rock n' roll, American suburbs, and then Egypt, the Pharaohs' capital, the holy city of the god Ptah."[59] The name was international. In addition to the Italians Sottsass, Branzi, Michele De Lucchi, and Matteo Thun, Memphis included two Americans, Graves and Peter Shire, the Japanese architect-designers Shiro Kuramata, Arata Isozaki, and Masanori Umeda, the Austrian Hans Hollein, George James Sowden of England, and Nathalie du Pasquier of France. Many of these designers sprawled in the boxing-ring conversation unit by Umeda that was exhibited at the Memphis inaugural show (fig. 106). In the mid-1980s, the Spaniards Oscar Tusquets, Jorge Pensi, and Javier Mariscal, who had benefited from the cultural efflorescence of Spain after Franco's death in 1975, were invited to join Memphis.

Memphis stood for quirky, animated surface decoration and intensely bright colors, effects enhanced through the startling juxtapositions of plastic laminates with luxurious materials. Memphis meant reconfigurations of conventional forms with structural and ornamental allusions to a panoply of historical styles. Such surprises can be seen in an interior of the mid-1980s with furnishings by Mariscal, Sottsass, Branzi, and Marco Zanini, all designed for Memphis (fig. 107). Through the "semantic confusion" of its mixtures of references to styles past and present, and to cultures high and low, Memphis challenged conventional good taste and insisted that no single standard could identify vital design.

The first Memphis exhibition, at the Milan Furniture Fair of 1981, included furniture, lighting, and ceramics: fifty-two works attracted 2,500 viewers on opening night. The group was already a success. Its lines were marketed worldwide and in showrooms designed by Memphis for its products in the United States and Japan, while growing demand took them from limited editions to mass production. So identified was Memphis with expensive and outré 1980s taste that its

fig. 106 ▶ Masanori Umeda, *Tawaraya* conversation unit, 1981. Memphis designers from left to right: Aldo Cibic, Andrea Branzi, Michele De Lucchi, Marco Zanini, Nathalie du Pasquier, George J. Sowden, Martine Bedin, Matteo Thun, and Ettore Sottsass.

wares furnished the nouveau-riche Los Angeles interior in the American comedy *Ruthless People*, produced in 1986 (fig. 108).[60] Although Sottsass began to exhibit apart from the group by 1985, and the collaborative effort dissolved by the end of the decade, Memphis continues to exist as a company today.

A bonus of the immediate commercial and critical success of Memphis was its encouragement to other manufacturers to sponsor vanguard designs. Not since the 1950s had architects made such names for themselves through their furniture, lighting, and housewares. Most Italian furniture designers of the twentieth century were also architects; now architects of other countries became widely known first through their furniture. Frank Gehry achieved his initial fame through his chairs rather than his buildings, remarking with wonder that in furniture, "I could design a shape and build it in the same day. Test it. Refine it. And the next day build another one...."[61] In 1979, Alessi commissioned silver tea and coffee services from eleven architects, including Hollein, Graves, Venturi, Aldo Rossi, and Alessandro Mendini. In 1982, Formica held a *Surface and Ornament Design* competition to promote Colorcore, its latest plastic laminate, and invited furniture designs from Venturi, Moore, Gehry, and Dan Friedman, among others (cat. 78). Two years later, Swid Powell, also an American firm, made its debut with tablewares designed by

Richard Meier, Gwathmey Siegel, and other architects. These companies gained the cachet of association with progressive architects, while the architects spread their design philosophy in miniature forms to audiences larger than those exposed to their buildings. Alessi's approach echoed that of Memphis: it sought designs with "SMI: Sensoriality, Memory, Imagination"—with affective codes that could tap unconscious memories and desires.[62] The best objects from these alliances had this resonance. They inspired long-term imaginative and emotional engagement from their owners.

Additional achievements of the 1980s in the world of Italian design included the opening of the Domus Academy in Milan in 1982. Led by the Studio Alchimia architect and theorist Andrea Branzi, it was one of the first schools of design in Italy. Branzi's *Modo* magazine, founded in 1977, was also an important forum for current design in the 1980s. Through the pages of Italian periodicals, the history of twentieth-century international design unfolded. *Domus* continued to wield influence, as did the journals *Casabella, Zodiac, Interni, Ottagono*, and *Abitare*. While the Triennale was held less frequently in the 1980s, the annual Salone del Mobile in Milan rose to become Italy's primary international design event and was dutifully documented and lavishly illustrated in each magazine. In 1987, the exhibition *Nouvelles Tendances: Les avant-gardes de la fin du XXᵉ siècle* at the Pompidou Center in Paris ratified the achievements of Italy in design (fig. 109). Sponsored by Abet Laminati, the Italian laminates manufacturer, the show underlined the creative synergy of the nation's companies and designers.

The Italian success helped draw attention to design elsewhere, and Japan in particular benefited from the market's internationalism. Since midcentury, Italian designers had accepted Japanese students, and the exchanges beginning then between Japan and Italy (and Japan and other countries) bore significant fruit in the 1980s. Toshiyuki Kita opened an office in Milan, and Cassina manufactured his *Wink* armchair (cat. 77). Sottsass visited Japan, appearing on Japanese television, and Memphis designs were widely sold in Japan, at the same time that Isozaki, Kuramata, and Umeda's designs were produced in Italy by Memphis. Japanese couturiers enjoyed international success, and commissioned Japanese designers to conceive interiors for their stores around the world. Kuramata designed eight for Issey Miyake (fig. 120), and his reputation and that of fellow Japanese designers was spread through internationally circulated exhibitions and books such as *Japan Style* (1980) and *Tokyo: Form and Spirit* (1986), exhibitions lauded for their minimalist beauty. Progressive Japanese designers embraced Post-Modernism's stylistic allusiveness, some emphasizing its roots in pop culture, others quoting and deconstructing modernist language. Expression was more diverse and eccentric than in Italy, as suggested by the artistic differences between Kita and Kuramata, for example. Execution remained thoughtful and refined.

While these designers gained world recognition for the imagination and careful finish of their furnishings, certain of Japan's consumer products industries won world dominance in the decade. The electronics manufacturers such as Nintendo and Sega led in satisfying the world craze for video games; and Sharp and Canon competed with IBM to produce and market the microchip-powered office equipment of choice around the world. Sony's Walkman portable cassette player, available in dozens of colors, and its compact disc player, introduced in 1985, once again changed the way we listen to music. These "lifestyle" luxuries were viewed as necessities by youthful consumers in particular. Their various changing tastes were anticipated by Japanese companies, which used design (increasingly assisted by computer technology) as an arm of marketing more swiftly and astutely than companies elsewhere.

Computer technology itself, pioneered by Japan and the United States, entered into businesses and homes worldwide in the 1980s. Invented in 1972, the "Minitel" was distributed with

fig. 108 ▲ Scene from *Ruthless People*, 1986, showing actor Danny DeVito seated on Michele De Lucchi's *Lido* sofa for Memphis. Set decoration by Anne McCulley.

French telephones in the early 1980s. Connected to a television, it allowed access to often-used data banks, such as train schedules, and served for sending and receiving telematic messages. IBM launched its personal computer in 1981; and Apple introduced its version of the PC in 1984, a friendlier system with a click-and-drag "mouse" and a screen menu of icons, the whole humanized by design.

In France, prosperity was most visible in Paris. In the 1980s, president François Mitterrand instigated mammoth building projects at the Grand Louvre and the Bibliothèque Nationale de France complex, among other cultural treasures. And the French government spent considerable sums to encourage native designers and the appreciation of French culture abroad. Designers filtered Post-Modernism through the artistic traditions of Surrealism and primitivism, and enjoyed the longtime association of French design with the luxury trades (fig. 110). At the highest end of the market were exquisitely contoured and finished works by Sylvain Dubuisson, while Philippe Starck captured global media attention with his svelte, deliciously disquieting designs for everything from a lemon squeezer to hotel interiors. He filled commissions from New York and Miami to Tokyo and Paris, and made his clever, stylish products available to households everywhere at a wide variety of prices (cat. 103-104). Intentionally shocking was the Neo-Primitivist movement, best exemplified by the designs of Elisabeth Garouste and Mattia Bonetti. This team managed to outrage both design professionals and the public beginning with their 1981 exhibition *The New Barbarians*, which evoked the French colonial past while incorporating found ingredients such as tree branches into chairs.

Toward the end of the decade, a reaction to such theatrical historicism set in, and some designers returned to social concerns. The ecological issues that had emerged in the 1970s, for instance, gained new strength and began to affect design in the second half of the 1980s, as previously unimaginable environmental tragedies occurred. Man-made disasters included the death of three thousand people from a toxic gas leak at the Union Carbide chemical plant in Bhopal, India, in 1984; the tragic radiation leaks at Chernobyl in the Soviet Ukraine in 1986; the release of a thousand tons of toxic chemicals into the Rhine River near Basel the same year; and the spill of crude oil by the tanker *Exxon Valdez* in Alaska in 1989. Such events, and long-term

fig. 109 ► Alessandro Mendini, *Memory Room*, in collaboration with Alchimia, Pier Carlo Bontempi, Giorgio Gregori, and Cristina Marino, for the exhibition *Nouvelles Tendances: les avant-gardes de la fin du XXᵉ siècle*, Georges Pompidou Center, Paris, 1987.

fig. 110 ▲ Garouste and Bonetti, salon, Christian Lacroix fashion house, Paris, 1987.

but perhaps more alarming phenomena such as global warming and holes in the ozone layer, led to the emergence of Green Design, reflecting international concern for the preservation of the environment. In 1986, The Design Centre in London hosted the exhibition *The Green Designer*, and *The Green Consumer Guide* was published in 1988. Both the exhibition and publication focused on the "energy-conscious design" of buildings and products. These movements were but the beginning of comparable, widespread design activities in the 1990s.

Before the decade came to an end, Post-Modernism had run its course, and reactions to its excesses had begun. The Memphis style had lent itself to cheap imitations with decorative features that were easily mimicked by lesser designers, leading to the rampant use of clichéd reproductions throughout the world. Describing the 1988 Salone del Mobile, a critic announced that "in place of Memphis' restless explosions . . . there appeared glimmers of what might be called 'design *dolce*,' a gentler approach more responsive to materials and to their evocative possibilities."[63] And just as everyone thought that Memphis and the openness to the use of ornament and the vernacular had killed Rationalism, that idiom began to reappear. As part of the Salone, an exhibition on the Rationalists was organized, for such designers as Mario Botta and Antonio Citterio had given fresh meaning to the principles of the interwar years. The article asserted that, as was inevitable after dominating for so many years, the "'Made in Italy' label [was] losing ground.... An invasion of foreigners is making itself felt even more strongly."[64] Spain, England, and Japan were identified as close contenders for Italy's high status as the international leader of design.

When "Black Monday" hit in late 1987, this crash of the world stock market sounded a warning. The bubble economy burst. Stock prices plunged nearly twice as far as they had in 1929, signaling that fear had overtaken greed among overleveraged investors. Massive interventions from the U.S. Federal Reserve and the American-backed International Monetary Fund, private banks, and corporations quelled the panic around the world, however, and the market regained its precrash level within two years. The high liquidity of Japanese investment institutions and their purchase of equity securities during the crisis enabled the country's economy to fare better than most; five weeks after the crash, Tokyo's market had fallen only 20 percent and by the year's end had achieved a 20 percent gain.

But designers and artists looked to the 1990s with new sobriety. In reaction to Post-Modernism were new voices anticipating the spirit of the following decade. Chief among these innovators was the Japanese designer Shiro Kuramata, whose "deconstructed" furniture defied convention in materials, form, and function (cat. 87, 101). Using expanded steel mesh and acrylic, Kuramata created dematerialized objects whose spiritual presence was a powerful antidote to the brash consumer materialism of the 1980s. These works were far from the extravagance of Memphis and Starck's conceptions. They forecast a fresh simplicity and transparency in the designs of the 1990s.

Gaetano **Pesce**

75. **Armchair: *I Feltri***

Designed 1986
Wool felt, polyester resin, hemp, cotton upholstery,
stainless steel
127.6 x 105.4 x 67.3 cm
Produced by Cassina S.p.A. (Meda Milano, Italy),
1986 to the present
D98.159.1

Upholstered in brilliantly hued quilted fabric, Pesce's
I Feltri (The Felts) armchairs have the casual chic
of the down-filled coats popular in the late 1970s
and early 1980s. Like the collars of those energy-
conscious garments, the chair backs can be turned
up or down depending on the warmth or look desired.
Their flexibility is made possible by Pesce's treatment
of the chairs' shell: the felt is precut, soaked with
varying amounts of polyester resin, and placed
in a mold to harden under high heat into a solid,
supporting base and a less rigid top. The quilted
upholstery is attached by snaps to the top and
bottom, which allow easy removal for cleaning
and replacement. Owners can also easily change
the chair back, which is another expression of
Pesce's desire to counter the uniformity of mass-
produced furnishings.

Notwithstanding the stylish look of *I Feltri*,
its manufacture is purposely low-tech. Felt itself is
a cheap, ancient, almost formless material made
of fibers held together with glue. Available in various
thicknesses and readily cut, it commended itself
as a sculptural substance in the 1960s and 1970s
to artists such as Joseph Beuys and Robert Morris
(fig. 111). Felt's antique associations attracted Pesce,
who also saw that it could be molded into his chairs
in developing countries with craft-based production
lines. Here too *I Feltri* demonstrates the designer's
social consciousness. Nonetheless, Cassina ended
up manufacturing the chairs in Italy. "I suggested it
be made in China," Pesce recalled. "But Cassina said,
'then what happens to our people here?'"[65]

In creating this chair, Pesce experimented with
a number of ideas to suggest it is a primal source
of comfort, partly originating in a culture of an earlier,
simpler time. In one prototype, the feet are a semicircle
of rubber, substituted for strength yet retaining
a "soft contact" with the floor. (Pesce wanted rigidity
only where structure was needed.) In another
prototype, the outer shell was bound to an inner one
with large over-cast stitches: they emphasized the
primitive associations of the felt form (fig. 112). In
the final design, the hemp stitching on the exterior
helps secure the resin-soaked seat, and it also adds
a handmade touch to the upholstery. These details,
the traditional material of felt, and the modern method
of hardening it with resin made a combination that
Pesce liked: "I wanted to re-suggest something
that had existed in our memory."[66]

fig. 111 ▼ Robert Morris, untitled felt sculpture, 1980.
Sonnabend Gallery, New York.

fig. 112 ▶ Pesce Ltd., c. 1986 publicity photograph showing
a sitter wrapped in a prototype for the *I Feltri* armchair.

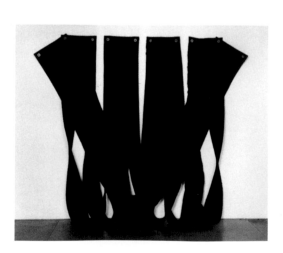

Gaetano **Pesce**

76. **Sofa:** *Tramonto a New York*

Designed 1980
Polyurethane foam, plywood, printed Dacron
upholstery
116.9 x 231.7 x 90.9 cm
Produced by Cassina S.p.A. (Meda Milano, Italy),
1980 to the present
D91.415.1

The metaphor of Pesce's title is meant to be bleak:
the sun is setting on New York, and its day as
a cultural capital is over. But his means are
characteristically bold and eye-catching. In this
cartoonlike sofa, Manhattan's skyline is made
of foam cushions covered in gray fabric with dark
checks imitating the skyscraper's signature grid
of windows. These cushions form three seats and
arms of different heights, while a scarlet-covered
cushion in the form of a setting sun unites them
with its semicircle—even more humorously shaped
in Pesce's poster for his designs (fig. 113).
Transpositions of unlikely objects into furniture typify
Pesce's invention, as seen in his chair-and-ottoman
pairs such as the humanoid *La Mamma* (cat. 40)
and the pillowy *Sit-Down* (cat. 51). The humor of
drastically altered scale—enlargement in those

chairs and miniaturization in this couch—makes
Pesce's socially critical messages charming and
more palatable. Explaining the genesis of *Sunset
in New York*, he said, "When I came to New York
for the first time, I found it full of energy. But on
a subsequent visit, I felt that vitality was less strong.
I thought the lack of it was a sign of the city's
decadence. Certainly New York was the capital
of the twentieth century, but . . . which city will be
the capital of the twenty-first . . .?"[67]

The Italian designer made these remarks in
1993, looking back on a decade in which North
America's earlier cultural dominance had been
challenged by Italian and German art, and its design
status by Italy and Japan. Resurgent capitalism
buoyed the 1980s economy worldwide and inspired
some correspondingly exuberant design, but Pesce
remained oppositional. No matter how visually
appealing, his furnishings challenge their potential
buyers. Although *Sunset in New York* lets its owner
play Master of the Universe by literally sitting on
the city, Pesce mocks the conformity of Modernist
corporate architecture with his printed fabric pattern
and repeated foam blocks. Later he included
the sofa in his own apartment in New York, and
accented its mockery by setting it against his
freeform, expressionist, poured acrylic-resin
floor decoration.

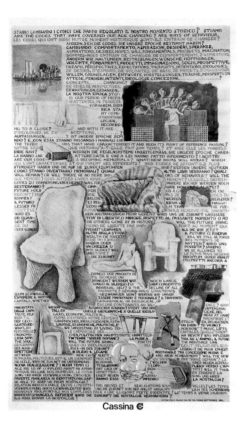

fig. 113 ▲ Pesce, *Milano Salone del Mobile* poster,
1980. Montreal Museum of Decorative Arts.

Toshiyuki **Kita**

77. **Armchair:** *Wink*

Designed 1980
Steel, polyurethane foam, Dacron, ABS plastic,
cotton fabric upholstery and slipcover
Extended:100 x 83.4 x 200 cm
Produced by Cassina S.p.A. (Meda Milano, Italy),
1980 to the present
D90.105.1

This brightly upholstered, legless chair, both
ingratiating and ingenious, created Kita's international
reputation as one of the most inventive of Japanese
furniture and product designers of the 1980s. The
fame was deserved.

The position of the chair seat can be adjusted by
a knob at the base, like the seat in a car or airplane.
The footrest when unfolded turns the chair into a
chaise longue. The two-part headrest can be bent
back for reclining or forward into a "winking" position
for more upright support.[68] The headrest parts also
resemble ears, and this, together with the various
Pop colors of the zip-on upholstery and slipcovers,
earned the chair the nickname "Mickey Mouse." That
Kita designed this in his native country after travel
and work in Italy (like many Japanese designers
of his generation) is not really paradoxical: from
the 1960s onward, American popular culture was
a passion among youths in both countries, and this
provided a counter-balance to their own strong,
craft-based traditions of high art. Around the world,
Pop aesthetics and icons like Disney's trademark
cartoon mouse survived well into the 1980s,
providing a parentage for Post-Modern furnishings
and fine arts.

In addition to creating in Pop language, Kita
was adept in designing rationalist seating systems
in metal, and in using traditional Japanese craft
media such as lacquer for tableware and paper
for lampshades (cat. 126). His facility with these
varied idioms is not unique among more recent
designers, and it responds to the current plurality
of advanced tastes.

Dan **Friedman**

78. **Table:** *Fountain*

Designed 1988
Surell, Colorcore, plywood
79.3 x 66.6 x 65.4 cm
Produced by Plexability Ltd. (New York, NY, USA), 1988
D90.209.1, gift of Formica Corporation

In the humorous, iconoclastic spirit of Pop art, Friedman designed this table as a show piece for *From Table to Tablescape,* a competition and traveling exhibition organized in 1988 by the well-known plastics manufacturer Formica Corporation. The company's goal was to display the qualities of its new "solid surfacing material" Surell, as well as its solid color substance called Colorcore, a laminate with uniform color through all its layers. In the 1920s, Formica invented its eponymous, trademarked material and, in the 1950s, it popularized the durable plastic sheets—generally laminated to plywood and available in a rainbow of colors, faux finishes, and vivid patterns. In the early 1980s, it launched Colorcore with a competition for which the architects Robert Venturi, Charles Moore, Frank Gehry, and other Americans produced designs. The 1988 contest presented Surell, a stonelike plastic sheet material that can be curved under heat, sawed and routed like wood, and fused to itself to create blocks for carving and polishing. *Fountain* exploits many of these properties, while displaying Friedman's signature teardrop forms.

Determining how the table stands on only two legs is part of its charm. One support is a sequence of stacked geometric solids, the other an elliptical cylinder striped with intrinsic color like Neapolitan ice cream. Historical allusions abound: the baluster forms recall Oskar Schlemmer's mecanomorphic costume designs of the 1920s; the amoeboid tabletop suggests a motif by Jean Arp or Joan Miró. And the forms and colors are wittily arranged, both vertically and horizontally. Nonetheless, the whole is relatively conservative in color and form compared to Friedman's other furnishings, which relate to those of the Memphis group, and his cacophonous graphic designs and interiors, all of which were widely admired in vanguard art circles of the 1980s.

Alessandro **Mendini** and Bruno **Gregori**

79. **Floor lamp:** *Atomaria*

Designed 1984
Lacquered wood, steel
189 x 40 x 40 cm
Produced by Zabro (Milan, Italy), 1984-88
D97.169.1

In this tall and planar lamp made for Nuova Alchimia, Mendini and Gregori emphasize decorative over functional values. It is shaped like a series of stylized fans springing from a small conical base. Pairs of little metal flags and small bulbs set in metal discs mark each step of the sides, and when lighted they further dramatize this Art Deco-flavored design, which recalls a sconce in a movie palace or salon of the late 1920s and 1930s.

Mendini introduced this type of fanlike form in a flag-bedecked lighting line of 1982 he called *Furniture Greenery* for its resemblance to artificial plants and flowers (fig. 114). Earlier, he used such flags in his *Banal Object* exhibition at the 1980 Venice Biennale, attaching them like arrows to emphasize the shapes of both anonymous appliances and classics of postwar Italian design.

For example, he added metal flags to the wooden uprights of Ponti's *Superleggera* chair and put a faux-marble finish on one of Colombo's stackable plastic chairs. That was the climax of his Anti-Design activity, when he believed that the "redesign" of existing works was the only defensible creativity in an age of over-production. Like the appropriation of photographic images in contemporary Post-Modern painting and camera art, Mendini's gestures declared that he saw Modernist originality as exhausted, yet ironic juxtapositions could illuminate otherwise unnoticed cultural codes. For Mendini, "design" did not mean making new kinds of functional objects, but underlining the meaning of existing types by adding symbols and decorative devices. Design was a system of free-floating signifiers, to be used in a socially critical, even nihilist spirit. The flags stress that *Atomaria*'s form derives not from function but from a historic style that also relates it to kitsch.

Mendini's critical position regarding design was publicized, beginning in 1978, through his affiliation with Studio Alchimia; he maintained his prominence in the radical group as it evolved into Zona Alchimia in 1983 and Nuova Alchimia in 1984-85. He and group members continue to design objects and conceive visionary architectural projects, all with an oppositional and anti-commercial stance.

fig. 114 ▲ Mendini and Gregori, *Furniture Greenery* exhibition, Gran Bazaar, Milan, 1982.

Ettore **Sottsass**

80. **Cabinet: *Dear Palladio (Give Me a Break!)***

Designed 1987
Alpi radica, ash, lacquered wood, Formica,
chromed steel, Grundig television set
196.8 x 190.5 x 60.5 cm
Produced by Renzo Brugola (Milan, Italy), 1987
D94.322.1, gift of Jean Boucher

Sottsass had this cabinet made for an influential
show of his work at the New York City art gallery
Blum-Helman in 1987 (fig. 115). His title for
the cabinet, a rebellious cry in English against Italy's
revered sixteenth-century architect, and the emblematic
arch and pediments applied to its facade, demonstrate
his flippant yet subtle historicism. The imposing form
of the piece, which is meant to be placed in the
center of the room, recalls his early insistence that
his furnishings are ritual tools in a domestic liturgy.
Palladio's symmetry, clear geometric forms, and
classical vocabulary of triangular and arch motifs
frame what Sottsass acknowledges is the psychic
center of the modern home, the television—the
global hearth of world communications. Amusingly
heavy and overbearing, this console is Sottsass'
answer to a container problem that most recognized
designers had ignored. Elevated on blocks, a plinth,
and small cylinders, it is his altar to the new
religion of TV.

For the press and for imitators, the attack of
the Memphis group on conventional Good Design
and good taste was epitomized by its use of plastic
laminates such as Formica, that kitchen-counter
covering identified with the 1950s.[69] Memphis
introduced it into fine furnishings and mischievously
juxtaposed it with expensive materials, as seen here.
Memphis artists printed their swarming, often
discordantly hued patterns on its slick surface, thus
challenging the moralistic absence of ornament and
the restrained color schemes of Modernism. In *Dear
Palladio*, Sottsass contrasts such patterns with the
luxury of exotic Alpi wood, enjoying what he called
the "semantic confusion" and socially leveling nature
of the effect.

fig. 115 ▲ *Dear Palladio* and other furniture installed in the exhibition *Ettore Sottsass*, Blum-Helman Gallery, New York, 1987.

Ettore **Sottsass**

81. **Cabinet: *Di Famiglia***

Designed 1985
Plastic-laminated plywood, alpica veneer,
lacquered poplar plywood
210 x 168 x 81 cm
Executed by Francesco Valtorta (Milan, Italy), 1985
D97.167.1

Di Famiglia (*Of the Family*) is a unique piece,
designed by Sottsass for *Le affinità elettive*,
the Memphis display at the 1985 Milan Triennale. It
reflects many aspects of Italian design of the 1980s.
"From the beginning," wrote Sottsass' friend Andrea
Branzi, "New Design [in Italy] was characterized by
an effort to renew the language of domestic objects
with new inspirations, deriving from irony, curiosity,
surprise, and friendliness."[70] Here Sottsass "renews"
both the cabinet and wardrobe types by startling
expansion and agglomeration. The size of a room
divider, this unit includes two cupboards, a shelf
(or bench) between them, and two lamps concealed
in the upper elements. One cupboard flaunts
decorative wood veneer, the other an intensely hued
plastic-laminate finish, while the horizontal wooden
members are all brightly painted. Almost nine feet tall,
Di Famiglia is an architectural piece, a doorwaylike
composition of bold upright rectangles around
a central void. Its contrasts of solid and space,
traditional and "vulgar" materials, noisy pattern
and plain painted surface constitute its visual
energy and demonstrate its purposeful clash of
semantic codes.

The "deconstruction" (or separation and analysis)
of these design languages was Sottsass' goal, and
one he shared with the successive radical design
groups with which he collaborated—first Superstudio,
then Studio Alchimia, and, most famously, Memphis,
founded in 1980. The earlier groups organized
themselves like political cells to foster critical
evaluation of current design. Memphis, on the other
hand, devoted itself primarily to commercial
production and thus won wide recognition through
the international circulation of its diverse lines—
furnishings, glassware, lighting, fabrics, etc. These
lines share characteristics with *Di Famiglia* of lively
decorated surfaces, mixtures of materials,
architectonic treatment of furnishing types, and fine
craftsmanship—a blend of high-quality execution
and sometimes outrageous style that assured
the celebrity of the group in the 1980s.

Ettore **Sottsass**

82. **Cabinet:** *Lemon Sherbet*
Designed 1987
Ash, mirror, Plexiglas, Formica
226 x 162 x 40 cm
Produced by Renzo Brugola (Milan, Italy), 1987
D88.135.1

Even more than *Di Famiglia* (cat. 81), *Lemon Sherbet* dominates its space by its sheer size and the dramatic play of solid and void in its eccentric asymmetry. Like a de Stijl construction, the open cabinets expand outward in their irregularly stepped rhythm, cantilevered out at the sides with a peculiar sense of fragile imbalance. These curious cubes are played against differentiated supports—a large mirrored cabinet evoking 1930s Hollywood, and a pair of disc-footed Plexiglas legs. Not least, the lemon-yellow paint on all the wood shelves contrasts with the other surfaces to effervescent effect.

In the early 1980s, high-end manufacturers such as Officina Alessi and Swid Powell commissioned tableware lines from architects, with results that—not surprisingly—resembled architecture. Indeed, Alessi called the designs it manufactured in 1983 by Michael Graves, Richard Meier, Robert Venturi, Charles Jencks, Aldo Rossi, and others "Tea and Coffee Piazzas." Such activity among those architects was then unusual, but not for Sottsass. He had always pursued his conceptions in all scales and media, from architecture to glass and ceramics, at the same time incorporating local traditions in his forms and fabrications. That the three Sottsass designs presented here in succession should resemble an altar, a portal, and a constructed sculpture suggests the breadth of his allusions, while his reworking of the conventions for wardrobes, cabinets, and shelving shows the bravura of his typological transformations. Like *Dear Palladio*, *Lemon Sherbet* was made specifically for Sottsass' 1987 exhibition in the Manhattan art gallery Blum-Helman, and was then produced in a limited edition.

Robert **Venturi**
and Denise **Scott Brown**

83. **Chair: *Queen Anne***
Designed 1984
Plywood, printed plastic laminate, rubber
98 x 69 x 63.5 cm
Produced by Knoll International
(New York, NY, USA), 1984-89
D85.117.1, gift of Knoll International

84. **Chair: *Art Deco***
Designed 1984
Plywood, printed plastic laminate, rubber
80.5 x 56.7 x 58 cm
Produced by Knoll International
(New York, NY, USA), 1984-89
D99.156.1

fig. 116 ▲ Knoll International, 1984 publicity photograph showing Venturi with the *Venturi* chair line.

fig. 117 ▲ Venturi, Scott Brown and Associates, 1999 photograph of the architects' living room showing the *Queen Anne* chair and Aulenti's *Pipistrello* lamp.

Venturi and Scott Brown's knowing combination of a Modernist technique—the machine molding of laminates pioneered by Aalto and the Eameses—and their faux-naive parody of historical styles help explain these chairs' high place in the Post-Modern canon. Of molded plywood covered with patterned plastic laminate, they look like seats for overgrown children. The back of the *Queen Anne* resembles a student's diagram or a Matisse-like sketch for a chair in the high style identified with the early eighteenth-century British monarch. So too, the form of the *Art Deco* chair has a charmingly naive simplicity.

Venturi, the design theorist and architect, and the architect and planner Scott Brown had pursued Post-Modernist ideas in both their buildings and writings before the term came into wide use. Here, in these examples from their first line of furniture, they realized those ideas in objects. The so-called "Venturi" line included nine different but comparable chairs, from *Chippendale*, *Sheraton*, and *Empire*, to *Gothic Revival* and *Art Deco* (fig. 116). Seen from the side, the thin profiles of all the chairs in the series prove to be similar, while "the fronts are signs," wrote Venturi and Scott Brown, "reminiscent of Western false-front stores."[71] The chair fronts' dictionary of grand manners and high styles underlines what Venturi and Scott Brown see as the equivalent value of all styles, old and new, as well as their intent to please.

The "Grandmother's Tablecloth" pattern printed on the *Queen Anne* chair, and also on Venturi tableware and fabrics, adds another set of references. The pastel roses suggest mass-marketed textiles of the 1920s, while the overlay of little parallel lines resembling chopsticks offers a contrast in energy. The radiating design on the *Art Deco* chair recalls that joyous love of decoration which challenged the International Style's puritanical stance. Thus Venturi and Scott Brown acknowledge the delight in decoration and nostalgia that underlie tastes at all levels. No wonder this line was successful: owners could enjoy the pleasures, forbidden by functionalism, of high- and lower-class ornament, along with the satisfaction of supporting contemporary design.

Massimo **Iosa Ghini**

85. **Bench:** *Vertigine*
Designed 1989
Chrome-plated steel, ash, leather upholstery
65 x 224 x 110 cm
Produced by Moroso (Milan, Italy) for Design Gallery
Milano (Milan, Italy), 1989
D94.200.1

From childhood onward, Iosa Ghini loved cartoons and drew his own, especially outer-space fantasies. The swooping curves and megalomaniac scale of his sources helped instill a taste that eventually led him to admire Futurist design, Italian Fascist architecture, and American streamlining of the 1930s. To promote that aesthetic of aerodynamics he cofounded the Bolidist design group in Milan in 1982 (from the Italian *bolide*, a *fast-moving object*). *Vertigine*, a Buck Rogers-like bench, is typical of Bolidist design: the seat juts forward; the back, without rear legs, is an opposing boomerang shape. Both forms are extensions of graphic marks into the third dimension, a visionary realm seen in his architectural renderings (fig. 118). The bench's fabrication is made possible through computer-assisted factory technology introduced in the 1980s; digitizing allows the reproduction of shapes previously possible only through handwork. The technology has also encouraged such anti-Rationalist designers as the Memphis group, with which Iosa Ghini exhibited in 1986. Speaking of their shared aesthetics, he said in 1988: "The first step of this new trend is to break the right angle and the straight line . . . in order to find the sinuous curve, the volute, the spiral, and shapes that can be obtained from complex equations, because now we have the possibility to memorize and to use them."[72]

Vertigine was produced in a limited edition and exhibited as part of a collection of wood and upholstered furniture, and silverware by Iosa Ghini to coincide with the 1989 Milan Furniture Fair. *Vertigine* (Italian for *Vertigo*) seems suitable as a name for this dizzying design, made in the capital of Italian Futurism and the home of Memphis.

fig. 118 ▲ Iosa Ghini, design of futuristic architecture, c. 1988. Studio Iosa Ghini, Milan.

fig. 119 ▲ Vladimir Tatlin, model of the *Monument to the Third International*, Eighth Congress of the Soviets, Moscow, 1920.

Mario **Cananzi**
and Roberto **Semprini**

86. **Sofa: *Tatlin***

Designed 1989
Lacquered wood, chrome-plated tubular steel,
polyurethane foam, cotton velvet upholstery
135.9 x 205.7 x 172.7 cm
Produced by Edra S.p.A. (Pisa, Italy),
1989 to the present
D93.258.1, gift of Maurice Forget

To identify the Modernist icon they evoke and amusingly transform, Cananzi and Semprini call this sofa *Tatlin*, referring to the Russian architect's most famous design, his 1919-20 *Monument to the Third International* (fig. 119). The Italian partners retain the spiral of the Constructivist's tribute to revolutionary Communism, but they seem to poke fun at that ideology by turning a conception for a giant steel and glass tower into a red velvet love seat, a staple of bourgeois Victorian interiors. Such mockery of old utopian ideals through transformation—a visionary building into a sofa—typifies much 1980s design. Another key aspect of Post-Modernism is the reexamination of a furniture type in form and function: here, seating for two or three people.

Tatlin's *Monument* was never built, but this sofa "is the symbol for a positive change in society," writes Stephen Hamel, a principal of its manufacturer Edra. "From a commercial standpoint, [it] perfectly suits waiting rooms, especially of lawyers and physicians, because people are not obliged to look each other in the face."[73] His words catch elements of *Tatlin*'s Post-Modernism: for the knowledgeable, it evokes the ironies of history while turning a symbol of revolution into a useful, saleable object—furniture for a waiting room.

Cananzi and Semprini's cultural insights were first enriched by their architectural training at the University of Florence; Cananzi went on to earn a master's degree in design at the Domus Academy in Milan, the city where the two now operate as partners. In 1986, Semprini joined the Bolidist group and collaborated on interior designs with its leader, Massimo Iosa Ghini. Both *Tatlin* and Iosa Ghini's *Vertigine* (cat. 85) can be described as *bolidi*, or fast-moving objects, emblematic of the group's fascination with shapes evocative of speed.

Shiro **Kuramata**

87. **Armchair: *How High the Moon***

Designed 1986
Nickel-plated steel mesh
72.4 x 95 x 81.8 cm
Produced by Vitra GmbH (Birsfelden, Switzerland),
1987 to the present
D90.114.1

Weightlessness and transparency are hallmarks of Kuramata's works. His furniture, objects, and interior designs epitomize the Japanese heritage of doing more with less, and they also evoke the European traditions of Modernism as well as American Minimalist sculpture of the 1960s and 1970s. Indeed, Kuramata's stature and his frames of reference were international: like his contemporaries and friends, the architects Tadao Ando and Arata Isozaki, he was equally admired in the United States, Europe, and Japan.

How High the Moon combines colliding Western associations: the archetypal overstuffed bourgeois armchair and the "primary structures" of vanguard American art. Just as artists such as Robert Morris challenged definitions of sculpture by reducing form to elemental geometries (fig. 121), so Kuramata challenges the concept of the soft Victorian chair by reducing its form to a few hard-edged, welded shapes and by making it from an industrial substance that dematerializes the chair. Steel mesh

is normally a reinforcement for plaster walls, hidden from sight, but it is undisguised here; it is the chair's sole material, and it allows moderately comfortable seating thanks to its resilience. Important to Kuramata are the optical properties of the mesh. It creates moiré patterns when seen in layers, as here, and the nickel plating makes the chair shimmer in changing light. Thus he mystifies Modernism and Western traditions, giving factory materials, industrial methods, and familiar forms an unexpected poetry.

Preceded by Frank Gehry, who openly used steel mesh in his architecture, Kuramata also employed this substance for the interiors of the Esprit boutique in Hong Kong in 1984 and the Issey Miyake boutique in the Seibu department store in Tokyo in 1987 (fig. 120). The refined expression Kuramata gave the gridded material suited those shops and their similarly minimalist fashions. His cantilevered armchair *Sing, Sing, Sing* showed his early adoption of steel mesh for furnishings; it turned the silhouette of Mies van der Rohe's *Brno* chair into one of winsome curls.

Though Kuramata's surprising transformations of industrial materials and conventional seating types identify him with Post-Modernism, his designs are suave rather than confrontational. Revealingly, the title *How High the Moon* comes from a refined composition by Duke Ellington, typifying the jazz that Kuramata heard and loved when he was growing up in Occupied Japan. Here too the designer makes an elegiac and lyrical connection with the past.

fig. 120 ▼ Kuramata, interior for Boutique Issey Miyake Men, Seibu Department Store, Tokyo, 1987.

fig. 121 ▼ Robert Morris, *Untitled (Quarter Round Mesh)*, 1967. Panza Collection, Solomon R. Guggenheim Museum, New York.

Shigeru **Uchida**

88. **Floor lamp:** *Tenderly*

Designed 1985
Steel with baked Melamine finish, aluminum
136.8 x 49.5 x 42 cm
Produced by Chairs (Tokyo, Japan), 1986-88
D92.192.1, gift of Toshiko Mori

An elegant exercise in attenuated geometry, this metal floor lamp adapts the concept of a professional photographer's adjustable light stand to domestic ends. *Tenderly* is composed of tall rods that telescope to create various heights, and a triangular light housing tops it off. The halogen light source is shielded by a metal grid, which can be tilted sideways. Uchida based his initial sketch for this tilting screen, he explained, on "the image of Japanese men holding up their sun visors to see who is good looking."[74]

The name *Tenderly* suggests the delicacy of the lamp's modulation of light and also Uchida's fondness for American popular music of the 1950s, a taste he shares with Shiro Kuramata, the Japanese designer who also finds poetic possibilities in metal mesh and other industrial materials. Like Kuramata, Uchida is celebrated for his commercial interiors, as well as his furniture designs. His conceptions for the chic New York City clothing store Charivari in 1984, and the Hotel Il Palazzo, Fukuoka, Japan, in 1989, demonstrate his skill in satisfying both Modernist and Post-Modernist schools as well as traditional Japanese design values. In all his work, Uchida focuses more on the relationships between his objects and space than on the objects themselves. *Tenderly*, for example, casts expressive diamond-patterned shadows on adjacent walls.

Alberto **Meda** and Paolo **Rizzatto**

89. **Hanging lamp: *Titania***

Designed 1989
Anodized aluminum, steel cable, polycarbonate filters
8 x 70 x 27 cm
Produced by Luceplan (Milan, Italy), 1990 to the present
D91.401.1

The name *Titania*, recalling Shakespeare's Queen of the Fairies, suits this lamp in its graceful elongated ellipse, its glistening anodized aluminum lattice, its adjustability to float at any height or angle, and the changeable colored light it can shed. To alter the lamp's angle from horizontal to diagonal or to nearly vertical, one easily adjusts the steel suspension cables which are set independently of the electrical connection. To alter the hue, the owner simply changes the silkscreened color filters on each side. If all that were not magic enough, the fixture is moderately priced.

Meda and Rizzatto's goal in *Titania* was to create a lamp that glows from all points of view but never produces glare. Therefore, the little halogen bulb is screened by seven elliptical elements; this allows both direct and diffused lighting. The resemblance of its skeleton to that of an airplane wing is no accident: Meda holds a degree in mechanical engineering and he has adopted materials and principles from aeronautic design for his conceptions of domestic items. "My interest lies in the expressive capacity of technologies that are adopted from specialized sectors," he says, "in order to enhance and improve the quality of daily objects."[75] That his solutions can take poetic forms is a bonus he does not expect.

Anodyzing, an electrolytic procedure that permanently coats and colors lightweight metals, became popular in 1950s design as a way of making aluminum vessels more attractive. The technique subsequently entered jewelry and flatware design, as well as other areas of metalwork, such as the lighting represented here.

Mario **Botta**

90. **Armchair: *Seconda***

Designed 1982
Epoxy-painted tubular steel, perforated sheet steel,
polyurethane foam, rubber upholstery
73 x 52 x 59.5 cm
Produced by Alias (Milan, Italy) for International
Contract Furnishings (New York, NY, USA),
1982 to the present
D85.120.1, gift of Luc d'Iberville-Moreau

figs. 122-123 ▲ Botta, axionometric projection and interior of a private residence, Morbio Superiore, Switzerland, 1982-83.

The philosopher William James proposed that there are two basic aesthetic responses: of recognition and surprise. Botta prompts both of them in this rectilinear armchair, apparently the epitome of Modernism. It was his second foray into furniture design, after an armless version of the same chair (*Primo*). *Seconda*'s bare, black metal skeleton, and the counterpoint of its crisp lines and the geometric forms of its seat and back evoke the language of the International Style. One expects *Seconda*'s metal structure to outline a cube, but the back and the front side are open. One also expects hard seating, but the seat is perforated metal, which is flexible, and the cylindrical back is a pair of foam cushions which rotate and softly give under pressure. Functionalist design, Botta seems to be saying, need not be rigid. Such design can respond to new industrial methods and materials, while satisfying one's senses of sight and touch. For Botta, Bauhaus language is still alive and available for personal inflection.

This attitude qualifies Botta as a late Modernist (if such definitions are useful), rather than a Post-Modern parodist of the idealistic International Style. A practicing architect and a professor of architecture, he is a member of the Tendenza movement in Italy, which holds that rationalist architecture has not reached its fullest realization. Botta wrote his master's thesis on the architect Carlo Scarpa, served under Louis Kahn, and worked in Le Corbusier's studio after the Frenchman's death. Le Corbusier's influence is evident in Botta's work, notably in his 1982-83 house at Morbio Superiore, Switzerland, where, fittingly enough, Botta placed *Seconda* chairs in a dining area facing onto a partly glass-enclosed terrace (figs. 122-123). Like the chair, the house facade is minimalist, tense, linear, and symmetrical, yet its curved elements subtly offset the rigidity of the dominant rectangles. In both cases, design is generated not primarily by function but by the symbolism of forms—the chair as an efficient, taut support, the house as a fortresslike villa with a view.

Andrea **Branzi**

91. **Bookcase:** *Magnolia*
Designed 1985
Chromium-plated steel, steel wire, glass, Abet plastic laminate-faced wood, plastic palm leaves
241.5 x 200 x 50 cm
Produced by Memphis Milano s.r.l.
(Pregnana Milanese, Italy), 1985 to the present
D90.220.1, gift of Jay Spectre*

Post-Modern furniture owes some of the impetus for its symbolic language to the comic substitutions of Pop art—a cactus for a coat stand, a baseball mitt for a chair. But the range of allusions in Branzi's bookcase suggests the growth in intellectual sophistication of design in Italy between the late 1960s and the 1980s. Here a pyramidal set of glass shelves hangs from steel-wire shrouds (like sailboat rigging) that extend from a pair of metal and plastic palm trees to a plastic laminate-covered wooden base. A remarkable adaptation of such engineering to shelving, this bookcase—the prototype for manufacture—is self-supporting, and it functions imaginatively as well as practically.

Dario Bartolini had designed similar trees as lighting in 1968 (fig. 145), and the Austrian architect Hans Hollein, a Memphis associate, used all-metal palms as decoration in his Austrian Travel Bureau, Vienna, in 1976-78, an early example of Post-Modern architecture (fig. 124). For Branzi, palms are identified with Egypt as well as California: there is an "international pop of palm trees" in nature itself. They also refer to "a pseudo-arabian world, which has been always excluded by design and the Modern Movement."[76] Thus this architect-theorist-designer happily included them in his structurally ingenious design, which the Memphis group whimsically named *Magnolia* (flower names were given to all the pieces in that year's collection).

In his defense of radical design, Branzi noted the diversification of markets in post-industrial society, reflecting different languages, fashions, traditions, and consumer needs. Inadequate responses to this, he found, were the "objectivity" and anonymity of Modernism, with its "drastic semantic reduction." Instead, he posited the need, "beyond questions of performance and service," for "emotional value . . . [which is] created not by the object's functionality, but by its expressive level. This latter feature is made up of the object's basic materials, its shape, weight, smell, tactile characteristics and perceptual presence: from high-tech to high touch."[77] In this vein, Branzi's bookcase combines several codes, just as its books would.

fig. 124 ▲ Hans Hollein, lobby and ticket counter, Austrian Travel Bureau Central Offices, Vienna, 1976-78.

Elisabeth **Garouste** and Mattia **Bonetti**

92. **Chair:** *Prince Impérial*

Designed 1985
Hand-painted found wood, found tree branches, raffia
132.7 x 43.5 x 44.8 cm
Executed by Elisabeth Garouste and Mattia Bonetti for Neotu (Paris, France), 1987 to the present
D93.251.1

This astonishing chair is one of the boldest reactions in the 1980s against functionalist aesthetics and the standardized look of industrial production. Garouste and Bonetti, who began collaborating on design projects in 1980, titled their first collection "The New Barbarians" and presented it in 1981 in a townhouse gallery on the Rue Royale (fig. 125). Much of their work in that decade similarly integrated the primitivist with the elegant. The *Prince Impérial* is one of the most literally barbaric of the pair's furnishings, reflecting their advocacy of historical references and a return to the "natural" (the back support is a real forked tree branch). With its African and Second Empire allusions, the chair could be a throne for the Prince Imperial, the ill-starred son of Napoleon III and the empress Eugénie, who spent his last days with the British military among the Zulus—a bizarre fact at the heart of Garouste and Bonetti's invention.

The partners' brightly painted furnishings show the influence of Surrealism as well as the overt illusionism of the theater, and by the late 1980s they added neo-Baroque decorative motifs to their repertory. Not surprisingly, their most visible success may have been the design of showrooms in 1987 for the extravagant couturier Christian Lacroix, who loves fantasy and rich cultural allusions (fig. 110). The team's passion for quotation—indeed narrative—typifies much Post-Modern design, especially in Europe, where the longing for magic and a sense of ritual in an increasingly alienated industrial society was seen in Neo-Expressionist art, from paintings and performances to furniture such as this.

fig. 125 ▲ Garouste and Bonetti, *The New Barbarians* exhibition, Jansen Gallery, Paris, 1981.

Andrea **Branzi**

93. **Sofa:** *Axale*

Designed 1988
Enameled aluminum, polyurethane foam, rubber, cotton/viscose upholstery
94.5 x 230 x 52 cm
Produced by Cassina S.p.A. (Meda Milano, Italy), 1988 to the present
D91.106.1, gift of Cassina S.p.A.

Primitive and industrial associations blend in this sofa, which is identified by the single, emphatic curve of its fabric-covered metal frame. An archer's bow inspired the C-shaped form, while the movable cushions that hang over it, covered in Jack Lenor Larsen fabric, suggest saddlebags. An early work with a bow structure was a "structural sculpture" by Branzi, intended to explore how "the stretched arch could be used as an expressive and structural base for a product" (fig. 126).[78] That sculpture—both African in flavor and abstract—is a handsome graphic design in its own right.

The sofa is part of a collection Branzi designed for Cassina with the goal of infusing industrially produced furniture with humanistic values. The designs, he said, are "archetypal objects that are almost mythical elaborations of primary structures, such as a bridge, an arch, the sea, a temple." These objects are intended to answer needs left unsatisfied by high-tech solutions because human beings, according to Branzi, "are able to create a richer and more complex rapport [with their possessions and places] than a simple functional and technical relationship; a rapport that consists of poetic, affective, symbolic, and psychological interchanges."[79] Thus *Axale* is richly coded with allusions to tribal and nomadic life—to the protection and beauty of a bow, to the versatility of a saddlebag. Yet its mass manufacture and modern materials of aluminum and polyurethane foam make it available to a wide and very modern audience.

fig. 126 ▲ Branzi in collaboration with the Centro Ricerche e Sviluppo Cassina, *Stretched Arch* sculpture, 1986-89. Milan, collection of the designer.

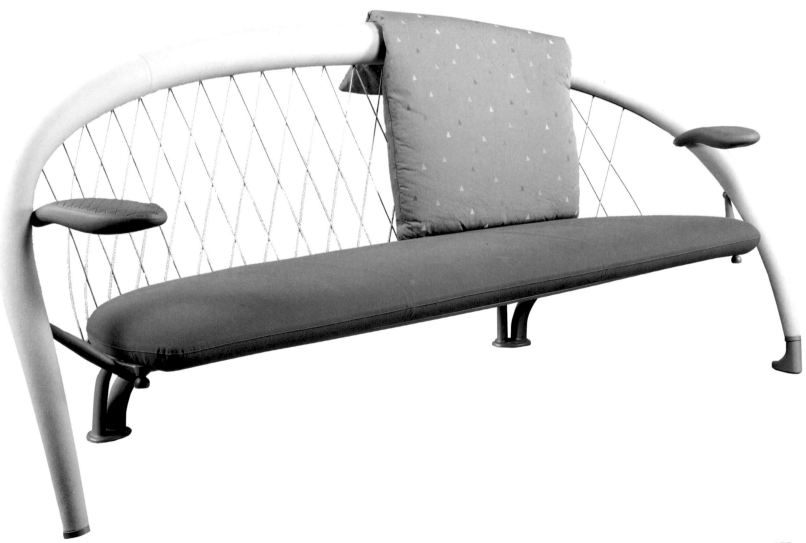

Tom **Dixon**

94. **Chair: *Fat***

Designed 1988
Steel, rush
81.9 x 71.8 x 83.8 cm
Executed by Tom Dixon, c. 1988; produced by Space
(London, England), 1989; by Cappellini S.p.A.
(Como, Italy), 1990 to the present
D93.250.1

The primitivist air of this low chair is created by its overall leaflike shape and the rush covering of its elliptical back and wide seat. Like an openwork sculpture, it displays its structure of curved steel rods and the evidence of its welds and joints, through which Dixon calls attention to his process of fabrication. How to apply rush to a steel frame was the technical challenge he set himself; usually such humble natural materials as rush, cane, and wicker are woven on a wooden structure. Typically, Dixon tackles the supposed limitations of materials as well as art and design types; his self-expression has found outlets in diverse media. In addition to furniture, he designs sculpture, lighting fixtures, installations, and stage sets. The *Fat* chair is a handcrafted prototype that became part of his first mass-produced collection, which was issued in 1990 and marked his transition from making one-off objects to serial production.

Dixon is part of a generation of British designers who emerged in the 1980s out of London's punk-rock scene. Building on British Pop, and like New York City's graffiti artists of the early 1980s, they helped create a style of rough, defiant, partly representational imagery applied to everything from T-shirts to nightclub decor. For this, Dixon could draw on his earlier training as a cartoonist and color-in artist for Disney Studios; to repair his motorcycle he learned to weld.

In 1985, he began designing chairs using scrap metals, forming a partnership he called Creative Salvage. Found materials are, of course, free, but for the Dixon team they were also ecologically correct. Further, their raw edges and gestural shapes critiqued the smug nostalgia of commercial British designers of the 1980s such as Laura Ashley and Terence Conran. Dixon replied to Victorian chintz with vital animal and vegetal forms close to early Abstract Expressionist art, and responded to neo-Scandinavian cabinetry with the moral superiority of recycled metals.

Oscar **Tusquets Blanca**

95. **Chair:** *Gaulino*
Designed 1987
Oak, plywood, leather upholstery
85.5 x 55 x 50.5 cm
Produced by Carlos Jané Camacho, S.A.
(Barcelona, Spain), 1987 to the present
D94.116.1, gift of Carlos Jané Camacho, S.A.

"There are too many tubular chairs with pipes, metal, and rubber," says this Catalan designer. Here he is delighted "to show the beauty of the texture of oak wood, which goes to make each piece different from the rest: a variation which stands out with the irregularities and folds of the leather upholstered seat."[80] These natural materials and the organic, somewhat bony form language of this chair associate it with Tusquets' countryman, the Art Nouveau architect Antoni Gaudí, and the Italian postwar designer Carlo Mollino. From their conjoined names Tusquets created the title *Gaulino* for this chair.

Tusquets was a prime mover in the emergence of Barcelona as a major design center in the 1980s, and critics have argued whether he or Ricardo Bofill is Spain's foremost architect-designer today. Tusquets began his career in the mid-1960s and has been recognized for work as various as his 1972 Belvedere de Regas building in Barcelona (a collaboration with Lluis Clotet) and his 1982 tea set commissioned by Alessi. These designs share a range of subtle stylistic allusions, and they reflect Tusquets' easy-going version of Post-Modernism. *Gaulino* also announces elements of much 1990s design in general: it will be unpretentious, recognizable in references, user-friendly.

Alex **Locadia**

96. **Speaker: *Iliad: The Trojan Horse***

Designed 1988
Anodized steel, rubber, Matsushita *Ramsa* audio
speaker, wood
183 x 42.6 x 54.5 cm
Executed for Gallery 91 (New York, NY, USA), 1988
D93.178.1, gift of Paul Leblanc

What is the shape of sound? This was the question
posed by Matsushita, the Japanese electronics
company, to Gallery 91 in New York City, which in
turn asked fifteen Western designers to incorporate
Matsushita's new *Ramsa* speakers—then the latest in
audio technology for home or commercial interior—
into a design of any form or size. The results were
sent on tour in 1989 in an exhibition entitled *Art of
Sound: Sculpture and Environment.*

Locadia, a New York City-based sculptor
and industrial designer, made no attempt to hide
the cylindrical speaker, but housed it in the "head"
of a six-foot-tall, somewhat intimidating construction.
The helmeted shape, adorned with an aerodynamic
"wing" containing the tweeter, stands on a tall wedge
that terminates in a spiky tripod reminiscent of
Calder's stabiles. The rubber rings around the "throat"
are intended to suggest the multiple necklaces
of Zulu tribespeople. The work is all black, like
most stereo equipment of the time, but there
the resemblance ends. The speaker relates not
to the Ulm school of purified, cubic design but to
comic-book fantasy and the customizing of hotrods
that Locadia worked at as a youth. Through the title,
Iliad: The Trojan Horse, he suggests that his creature
contains unsuspected foreign power: that of sound.[81]

Such expressive conceits were facilitated by
the increasing miniaturization of audio components
since the 1950s, which severed the once-necessary
formal relation between the container and its contents.
Manufacturers were therefore able to house the
components easily and to focus more attention on
producing eye-catching, saleable designs. That was
Matsushita's goal in this venture, and it received a
range of novel conceptions, from single sculptural
objects to full environments, reflecting the growing
taste among music aficionados for surrounding
sound and among gallery-goers for art installations.
None of the speakers were conceived as an
unobtrusive and harmonious ingredient of interior
decor, as they might have been in the 1950s.
Rather, their variety reflects the stylistic heterogeneity
of interiors in the 1980s and the eagerness of
manufacturers to produce novel packaging to pique
every taste.

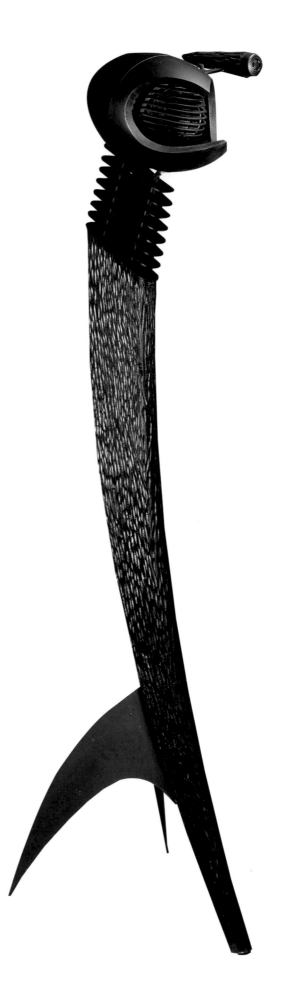

Forrest **Myers**

97. **Stool:** *Thicket*
Designed 1988
Anodized aluminum
59 x 57 x 56.5 cm
Executed by Forrest Myers (New York, NY, USA),
1988
D93.170.1, gift of Paul Leblanc

Aptly named *Thicket*, this stool is made of gleaming purple and green wires of various diameters, meandering and intertwining without evident beginning or end. This imploding mass has the vitality of the mangrove vines around Key West, Florida, where Myers grew up. In photographs, the piece appears nearly shapeless, for the plane of the seat is less noticeable than the whole gnarled nest of wires. Such amorphousness may repel, yet the sheen of the wire and its chemically induced colors attract the eye. Myers has turned an artist's doodling into sculptural seating.

Viewing *Thicket*, one can well believe that Myers came of age as a sculptor among those associated with Abstract Expressionism, such as David Smith and Mark di Suvero. These two men were his mentors, in addition to Alexander Calder, famed for his wire mobiles and sheet-steel stabiles, and John Chamberlain, who used crushed cars in his assemblages of the late 1950s. Myers designed his first useful sculpture in 1964; his pieces folded from single sheets of aluminum led to his first design exhibition, in 1981, at Art et Industrie, a New York City gallery specializing in one-off and limited-edition designs by artists. He has continued to create "sculpture that people can actually sit on." As he happily remarked, "Design people can say it is not furniture and the sculpture community can say it is not art."[82] The openwork aesthetic of *Thicket* is continuous with that of his nearly forty-year oeuvre, and it foretells the quirky, dematerialized furnishings that appear in the 1990s.

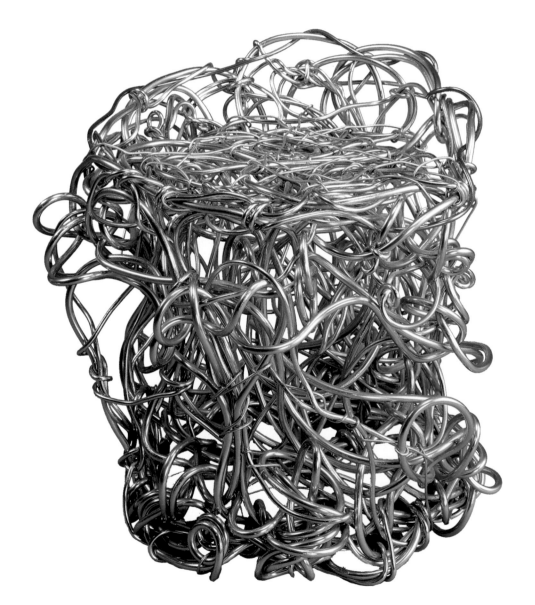

Ron **Arad**

98. **Armchair:** *Big Easy Volume Two* **(with BBC Arms)**

Designed 1988
Mild steel
101.9 x 136 x 97.8 cm
Executed by One-Off Ltd. (London, England), 1989
D90.200.1, gift of Paul Leblanc

Trained as an architect, Arad has long been fascinated with the philosophical and sculptural aspects of furniture design. His version of high-tech language is subversive, however, for his one-of-a-kind designs challenge the credos of Modernism—its ethics of functionalism for mass production, purified aesthetics, and truth to materials. His designs also defy bourgeois standards—the pursuit of ornament and comfort, especially while watching the BBC. This armchair, exploiting the flexibility of sheet steel, simultaneously mocks the middle-brow image of an inviting, overstuffed, plush armchair by transforming it into a hollow form in a cold, hard material. Yet despite the apparent threat of its seemingly sharp edges, the chair does allow sitting—if not with Victorian ease. More obscurely, the chair silhouette was

inspired by the three-part shape of the letter *Shin* in Hebrew, an alphabet that the Israeli-born designer explored for the shapes of this and eight other chairs he designed between 1986 and 1992 (fig. 127).

Expectations of form, material, and function are all inverted in Arad's series of Dada-spirited armchairs, in which no two examples of the same model are alike (fig. 128). Variations occur during welding and are accentuated by polishing, which creates an industrial version of freehand line drawings contrasting with the blackened steel. Sand, which partly fills some of the chairs in the series (though not this one), allows the user to shift the seat's center of gravity and thus the chair's uprightness. The user and the environment are reflected in distorted form in the chairs' irregular surfaces. All of these elements contribute to Arad's idiosyncratic, one-off expressions, yet paradoxically he has realized them through industrial materials and methods.

"One-Off" was the name Arad gave the alternative design studio and workshop he cofounded in 1981 and closed in 1993. The manufacturer of limited editions as well as unique pieces, Ron Arad Associates continues to give Arad a physical forum in London, from which he exercises important critical influence on design.

fig. 127 ▲ Raymond Guidot, *A Language of Forms Rooted in Ancient Hebrew Writing*, c. 1992.

fig. 128 ▲ Prototypes of *Big Easy Volume Two* armchairs as photographed in Arad's London studio, 1988.

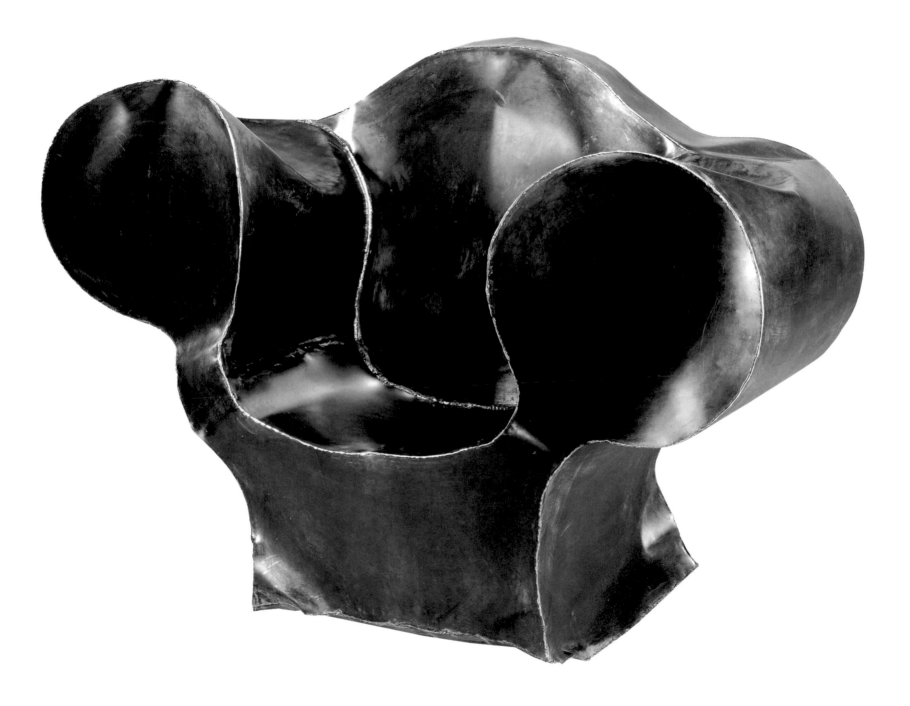

Sinya **Okayama**

99. **Stool:** *Kazenoko*

Designed 1984
Painted steel, rubber laminate
42 x 47 x 30.5 cm
Produced by Sinya Collections (Osaka, Japan)
and Interior Object Inc. (Tokyo, Japan),
1984 to the present
D93.125.1, gift of Sinya Okayama through Gallery 91

This stool's poetic title, *Kazenoko* (*Child of the Wind*),
suits its diminutive stature, its toylike ball feet,
and the stance of its third leg, extended as if bracing
against the weather. That leg has a wavy projection
at its top evoking a windblown banner, and the seat,
covered with ridged rubber laminate, swells
somewhat aerodynamically from this point into
a droplet shape. Japanese consumers can "read"
the stool easily: it was inspired by the Japanese
pictograph for "child of the wind," a Japanese
metaphor for a tough kid (able to withstand rough
weather), and it inaugurated Okayama's series of
furnishings with such linguistic sources. His sketch
for *Kazenoko* (fig. 129) conveys the whimsy and
charm of his conception.

   Shown in a Toronto gallery of art and design in
1984, the stool was admired by Alessandro Mendini,
a leading member of the Studio Alchimia group,
who invited Okayama to collaborate with him in
Milan on a furniture line. The Japanese and Italian
designers were equally interested in sign systems as
inspirations for the forms of objects, while Okayama
found in Milan's individualistic design milieu more
openness to experiment than he did in Japan.
Okayama's *Poetical Objects*, including lighting
fixtures and a chair, were shown by Nuova Alchimia
in Milan in 1985.

fig. 129 ▲ Okayama, drawing for the *Kazenoko* stool,
1984. Osaka, collection of the designer.

Ingo **Maurer**

100. **Table lamp:** *Fukushú*

Designed 1984
Nickel-plated iron, Makrolon plastic
61.2 x 35.5 x 9.9 cm
Produced by Design M (Munich, Germany),
1984 to the present
D89.117.1, gift of Design M

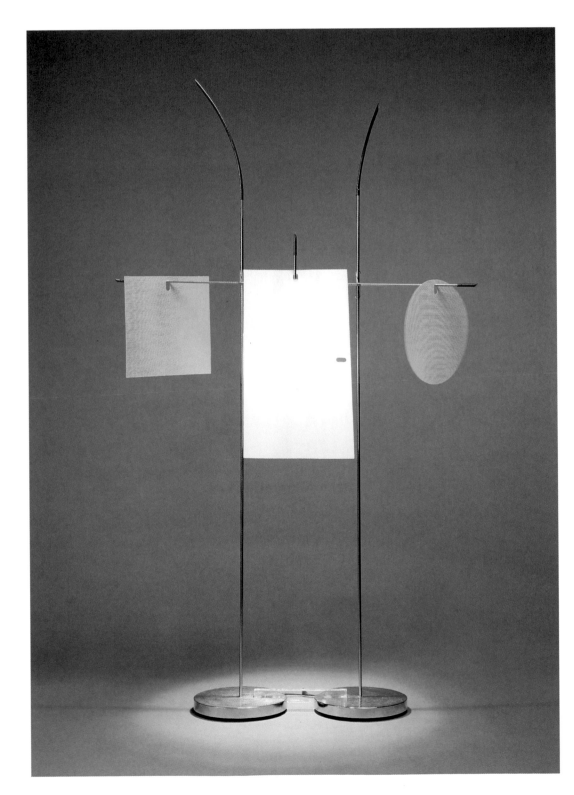

A Minimalist yet a playful fantasist in his aesthetics, Maurer enjoys the small scale and potential dematerialization that halogen lighting permits designers. *Fukushú*, with its pair of thin red- and blue-tipped rods on shiny disc feet, resembles a Japanese toy robot or a humorous table sculpture. The halogen fixture, with its transformer-sensor-dimmer, hangs on a horizontal bar at the center, and the owner can adjust the plastic reflectors. The work as a whole thus responds not only to the owner's lighting needs but to his or her tastes in abstraction. *Fukushú*, which means "review" in Japanese, invites another look (although Maurer says he chose the word and added the accent without concern for their meaning).[83]

Ingo Maurer's allowance for an individual's spontaneous intervention typifies much design of the 1980s, whether the product involves low-tech processes or high-tech materials, both of which are present here. Gone from this lamp is any admiration for the fixed and Platonic perfection of a Modernist object type. It is revealing that design innovations of the decade occurred especially in lighting. The field combines aspects of theater and sculpture, and it can affect mood and spatial perception with almost immaterial means. Later in the 1980s, Maurer developed lamps that could be turned on and regulated by touching them anywhere. These typically involve and amuse his usual patrons, while tactfully serving those with limited manual dexterity. In this sensitivity, his designs display concerns that were nascent in the 1970s and that would become broad issues in the 1990s.

Shiro **Kuramata**

101. **Armchair:** *Miss Blanche*

Designed 1988
Acrylic, paper roses, aluminum with stained
alumite finish
94 x 63 x 61 cm
Produced by Ishimaru Ltd. (Tokyo, Japan),
1988 to the present
D98.144.1

"My strongest desire is to be free of gravity, free
of bondage. I want to float," said Kuramata.[84] So
red roses float in the acrylic planes that compose
Miss Blanche, inspired by the corsage worn by the
faded New Orleans belle Blanche DuBois in the film
of Tennessee Williams' *A Streetcar Named Desire*.
As he often did, the Japanese designer confounded
expectations of his materials, having the artificial
flowers embalmed in clear plastic, and thus risking
but not succumbing to an association with kitsch.

Acrylic, available from the 1940s, had entered
furniture and lamp design in the 1960s. Here
Kuramata exploited its strength and transparency
as a medium for the roses, which serve as three-
dimensional chintz, casting shadows on the floor
and defying the Modernist taboo against ornament.
This chair's blend of wit and nostalgic charm calls
to mind the theatrical gestures and disguises of
Kuramata's idol, Marcel Duchamp: *Miss Blanche*
is an equivalent to the Dadaist's personification
as Rrose Selavy, half-mocking and half-extending
the lovelorn tradition. A year after conceiving this
chair, Kuramata explored the idea further in an
almost wholly acrylic bar interior he designed in
the Japanese city of Fukuoka: there, roses float
in acrylic columns (fig. 130).

Such allusiveness had paved Kuramata's way
to Memphis in 1981, when he participated in
the group's first exhibition in Milan. He remained
a member and considered Ettore Sottsass a mentor.
The echoes of Art Deco styling in this armchair's
wedge-shaped back and arms harmonize with the
Memphis group's retrospective historicism, as does
the chair's transmutation of materials and novel
coloration: its legs are pink-stained aluminum.
Nonetheless, before joining Memphis, Kuramata
had already pursued transparency to an extreme.
His one-of-a-kind *Glass Chair* of 1976 is solely
of glass, six flat sheets held together at their edges
by an industrial-strength glue. Like *Glass Chair*
and all Kuramata's designs, *Miss Blanche* seems
apparitional: no signs of labor remain on its simple
forms, and it floats with the completeness and
mystery of a magic trick.

fig. 130 ▲ Kuramata, interior of the Oblomov Bar,
Fukuoka, Japan, 1989.

Masayuki **Kurokawa**

102. **Table lamp:** *Lavinia*
Designed 1988
Painted aluminum
47 x 50.8 x 59 cm
Produced by Artemide S.p.A.
(Pregnana Milanese, Italy), 1988-92
D94.167.1

A Tokyo-based architect and industrial designer, Kurokawa works with geometries for his lamps, clocks, and other tablewares, but varies them with contrasts of textures and materials. His sensitivity to line typifies his gifts as a draftsmanlike sculptor, visible in the floating, eggshell-like shade of *Lavinia* and the forward tilt of its conical base. The all-white lamp hovers between space-age and natural associations: was it inspired by a rocket fuselage or a mushroom? This combination of futuristic aura with refined proportions and perfect industrial finish is characteristic of much Japanese design and has commended it to Italian manufacturers since the 1960s. Kurokawa's lamp was produced by Artemide as well as exhibited in international galleries of art furnishings. This suggests the range of consumers he has pleased with the subtlety of his contouring and the majesty of this expansive form.

Kurokawa first won prizes in the late 1960s for his architectural designs for prefabricated houses with novel uses of wood, concrete, and steel. Innovative handling of materials also characterizes his product design, which he began in the 1970s, and can be seen in his desk accessories in rubber and his *Cobra* lamps in Neoprene (cat. 70-71). Objects made in the 1980s such as *Lavinia* were created partly in response to the growth of Japanese taste for embellishing "the domestic landscape" in upscale homes. Whether candle holders or rice cookers, his designs are simplified shapes, with delicate contouring and smooth surfaces.

Philippe **Starck**

103. **Armchair: *Richard III***

Designed 1984
Polyurethane, metallic polyurethane enamel,
expanded polyurethane foam, Dacron, leather
upholstery
92 x 93 x 80 cm
Produced by Baleri Italia S.p.A. (Milan, Italy),
1985 to the present
D90.104.1

fig. 131 ▲ Starck, room in Mme Danielle Mitterrand's suite, Élysée Palace, Paris, c. 1984.

Except for its back legs, this armchair was molded as one piece of plastic, which is enameled a metallic silver and given a black leather seat cushion. The effect is intentionally somewhat sinister: from an angle the overstuffed form reveals itself as hollow, its stage-set thinness accentuated by the rear peg legs. One recalls that Richard III, the chair's royal namesake, was a crippled hunchback who used deceit, among other devices, to take the British throne. With Post-Modern tongue in cheek, Starck mocks the club chair and its outdated posh associations: "You always found club armchairs sitting on pavements when you came out of nightclubs at dawn," he said, "all that solid bourgeois comfort, out on the street." Using plastic technology to save space and weight, he believed he was playing "a dialectical game about topology and social representation. It has lost the connotations of a club chair, but still is one."[85] *Richard III* and other startling reconfigurations of traditional furniture types created much of the Frenchman's early success.

Starck began his meteoric career as artistic director of the high fashion house of Pierre Cardin, where he designed sixty-five furnishings (a remarkably large number in a short time) in the mid-1970s. In 1981, he was chosen, with five other young French designers, to decorate the private apartments of President François Mitterrand at the Élysée Palace, a government initiative that focused needed attention on new French design. Placed in a corner of one of Mme Mitterrand's rooms, *Richard III* is less ironic in effect than its regal location might promise: it does not show its peg legs and it is fully upholstered in leather (fig. 131). Capitalizing on the honor of the association, Starck sold his Élysée designs through mail-order catalogues and other channels, assuring that his elegant yet discomfiting idiom gained wider exposure. His subsequent commissions, for the interiors and accoutrements of stylish clubs, cafés, and hotels, have brought him international recognition, indicating the eternal appeal—known to the Surrealists, his artistic forebears—of the slightly outrageous.

Philippe **Starck**

104. **Coffee table**

Designed 1985
Glass
48.3 x 150 x 150 cm
Executed by Daum Cristal (Nancy, France), 1985
D91.394.1, gift of Lilliana and David Simpson

This low, all-glass table displays Starck's zoomorphic imagination in its bull's-horn-like legs, and his ability to draw on the best in French craftsmanship to realize his conceptions. Under his direction, glassblowers at the august firm of Daum Cristal made three of the hollow legs in clear glass, then created the fourth as an open-mouthed, green-tinted receptacle for fresh or dried flowers. The table was intended for the Royalton Hotel, one of Starck's most publicized commissions in New York City, but the idea was never realized in series. Nevertheless, his bull's-horn legs for furnishings and lighting appear in many guest rooms and the hotel's lobby. Such a svelte and luxurious reworking of conventions helps account for the designer's fame. "A piece of furniture is inevitably symbolic," he says. "Modernity is not expressed within a formal context, it is inevitably linked to social life, to materials, to manufacture."[86]

In general, Starck's stylistic and symbolic sources lie in nature and high art, in the aggressive yet alluring forms of animal horns and crustaceans, the polish and refinement of Brancusi's sculpture. Such shapes are visible in this table and his *Ara* lamp of 1988, for example, and he used two such lamps to turn himself into a Minotaur in a portrait photograph (fig. 132). Regarding his designs, the manufacturer Alberto Alessi remarked: "It seems clear to me that 'Beauty' is the wrong word to describe them, and that a more appropriate one should be looked for in the zone of 'Perturbation-Uneasiness-Fear. . . . This makes him a courageous tightrope-walker, grappling with the great mystery of the affections, and in particular with the code of life and death."[87]

fig. 132 ▲ Jean-Baptiste Mondino, portrait of Starck with his *Ara* table lamps, 1988.

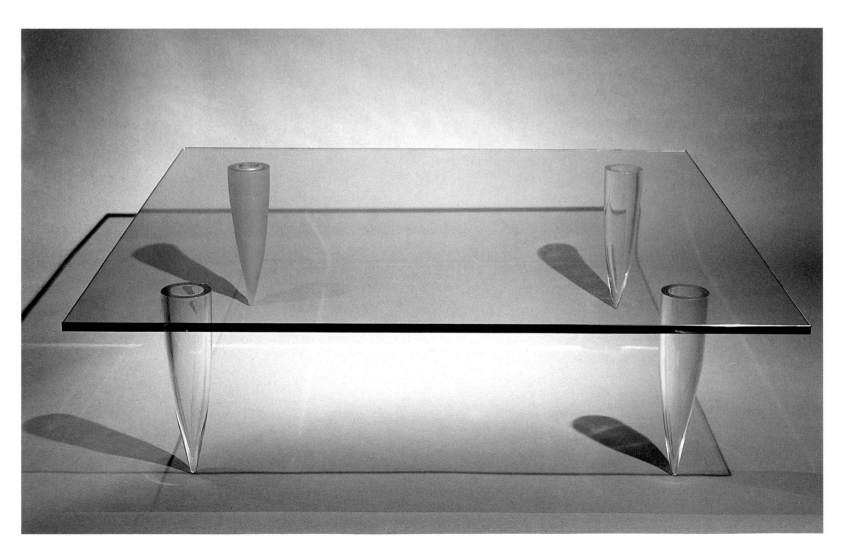

189

The 1990s
Materials
and Dematerialization

THE 1990S SAW "THE BEST OF TIMES AND THE WORST OF TIMES." THE END OF THE COLD WAR CREATED A resurgence of optimism throughout the world, yet new tensions replaced old ones. Eastern European countries were liberated from Soviet power and began the process of developing democracies; East and West Germany were reunified. The European Economic Community was established with the promise of a new unity and prosperity for member nations and saw the liberation of countries from the former Eastern Bloc. Balancing this was the rise of independent groups calling for cultural and political separation within the newly reconfigured Europe, ranging from the splitting apart of Czechoslovakia and Yugoslavia, and the devolution of Scotland, to the demands of separatists in Languedoc, Corsica, and Brittany in France, as well as in the Basque region of Spain. Yet despite such political rifts, the European Community, later known as the European Union, has struggled to establish a single market currency, even in the face of dissension from Denmark and Great Britain. Elsewhere, there are similar signs of optimism. The symbol of apartheid's injustice, Nelson Mandela, was elected president in the new South Africa. Taiwan held its first democratic election, but now that island faces renewed threats from China.

Throughout the world, the forces of ethnicity and regionalism have bloodied relations where there was once unity. In the 1990s, those forces led to some of the most appalling atrocities ever inflicted by human beings on one another. Millions of Africans perished in genocidal tribal conflicts in Rwanda and Somalia; civil war tore Zaire, Liberia, Sierra Leone, and Nigeria; and AIDS and famine disproportionately ravaged that continent. In 1992, civil war erupted after four of the six republics of Yugoslavia declared their independence; and by 1998 the murder and eviction of Muslims conducted by Serbs and Croats in that region escalated to massive proportions. Despite the intervention of NATO forces, the West was forced to remember the limits of technology: its superior military hardware could not enforce lasting solutions.

A renewed realization of the cyclical nature of economies dawned at the beginning of the decade. What financial observers called the Predator's Ball of the 1980s had a morning after, well after the 1987 stock market crash, in the recession of 1990-91. Economic giants of the 1980s were humbled, including Japan, by overleveraged real estate and currency speculation, and Germany in part by the costs of reunifying the country. On July 1, 1997, Great Britain ceded control over Hong Kong to China in a lavish ceremony that was shortly overshadowed by the collapse of Thailand's economy, whose stabilization required emergency International Monetary Fund loans. In 1998, the crash of stock markets across East Asia brought the region into its greatest economic crisis since World War II amid the speculative sales of national currencies: the Japanese yen slumped badly due to economic recession; astronomical costs of living and a plummeting currency in Indonesia led to looting and the forced dismissal of President Suharto after thirty-two years in office. Such economic changes gave urgency to older concerns about wasteful production, disappearing natural resources, the fragile environment, and relations between industrialized and Third World countries. The search for solutions was complicated by the often strident babel of multiculturalism.

Computer technology and global communications, which grew exponentially in the decade, lightened designers' work, but the majority of the designers realized their responsibilities were heavier, if conferences, special issues, and new books are any barometer of what was being discussed. The 1980s had fostered design's affiliation with fashion and art; the 1990s reawakened its social consciousness. Prosperity returned in the second half of the decade, and the Dow Jones industrial average broke 11,000, less than twenty years after it touched 1,000, but the design and art masquerade of the 1980s did not resume.

When the couturier Karl Lagerfeld, a pioneer supporter of Memphis, sold his collection in 1991, the auction marked the end of an era and the dominance of that design movement.[88]

fig. 133 ► Jean Nouvel, Cartier Foundation for Contemporary Art, Paris, 1994, showing exterior curtain wall.

Although design of the 1990s had the plurality of styles that had typified the field since the 1960s, transparency and minimalism represented one pole of expression. Among what could be called Neo-Minimalists, the cacophonous patterns and colors of Memphis ceded to unadorned planar surfaces, soft and translucent hues, and simplified silhouettes. The ornamented facades of buildings and cabinets went the way of the ornate couture worn on television's internationally popular *Dynasty* and *Dallas*. In the aesthetic of lightness, transparency, and simplicity that characterized an aspect of the decade, one might even find a yearning for things of the spirit, as materialism, the opiate of the West, lost favor. The Mardi Gras celebration of material possessions from the 1950s through the 1980s was over for a time, and thinking consumers sought values of quality over quantity in their purchases.

The Museum of Modern Art's exhibition *Light Constructions* (1995) used its punning title to describe an international style of contemporary architecture in which buildings are seemingly both lightweight and filled ingeniously with light in various forms. The architectural reinterpretation of the work of early Modernists showed a sensibility that was also apparent in the design world. Many of the means were similar to those of the interwar generation, but the goals differed. As in the architect Jean Nouvel's building for the Cartier Foundation for Contemporary Art in Paris (fig. 133), the curtain wall is not part of the structure of the building, as it would have been in a work by Mies van der Rohe, but, instead, a separate veil set in front. It engages the viewer in an optical game of reading superimposed reflections and deformations that relate solid and void, interior and exterior, building and environment, yet make that relation ambiguous and contingent. Similarly, Karim Rashid's three-tiered glass coffee table (cat. 129) lends itself to shifting perceptions, while challenging one's grasp of its conception.

Mirrorlike surfaces, seen in architecture of the 1980s, also migrated to design, and their silvery beauty and intriguing sensory confusions became positive features of furnishings by such designers as Andrea Anastasio (cat. 128) and Ron Arad. Arad inaugurated the Cartier Foundation's exhibition program by filling the entrance level with mirror-polished tables that challenged the identification of the ceiling and floor (fig. 134). Foremost among dematerializing designers was Shiro Kuramata, whose furniture and interiors were made from transparent acrylic: the magical results are physically strong and heavy but visually evanescent, defined less by their simplified forms than by ambient light and the viewer's vantage point (cat. 125).

A Neo-Minimalist aesthetic, partly in reaction to Memphis, also inspired designers as different as Jasper Morrison in Great Britain and Antonio Citterio of Italy. Morrison's pared-down, straightforward designs for furniture in wood, which he introduced in the 1980s, asked for comparison with such designs of the 1950s as Gio Ponti's *Superleggera* chair (cat. 18), and they brought him international attention in the 1990s. In 1999, he was invited to be guest editor of the *International Design Yearbook*, selecting what he considered the significant products of the year. Morrison opined that what "led to modernism's temporary downfall was [its lack of] humor, or at least a lightness of touch which took into account that while a product was born to industry, it was destined to spend the rest of its life with people, who might not be interested in the dry logic of manufacturing solutions. . . . Looking back there was nothing wrong with modernism, it just needed an oil change."[89] Also participating in the postwar revival was The Knoll Group, which reintroduced its designs from the 1950s. Functional above all and also sophisticated in their allusions, revisions of Modernism by Morrison, The Knoll Group, and others have been one of the most important aspects of design in this decade.

Finding inspiration in postwar design also bore fruit on a popular level, as the utilitarian simplicities of "Scandinavian Modern" reached into millions of homes through the IKEA chain of international stores and mail-order system. The company, founded in the 1950s, was offering

fig. 134 ► Ron Arad, installation of forty mirror-polished stainless steel tables on the entrance level of the Cartier Foundation for Contemporary Art, Paris, 1994.

over twelve thousand home products by the 1990s, selling its low-cost but quality furniture and housewares in twenty-six nations.[90] Thanks to IKEA's skills in distribution, Good Design as defined in the 1950s at last found its intended audience—although one that demanded less refinement and durability than its grandparents had.

Modest cost was not the only benefit of Good Design as revisited in the 1990s. The decade's advocacy of formal reduction in some cases went hand in hand with the acceleration of the Green Design movement. The issue of responsibility to the environment, recognized in the 1970s, was of wide concern in the 1990s, as governments, designers, and consumers took the need to conserve resources and nature more seriously. In industrialized countries, recycling laws became ubiquitous: by the middle of the decade, some 6,600 cities and towns in the United States were estimated to have such programs, and the federal Environment Protection Agency asserted that approximately one-fifth of waste products were being recycled. Environmentally conscious design added value to manufactures; according to the *Green Newsletter*, by 1994, 10.5 percent of new products claimed a green feature.[91]

Epitomizing environmentally conscious design in the decade, as well as idiosyncratic minimalism, was Droog Design, introduced at the 1993 Salone del Mobile in Milan. A loose organization of designers with a shared mission of experimentation, this Dutch collaborative brought the Netherlands into the forefront of global design. Droog designs in furnishings, lighting, and housewares were developed apart from their financial potential but, nevertheless, they have proved moderately successful commercially and are manufactured in the Netherlands and Italy. "Droog" signifies "dry" in Dutch, a word with connotations the group wanted its work to evoke: "Strong and clear like a good Martini, the desert, or a pointed remark in a conversation."[92] The group saw itself as typical of the 1990s in its oppositional stance and refusal to adopt a single program. "Our products challenge that culture, run counter to it—in other words, derive their recalcitrance from it," said Renny Ramakers. "We certainly don't see them as the definitive solution to a problem or the one direction to take but as the door to any number of possibilities."[93] Thus recycling was the theme of the chest of drawers made from old drawers piled and belted together (cat. 111) and a hanging lamp of recycled milk bottles by Tejo Remy (cat. 110), whereas Marcel Wanders' *Knotted Chair* was of high-tech Aramid fibers (cat. 109). Despite their disparate styles and materials, these pieces showed a shared desire to give design humanistic values. Found objects were introduced to art by Dada and popularized by Pop, but for Droog they were not nihilistic but moralistic: they proclaimed "Waste not, Want not" to a culture of stupefying overabundance.

Droog ignored the traditional identification of important design with a single, signature style. For this it drew on precedents in the art world of the 1980s as, for example, in the changes of idiom by the German painter Sigmar Polke which epitomized the Post-Modern denial of aesthetic hierarchies. Nonetheless, the design market of the 1990s and celebrity-hungry media still supported superstars such as Philippe Starck, whose work presented an identifiable image of elegance and wit (cat. 114). Starck's glamorous interiors for hotels, restaurants, and boutiques were built throughout the world and often published, making the designer a cult figure. Not content to remain in his native France, in 1999 Starck moved to New York, which he perceived to be the world's center for promoting and selling new design.

Even more mobile was the Czech-born Bořek Šípek who, like Starck, pursued a Surrealist poetry of organicism, but with the Baroque accent of Middle Europe. Šípek's relocations, from the Netherlands to Germany and back to the Czech Republic, symbolize the mobility of designers in reunited, post-Cold War Europe.

The stylistic exuberance of Starck and Šípek was shared by British designers who emerged in the 1980s from the "one-off" art traditions of punk culture, such as Ron Arad, Tom Dixon, Nigel Coates, and Marc Newson. While they couched their expressionism largely in welded-metal sculptural forms, veteran Italian designers including Gaetano Pesce and Alessandro Mendini showed sustained allegiance to painterly and decorative modes. Whereas neo-minimalism in design revised Modernist architectural models and their functionalist values, the expressionist vein drew strength from subjective currents in 1980s painting and sculpture.

In this vein, Pesce conceived one of the most radical interiors of the 1990s, the Manhattan facility of Chiat/Day, the advertising agency's office completed in 1994 (and, sadly, demolished when Chiat/Day later moved). The interior can be seen as an extension of the open planning initiated in workplaces of the 1960s and also as an example of the new spaces made possible by the computer. The facility had no offices at all. Employees met via laptop computer communication and cellular phones and in areas allocated according to the account they were working on. The elimination of personal space was seen as positive, countering territoriality and competitive status seeking and refocusing attention on the tasks at hand. Signs of creativity were everywhere. Pesce covered all surfaces—floors, ceilings, walls—with his childlike paintings in vivid hues of poured resins, the idiom of his furnishings of the 1980s and 1990s (cat. 75, 116). The paintings combined meaning and decoration: a big arrow on the floor pointed from the elevator to the reception desk; a conference room festooned with lamps suggested ideas lighting up (fig. 135). To clients, the design identified the agency with innovation and artistic daring. To the agency director Jay Chiat and Pesce, the space was a village fostering communal activity, its energy level raised by the speed of computer technology. For them, the "virtual office" created in cyberspace focused attention "not on what people have, but what they do."[94] The design of the space and furnishings was liberated to address the employees' and the clients' social and cultural needs and desires. Pesce's Chiat/Day interior represented an extreme in the exploitation

of the separation between the functional and the symbolic. This awareness of the importance of
symbolism in furnishing and product designs—and even of the symbolism of the functionalist
look—has been an important theme in design since the 1960s.

The computer also revolutionized design as a whole in the 1990s. It became the accepted
tool, with the Internet as its instant and global communication link. The design process was for-
ever altered. A wide variety of design software was developed, which speeded the generation
of design and reduced costs. No longer drawn laboriously by hand, design concepts were
explored via computer-generated images which showed virtual objects in three dimensions and
calculated the behavior of their materials. This also eased communication with colleagues and
clients and eliminated the need for making all but the final models and prototypes. Greater
experimentation was possible because problems were solved early in the design process and
thus performance could be tested, avoiding costly mistakes. In addition, computer-aided design
and molding (CAD/CAM) allowed specifications and tooling to be changed quickly during
manufacture. Products could be altered to suit changing needs and niche markets, ending the
uniformity once intrinsic to factory output. The convenience of systems such as CAD has been
condemned for contributing to the glut of objects on today's marketplace, but the growing ubiq-
uity of design software has also refocused attention on the quality of each conception and on
the need for thoughtful design programs.

The computer whetted the world's appetite for information, an appetite already evident in the realms of art and culture in the burgeoning of museums, galleries, and publishing since the 1980s. In the 1990s, understanding of modern design was enhanced as important exhibitions of it were organized and in some cases toured. Compared to the Good Design shows of the 1950s, these demonstrated the rise in the reputation of designers and the increased sophistication of museum practices. Following European curatorial customs, the Georges Pompidou Center in Paris invited important individual designers to participate in the planning and installation of retrospectives of their own work. Sottsass was honored in 1994, and Pesce's 1996 retrospective, *The Time of Questions*, incorporated his creative use of resin in his floor "paintings" as well as in many of his objects on view. In 1997-98, the Hara Museum of Contemporary Art in Tokyo circulated an impressive retrospective of Shiro Kuramata worldwide.

The 1990s also saw the further development of museums specifically for modern and contemporary design. Notable was the creation in 1989 of the Design Museum in London, now independent of its parent institution, the Victoria & Albert Museum; design museums in Toronto and Chicago were also established. In 1990, the Vitra Design Museum, using the corporate collection of the Vitra furniture manufacturing company, opened the doors of its new Frank Gehry building in Weil am Rhein, Germany, to the public, and began originating and circulating exhibitions of twentieth-century furnishings, as well as hosting summer workshops in France with leading designers. In Italy, serious steps were taken to found a design museum in the extensive buildings of the Milan Triennale. Three exhibitions were held to explore how design should be collected and displayed, and a permanent collection was inaugurated. In 1996, Andrea Branzi staged the survey *Italian Design 1964-1972*, and he followed this with an exhibition focusing on the period 1973-1990. Twentieth-century design was being codified and institutionalized.

Meanwhile, current design has remained vital. The nineteenth Milan Triennale was held in the spring of 1996. Exhibitions modeled on the Triennale, such as the furniture trade fairs of Cologne and Barcelona, also became significant in the last years of the decade. And the New York

Furniture Fair, which had once been a pallid echo of Milan, sparked off-site (or "off") exhibitions that were coordinated by the New Museum of Contemporary Art, an institution devoted to the innovative art of today. These events signaled the art world's recognition of quality in current design, and they revived public interest in the subject.

The Milan furniture fair, the Salone del Mobile, held annually since 1961, continued to be a focal point for new creative design in the 1990s. Related exhibitions outside the official area, in both showrooms and alternative exhibition spaces, increased excitement for the Salone. Of the "off" exhibitions, some of the most creative were those mounted by Design Gallery Milano, while off-site and at the Triennale, well-received installations were co-organized by Ingo Maurer and Ron Arad (fig. 136). The contrast of Maurer's magical lighting with Arad's boldly sculptural furnishings sharpened interest in their ceaseless invention.

The last Milan furniture fair of the millennium included many familiar names. An exhibition of designs by Sottsass, then in his eighty-second year, indicated the astonishing energy of his last three decades of work. Recent and new minimalists were shown, including Jasper Morrison, Antonio Citterio, and the Belgian Marten van Severen, and their bare-boned, beautifully crafted furniture was much praised. The austere yet individualized and subtle designs of those younger designers who had rediscovered Modernism in the 1990s—its style and aspects of its idealism—were a promising indication of the future.

Also prophetic was a 1999 project involving the Droog collective in the historic town of Oranienbaum, once behind the Iron Curtain and now part of reunified Germany. To revive its severely depressed economy and renew its cultural identity, the town invited Droog to propose designs to be made with local materials by local manufacturers. Droog's slogan, reviving that of the 1970s, was "act locally, think globally." All of its many design ideas were appealingly modest in form and environmentally engaged: for example, a lollipop of local orange candy came on a prettily curved poplar stick with an orange seed. The packaging suggested you eat the candy and plant the seed, with the hope that it would grow into a tree. "Restoration, revival and innovation are the three pillars supporting the [Droog] concept," wrote one of the Oranienbaum organizers, "the guiding purpose of which was to give the complex its soul back."[95] His belief, on the eve of a new millennium, that design could restore a community's soul was profoundly uplifting.

Frank O. **Gehry**

105. **Armchair: *Power Play***

Designed 1990
Maple-faced plywood
94.5 x 88.5 x 65 cm
Executed by Gehry Studio (Los Angeles, CA, USA), 1990
D92.111.1, gift of Frank Gehry and The Knoll Group

Ever-inventive with unlikely materials and methods, Gehry was inspired by bushel baskets of thin, woven bentwood to create a line of chairs and tables for The Knoll Group. The vernacular craft, still in use, produces strong but lightweight, inexpensive containers for vegetables and fruit. Gehry used it to improve on the Modernist tradition of bentwood furniture, which descends from Thonet to Aalto and the Eameses. After trying out more than a hundred prototypes (of which this is one), he and the engineers at The Knoll Group arrived at a series of five chairs and a table which have been produced from 1991 to the present (fig. 138). In production, this armchair (on the far left) differs from the prototype in its more splayed silhouette, the elimination of the basket weaving in the seat, and the structure of the arms and legs. Earlier bentwood furniture, Gehry pointed out, "always had a heavy substructure and thin webbing, or an intermediary structure for the seating. The difference in my chairs is that the [support] structure and the seat are formed of the same lightweight slender wood strips, which serve both functions. The material forms a single and continuous idea." Gehry experimented boldly with the bentwood as he discovered its strength,

and he gave the pliant strips an airy curvilinearity. Yet this beauty derives from function, in the spirit of Modernist design. "The swirls and curves of my chairs are structural and they grow out of necessity," Gehry said.[96] The maple, sealed with an environmentally friendly water-based finish, and its weaving have a reassuring familiarity, yet the forms Gehry gives the bentwood are open, springy, and contemporary, reworking traditional furniture types with easy grace.

Gehry's art conceals his work, which is part of its charm. Forty-one pieces of bentwood and 130 glue joints were needed to create this armchair in manufacture, but one focuses instead on its adroit internal spatial relations and its arabesque of lines. Gehry's alchemy with the thin laminate is more obvious: one marvels at its strength, as one does with the cardboard of his *Easy Edges* chairs (cat. 54). Both furniture lines are ecologically sensitive, using modest materials; both join low-tech associations with high-tech methods of mass production. If the *Easy Edges* chairs have a Dada impudence, his bentwood furniture is perhaps nostalgic—with some of the retrospectiveness of design at the end of the millennium.

fig. 137 ◄ The Knoll Group, 1992 publicity photograph showing the *Power Play* armchairs and companion coffee table.

fig. 138 ▲ The Knoll Group, 1992 publicity photograph showing some of the *Power Play* chairs, an ottoman, and a table.

Ron **Arad**

106. **Bookcase: *One Way or Another***

Designed 1993
Steel
255 x 180 x 30 cm
Executed by One-Off Ltd. (London, England), 1993
D93.311.1, gift of Mr. and Mrs. Roger Labbé

Arad's ribbonlike bookcase of blackened, tempered sheet steel tends to sway depending on the weight and position of what is placed in it—hence its name (provided by Arad's young daughter). This variability is a result of its quirky shape and material, and it is an aspect of Arad's idiosyncratic design in general. Just as the sand inside some of his sheet metal *Big Easy* armchairs allows the owner to shift their center of gravity, so this bookcase responds to the user and his or her collection of objects while otherwise denying all expectations of the form. Rejecting the grid of conventional shelving or even right angles, the bookcase nevertheless actually functions as storage, while it dominates its environment by its large scale and doodlelike shape.

A purposely shocking designer and theorist in the 1980s, Arad created marginally more appealing furnishings and interiors in the 1990s at the same time that a growing client list learned to like his challenges. Inspired by the curvaceous shapes of pappardelle noodles, he made sheet steel in more irregular configurations into chair, lectern, and chaise longue forms (fig. 139). The continuous S-curves of *One Way or Another* and its family of steel bookcases led to his first commercial venture, the *Bookworm* bookcase manufactured by Kartell in translucent plastic of various colors (fig. 140). The plastic shelving can be bought by measure and installed in the configuration decided by the owner; it was a popular success from its introduction in 1994. *One Way or Another*, the series of *Papardelle* chairs, and the plastic *Bookworm* are all sleeker and less threatening than his work of the 1980s. On his metal pieces, the marks of their welding are smoothed away and their surfaces are glamorously shiny. They too represent Arad's exploration of the properties of sheet steel, including its ability to extend drawing into three dimensions. The metal's springiness introduces an amusing kineticism to furniture forms and materials that one normally expects to be rigid.

fig. 139 ▲ Arad, *London Papardelle* chair, 1992. Montreal Museum of Decorative Arts.

fig. 140 ▲ Topdeq, 1996 publicity photograph showing Arad's *Bookworm* shelf and the *Titania* lamp by Alberto Meda and Paolo Rizzatto.

Marc **Newson**

107. Chair: _Wicker Chair_
Designed 1990
Wicker, steel
77 x 66 x 88 cm
Produced by Idée Co., Ltd. (Tokyo, Japan),
1992 to the present
D99.166.1

Looking more like a basket or a stocking than a chair, Newson's wicker seat seems to be a single piece of weaving voluptuously curved in three directions. Underneath, though, is a steel frame, and a steel strut at the back gives additional support. Signatures of his style are the chair's pinched waist, the continuity of its seat and support, here eliminating legs, and its allusions to the streamlining of 1950s industrial forms. Also available in a reclining format and in felt (over reinforced fiberglass and aluminum), the design marries a traditional material with an aerodynamic shape, a combination of low and high tech characteristic of much 1990s design. Using wicker and felt may reflect the strained economy of the early part of the decade, since those materials allow cheaper production and less skilled labor. But, as designers such as Pesce and Arad found, they also permit forms of continuous curvilinearity, satisfying tastes both nostalgic and futuristic.

Newson began his career as a jewelry designer, and then worked with Arad in London and at length in Japan for the manufacturer Idée. The craftsmanship and draftsmanship that this background fostered are evident in his understanding of weaving and the contour of this chair. It was preceded by boldly curved designs of the late 1980s with names like _Embryo_ and _Orgone_, in which Newson celebrated the surfer culture of his native Sydney, Australia, as well as _moderne_ sculptures of the 1930s by artists such as Alexander Archipenko. Such designs by Newson, executed in sheet metal, drew the attention of Arad and Starck, who helped make him a celebrity by the time he was twenty-two.

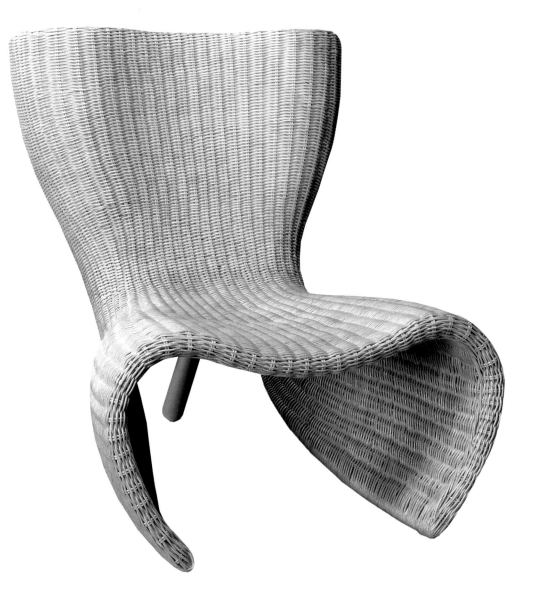

David **Palterer**

108. **Armchairs:** *Tritrono*

Designed 1990
Ebonized ash
71.7 x 72.3 x 72 cm; 71.7 x 76 x 73.5 cm;
71.7x 74.5 x 84.5 cm
Executed by David Palterer for Galleria Paola
e Rossella Colombari (Milan, Italy), 1990
D91.409.1-3

The name *Tritrono* describes this composition of chairs: *trono* means *throne* in Italian, and when placed together, these chairs become a Post-Modern tripartite throne. The shelf-like extensions from their crest rails compose one horizontal surface when they are placed back to back, turning the group into an elaborate table form. Here Palterer wittily demonstrates that any chair can function in groups and alone, while he quotes a flirtatious nineteenth-century settee type and inverts the 1950s idea of sectional seating. In midcentury suburban homes, modular, foam rubber sofa sections fitted together to create conversation areas. In *Tritrono*, however, Palterer's spiny wooden chairs become one only when they face outward, a metaphor for the oppositions within unity that typify much current cultural experience.

As for process, Palterer prefers to work in an organic way, as if sculpting a figure. "A work is like a person: you're doing the bust, then you do the legs, because everything is done together."[97] This is the attitude of an artist—indeed he carved these three chairs himself as part of a handcrafted limited edition. It may seem paradoxical, therefore, that this Israeli-born artist was trained as an architect at the University of Florence, and taught there while also designing buildings, interiors, and products. Yet the architectural training that evolved in Italy in the 1970s and 1980s stressed theory over practice, coming out of the Anti-Design movement. Like his Italian colleagues, Palterer is interested in the deconstruction of norms and expectations in design, including even the placement of chair legs. Here the sitter must straddle the front leg, because the seat is turned at a forty-five-degree angle to the back. "Typologies and tastes . . . are too often determined by a social order and by obsessively repetitive processes," he said in 1994.[98] This is a far cry from older, functionalist theory—just as *Tritrono* is a far cry from conventional seating.

Marcel **Wanders**

109. **Chair: *Geknoopte stoel***

Designed 1995
Carbon and Aramid fibers, epoxy
74.8 x 50.5 x 66 cm
Produced by Cappellini S.p.A. (Como, Italy),
1996 to the present
D99.138.1, gift of Cappellini S.p.A.

An ancient craft meets today's technology in this small, low chair, which has become an icon of Droog design. Conceived by Marcel Wanders, the *Geknoopte stoel (Knotted Chair)* is made by macramé or knotting string—that tool-free, Third-World method of weaving adopted by flower children worldwide in the late 1960s. The material used for Wanders' macramé, however, is strictly datable to 1995 in the West, when he invented this carbon fiber rope in a sleeve of Aramid fibers. In his process, it is knotted by an individual worker into a limp chair shape and then, at the Cappellini plant, soaked in liquid epoxy, hung in a frame in the form desired, and dried at eighty degrees centigrade. Lightweight and lacy, the finished chair is both rigid and very strong.

The processes and form of Wanders' chair came during experimentation in his studio and at the Laboratory for Aeronautics and Astronautics of the T.U. Polytechnic in Delft. Wanders had the idea of translating macramé to furniture, and sought a mass-produceable design that would look old, so that it would not soon appear out of date, and that would appear and actually be handmade. "I want to make objects that last long," he writes, ". . . that communicate positive messages . . . products that tell me, '. . . I am made with great care and love, by someone who liked to make me. I am there to grow old together with you.'"[99]

In fact, Wanders' chair does appear unassuming and faintly familiar, not drastically new. The quiet surprise it offers is the transformation of normally boneless macramé, most often seen in slings for hanging flower pots, into a strong seating material.

fig. 141 ▲ Wanders' living room, Amsterdam, showing his *Geknoopte stoel* and *Shadow* and *Set-up Shades* lamps, as well as Starck's *Bubu 1er*, 1997.

Tejo **Remy**

110. **Hanging lamp:** *Melkflessenlamp*
Designed 1991
Sandblasted glass milk bottles, stainless steel
28.5 x 36 x 36 cm
Produced by DMD (Development Manufacturing
Distribution Rotterdam BV) (Voorburg,
the Netherlands), 1993 to the present
D99.124.1, gift of Murray Moss

Remy designed this lamp of recycled milk bottles
as well as the chest of drawers (cat. 111) and
a chair of rags for his final exams in design at the
Utrecht College for the Fine Arts in 1991. Using
Robinson Crusoe's island as an image was the self-
imposed task, and Remy improvised with materials
at hand. He intended his designs to counter the
decorative abundance and costly materials of many
furnishings of the 1980s, as well as the glut of
different products serving the same purpose. He also
wanted to exploit the humble lyricism of his chosen
ingredients, their memories of the past, as Remy put
it, like those of old American patchwork quilts.[100]
His materials are not castoffs of sophisticated
contemporary technology but of older processes
from a simpler time: these bottles are reminders of
home delivery and of the Netherlands' wonderfully
rich milk, which adults have traditionally enjoyed as
much as their children do.

The straightforwardness of the assembly of
the *Melkflessenlamp* (*Milkbottle Lamp)* is part of its
sober appeal. Four rows of bottles appear three
deep, as they do in a Dutch milk crate. They were
frosted by the manufacturer to diffuse the light and
imitate older bottles; special stainless-steel fittings
replace the original caps, and hold the sockets and
bulbs. Whether or not the rationality of the piece
can be associated with the de Stijl tradition in the
Netherlands and the Calvinist strictness attributed
to the Dutch national character, as some observers
claim,[101] Remy's lamp reflects the new frankness in
design that would inspire the formation of the Droog
collaborative in 1993. No displays of technical
ingenuity and no intricate transformations are
evident here: the milk bottles merely hang down
and light up.

fig. 142 ▲ The home of Thomas Niddershoven
and Nikki Gonnissen (two members of Droog Design),
Amsterdam, 1996, showing the *Melkflessenlamp*.

Tejo **Remy**

111. **Chest of drawers: *You Can't Lay Down Your Memories***

Designed 1991
Maple, recycled wood, plastic, metal,
and cardboard drawers, cotton belt
134.5 x 136 x 69 cm
Produced by Droog Design (Amsterdam,
the Netherlands), 1991 to the present
D99.159.1

Composing this chest are twenty drawers from old and recently made furniture in different sizes and as many different facings, held together by a furniture mover's belt. At the end of the twentieth century, no better metaphor may be found for the sense of life's transience, of the temporary nature of ownership, and the contingency of commodities themselves. Evoking a moving man's bundle or a 1950s assemblage of found objects like those by Arman, this poetically named chest of drawers nonetheless functions as storage. This is one of the achievements of the much-heralded Dutch collective, Droog Design, with which Tejo Remy has been associated: its furnishings are down-to-earth and rich in social comment. They are as easily fabricated as they are put together and disassembled by the client, and thus suit a fluid lifestyle of changing needs and locations (fig. 143).

Choosing discarded, everyday furniture parts and disdaining manufacturing reflects Droog's attitudes toward the environment and technology. This chest's components are virtuous as recycled objects and also resonant through their marks of age and use, summoning up the offices and homes of bygone ages. Finishing the drawers for this chest simply required giving each a complete wooden sleeve. Thus the chest in its simplicity makes a large-scale claim as both art and socially aware design. This is a one-of-a-kind piece, yet consumers can order a similar chest designed on the same principles. It may include different components and it is shipped unassembled, leaving consumers the freedom to arrange it at will, and include pieces of their own. One owner even added a television.

Typical of Droog is the collective's more conceptual than commercial approach: many of its pieces are limited runs, like this one, or one-offs, as well as prototypes for mass production. There is no manifesto or set of problem-solving devices. Although such gently Dadaist pieces as Remy's were popular from the start, the designers linked with Droog have since moved on to use synthetics and explore decoration. Such individualism and low-key experiment also distinguish Droog from earlier design groups, such as Memphis, which were equally well received but made an immediate impact through canny marketing and an emphasis on sensational aspects of style.

fig. 143 ▲ Remy's *You Can't Lay Down Your Memories* chest of drawers being assembled at the home of Thomas Niddershoven and Nikki Gonnissen, Amsterdam, 1996.

Fernando and Humberto
Campana

112. Tables
Designed 1995
Plastic, aluminum pizza pans, aluminum
44.5 x 41 x 41 cm
Produced by Fernando and Humberto Campana
(São Paulo, Brazil), 1995 to the present
D99.105.1; D99.125.1

Made with two aluminum pizza pans, these inflatable tables epitomize many aspects of furnishings in the 1990s: the minimalism, the "no-design" design, and the stress on usefulness. After opening the slender shipping carton, the customer can blow up a table for use, and he or she can deflate it with equal ease for quick packing. The Campana brothers' work

has little of the obvious humor of the inflatable furnishings of the 1960s like *Blow* (cat. 43), which imitated beach toys. Nor are the pizza pans identifiable as such, and thus they lack any Dada shock value as obvious readymades. Rather, this is a simple, unadorned cylinder in a cheerful color of transparent plastic, which can lay full claim to the 1990s' favorite quality—lightness. It is literally made of air. This and contemporary designs by the Campanas, such as a chair of woven plastic garden hose and a screen criss-crossed by plastic string, are most notable for their refusals—of ornament, allusion, complexity of form, weight, apparent value. Like the cargo pants and little slip dresses that swept 1990s fashion from Paris to chain stores, they announce that the owner is superior to the ostentation that typified design developments in the 1980s. The inflatable table also has the merit of moderate price: under $100 (USA) in 1999.

Ali **Tayar**

113. **Coffee table: *NEA Table I***

Designed 1995
Recycled particle-board palette, aluminum, glass
32.2 x 121.7 x 101.5 cm
Executed by Ali Tayar (New York, NY, USA), 1995
D97.130.1, gift of Ali Tayar

Tayar named this prototype for a coffee table after the NEA, the National Endowment for the Arts, because the United States government agency subsidized the project that led to this design. He defined his research purpose as "to explore the potential of molded particle board as a new material for furniture design," having been inspired by a pallet of the wood composite that he found discarded outside his studio door.[102]

Particle board, a wood composite compressed with resin, comes in various densities according to the different calibers of the wood shavings or chips utilized. It was introduced in the late 1970s as a cheap alternative to wood and plywood in mass construction, and is both durable and environmentally sound. Tayar employed not the familiar sheet type used for building but the stock pallet itself, a rough, molded slab grooved for strength and designed to help transport crates. It is a commercial product that costs about $5 (USA).

Tayar confronted the pallet's coarseness head-on, covering it with glass to provide a level surface that also reveals it. He fitted the nine stumps on its bottom (which normally allow space for a fork lift to be inserted) with clawlike aluminum legs that he had sand-cast at Lowe-Tech, Owlshead, Maine. The total has the tribal air of a work by Garouste and Bonetti, but Tayar's goal is a different consumer from theirs, one whom he hopes to reach through mass production. "I don't want to be known as the guy who made cool furniture for rich people. You should be able to order my things out of a catalogue just like IKEA," he said, referring to the Scandinavian chain of stores selling modestly priced furniture.[103] His concern for the consumer and his use of a waste material place Tayar among the environmentally conscious designers of the decade, which was acknowledged by the inclusion of a variant of the table in The Museum of Modern Art's lively survey of 1995, *Mutant Materials in Contemporary Design*. Ironically, though, the table has not yet found a manufacturer.

Philippe **Starck**

114. **Stools/coffee tables:** *Bubu 1ᵉʳ*

Designed 1991
Polypropylene
44 x 32.5 x 32.5 cm
Produced by OWO (Pisa, Italy), 1992-95;
by XO (Servon, France), 1996 to the present
D95.103.1; D99.139.1-2

Starck's characteristic playfulness with furnishing types continues in these chunky stools/coffee tables. Their cylindrical primitivism, like tribal stools cut from tree trunks, is underlined by their name, which evokes Ubu Roi, the squat, comic tyrant created by the playwright Alfred Jarry and beloved by the Surrealists. *Bubu* also suggests the English slang "booboo" for a mistake and, indeed, Starck defies expectations: *Bubu 1ᵉʳ* appears heavy and solid, but one can lift it easily by hooking a finger through the hole in its top. The top comes off and the interior is hollow, allowing storage. Furthermore, the stool is strong enough to sit on.

In the 1990s, plastics such as the polypropylene of *Bubu 1ᵉʳ* were used less apologetically in design, as oil supplies were gradually reestablished, thanks to conservation and the discovery of new fields.

For Starck, trees are a more fragile resource than oil, and preserving them was one of his pleas to designers in the early part of the decade, as he urged them to rein in their excesses and focus on their social obligations. His message has the sobriety of the end of the century. By the mid-1990s he was vowing to give up interior design (he didn't) and to devote himself to creating architecture and industrial products, a decision encouraged by his appointment in 1995 as design director for domestic electronics for the Thomson Group, parent to RCA, Telefunken, and other companies. Thus *Bubu 1ᵉʳ* should be seen within his new definition of design not "as the tool of the consumer, but as a service to society." If a product is necessary at all, he said, it "must involve the minimum use of raw materials and contain a maximum of human values."[104] Starck's little creation fits his criteria.

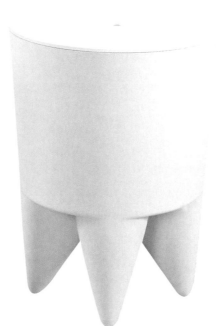

Alessandro **Mendini**

115. **Chest of drawers:** *Nigritella Nigra*

Designed 1993
Lacquered and stained mahogany, Abet plastic
laminate, gold leaf, glass mosaic tile
110 x 97 x 50 cm
Produced for Design Gallery Milano (Milan, Italy),
1993
D94.318.1, gift of Caroline Moreau

This ziggurat-like chest of drawers, named after a European black orchid, is both exotic and retrospective: it enjoys a pile-up of diverse patterns typical of Post-Modernism and it also recalls the centuries-old north Italian craft of covering small boxes and stationery items with elaborately figured papers. Mendini is inventive in enlarging and transforming what might be a chic tabletop arrangement into functional storage. Each wooden box was made and decorated separately; then the total was assembled and screwed together.

fig. 144 ▲ Mendini, drawing for *Nigritella Nigra* chest of drawers, 1993. Atelier Mendini, Milan.

The patterns progress architecturally from complex ones below to simpler geometrics in the main four boxes, and they vary in their techniques. The base is of gold-colored plastic laminate with a fillet of glass mosaic; the first drawer from the bottom is faced with inlaid wood; the second is covered with another Abet laminate; the exterior of the third is lacquered to simulate ceramic; the fourth is lacquered and gold leafed. The crowning box has a naive pastel abstraction originally drawn by a psychiatric patient and reproduced here in plastic.

This elaborate display of craftsmanship and patterning links the work, issued in an edition of twelve, to the luxuriousness of much Post-Modern design in Italy. What separates it from many pieces of the 1980s made by Mendini and his colleagues at Studio Alchimia is the repetition of its simple forms and the appearance of pattern and material classification—including "Neoclassical," "ethnic," and "psychological" categories, as indicated in one of Mendini's preliminary drawings (fig. 144). Geometric and additive, the work resembles not only a step pyramid, to be admired for the historical allusions of its shape and decorations, but also a stack of handsome gift boxes.

Gaetano **Pesce**

116. **Table lamp:** *Spaghetti*

Designed 1997
Polyurethane resin
24.5 x 66 x 66 cm
Produced by Fish Design (New York, NY, USA),
1997 to the present
D97.138.1

117. **Table lamp:** *Rag Lamp No. 7*

Designed 1997
Polyurethane resin, steel
45.5 x 50 x 49 cm
Produced by Fish Design (New York, NY, USA),
1997 to the present
D97.137.1

118. **Table lamp:** *Verbal Abuse*

Designed 1993
Polyurethane resin, lead, graphite fishing rods,
steel rods
65 x 37 x 63 cm
Executed by Fish Design (New York, NY, USA),
1997
D98.169.1

A lamp that looks like a bowl of spaghetti, a twisted rag, or a looming, big-footed cartoon figure: these are the latest instances of Pesce's light-hearted transformations, made possible by his use of polyurethane resin, a material he employed to painterly effect in the installation he designed for his retrospective at the Georges Pompidou Center in 1996. Shaping functional items to resemble foodstuffs or playful objects began for various designers in the 1960s when Pesce made his debut, and he is one of the few who continues to mine this vein of purposely unpretentious, fun-loving design. His reinterpretations of the lamp form are expressive and childlike, whether they are intended for adults' or children's use. For his candy-bright colors and his use of jellylike resins, the *New York Times* jokingly awarded its "Gummi Bear" prize to his designs at the 1999 Milan Furniture Fair.[105]

The *Spaghetti* and *Rag* lamps are part of Pesce's Fish Design Collection, a diversified series of cast-resin pieces, in which the overall forms of each model are constant, but no two results are alike. The idiosyncrasies of execution assure the buyer unique products. *Verbal Abuse*, by contrast, was made in only a few examples, and its humanoid form and behavior are more complex. Two graphite fishing rods, strong and flexible, are set between three steel rods and inserted into a pair of lead feet; the five are held together by a "body" of red poured resin and a horizontal wire representing the arms, placed at the level of the sensor light switch. The red body and light-bulb head are bowed by lead weights at the end of two chains. The total, according to Pesce, represents a victim of verbal abuse, a person trying to please. Resembling both a painting in its poured resin and a sculpture, the lamp is also springy and responsive to touch. Its incorporation of movement characterizes many of Pesce's designs, which avoid the rigidity of most functional objects and call up associations with our yielding bodies.

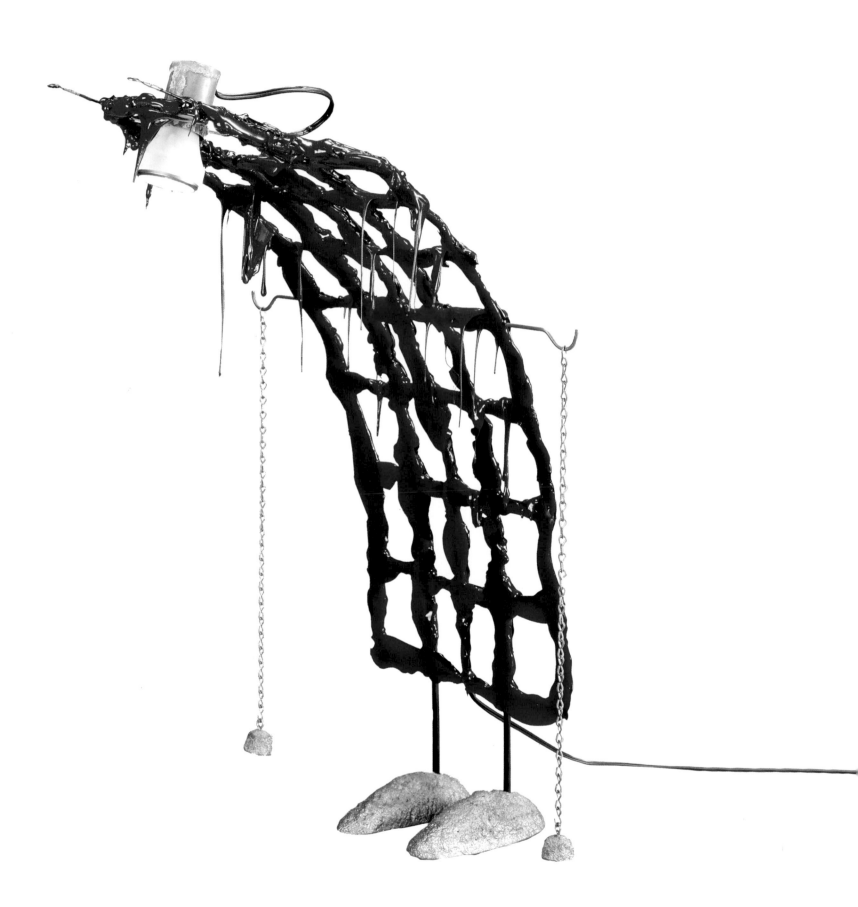

Gaetano **Pesce**

119. **Tables: *Triple Play I***

Designed 1992
Polyurethane resin, steel, rubber
24.2 x 42.1 x 42.1 cm; 31.2 x 43.3 x 42 cm;
38.2 x 42.3 x 44 cm
Produced by Fish Design (Mexico), 1992;
by Fish Design (New York, NY, USA),
1995 to the present
D95.208.1-3

Pesce's simple idea for a trio of occasional nesting tables yields visually complex results in *Triple Play I*. The legs and base of each table are formed of two sets of three U shapes of steel wire crossing one another at right angles. Rubber unites each set of feet. Each tabletop is a pancake of liquid resin in one of the primary colors; they are freely poured and allowed to set with irregular edges. Resembling outer-space

spiders, the tables look like what a child might make —if he or she knew the properties of the synthetic substance. The multiplicity of the spiny legs, especially noticeable when the tables are stacked, and the contrast between them and the small "bodies" of the tabletops, increase the tables' insectile associations, yet they are friendly in their small size and bright primary colors.

Triple Play I is part of Pesce's Fish Design Collection (*pesce* means *fish* in Italian), which began in 1992, a line of inexpensive lamps, vases, and other household objects that grew out of his desire to create affordable art for young people and that he initially had manufactured in Mexico. Whereas conventional manufacturing of plastics aims for uniformly smooth, perfected execution of preconceived forms, Pesce welcomed the unforeseen differences that result from the rudimentary equipment used and the workers' various ways of pouring the pigmented resin into the mold. This assured every consumer a unique Pesce.

fig. 145 ▲ Fulvio Ferrari and Toni Cordero, living room of Ferrari's apartment, Turin, 1998, showing Pesce's *Triple Play I* nesting tables and Dario Bartolini's *Sanremo* lamp.

Jacopo **Foggini**

120. **Floor lamp:** *Dancing Sculpture*

Designed 1998
Methacrylate, lacquered wood, iron
178.5 x 64 x 65 cm
Executed by Jacopo Foggini for Design Gallery
Milano (Milan, Italy), 1998
D98.134.1

Resin methacrylate, the plastic used for reflectors and road signs, transcends its industrial origins in Foggini's fantastical lamps. The Italian sculptor, born into a family of artists, soon learned the characteristics of clay, wood, bronze, iron, and glass, but he found his most spectacular idiom through methacrylate, which he melts at a high temperature and then turns into translucent, brilliantly colored filaments. He then spins these filaments into attenuated, organic, vaselike shapes in limited editions. One of ten exemplars, *Dancing Sculpture* gathers and intensifies ambient light (as a highway reflector does) and emits light from a bulb from within, while its coils glisten with a quick calligraphy. In addition, the lamp rests on a motor that allows it to rotate by remote control. Some of Foggini's "light sculptures" are regular and circular; others tower ten feet high like precarious totems. For exhibition purposes, he places them in darkened installations so that their intense colors radiate more dramatically (fig. 146).

Showing his work for the first time at the Salon International du Luminaire in Paris in 1993, Foggini was quickly accepted by the worlds of European fashion and art. Although his artistic use of methacrylate is unique to date, his creation of functional artworks can be related to that of glass artists who have emerged since the 1980s, such as Dale Chihuly in the United States, and the experience of artists in Italy where government sponsorship of collaborations between artists and traditional glasshouses, including those of Murano, has encouraged sculptors and designers to create luminous objects that can serve as lamps or vessels while they dazzle the eye.

Antonio **Citterio**
and Glen Oliver **Löw**

121. **Table:** *Battista*

Designed 1991
Thermoplastic technopolymer, steel, aluminum, rubber
Extended: 68.5 x 100 x 54.5 cm
Folded: 68.5 x 20.3 x 54.5 cm
Produced by Kartell S.p.A. (Milan, Italy),
1991 to the present
D95.194.1

Battista's resemblance to hospital gurneys and food trolleys typifies the frankly utilitarian appearance of many designs in the 1990s.[106] The ingenious aluminum accordion supports of the table top allow the piece of furniture to shrink to one-fifth its length, and to fold for storage. Such flexibility makes it highly adaptable to changing needs and locations. The large, custom-made wheels, a Citterio and Löw hallmark, give it complete mobility. Indeed, this table has all the advantages of a cart, while its elegant simplicity and refinement of finish associate it with early Modernist furnishings.

Such work by Citterio (who has designed without his partner Löw), Vico Magistretti, and a selection of international designers was labeled "anonymity with attitude" by Philippe Starck.[107] As guest editor, he selected the *Battista* table for inclusion in the *International Design Yearbook* of 1997. Minimal in form and undecorated, such pieces are meant to harmonize with almost any interior, and they respond to the consumer's increased need for flexibility and mobility.

It is no accident that *Battista* is manufactured by Kartell, a company that led other Italian manufacturers in the 1990s in its eagerness to sweep away what were then seen as the extremes of the 1980s. Kartell's reissue of Gino Colombini's functionalist kitchen equipment of the 1960s, but in recycled plastics, was symptomatic of the new stance of the decade. Citterio has been quoted as sharing such ideals: he prefers "not to work in the area of elite consumption," insisting instead that "you need to know what simple solutions people require every day."[108]

fig. 147 ▲ Willem Jan Neutelings, living room and terrace of an apartment in Berchem, Belgium, 1993, showing Citterio and Löw's *Battista* table.

Donald **Chadwick**
and William **Stumpf**

122. **Chair: *Aeron***
Designed 1992
Glass-reinforced polyester, aluminum, Hytrel polymer,
polyester, Lycra, leather
97 x 67 x 71 cm
Produced by Herman Miller, Inc. (Zeeland, MI, USA),
1994 to the present
D99.100.1, gift of Herman Miller, Inc.

Comfort and adaptability are the keynotes of the *Aeron* office chair, which supports the worker on a translucent fiber net originally used for car seats. This fabric, woven with a polyester elastomer, can change its shape to respond to the sitter's weight, thus minimizing strain. When the sitter stands up, the elastomer's memory erases the deformation. Cushions are unnecessary, and the thin mesh can breathe, eliminating the heat buildup of conventional seating. The chair's seat height can be adjusted for a wide range of preferences, occupations, and anatomies, and it can recline for relaxation as well as tilt forward for those who, for example, use microscopes. The armrests swing inward for keyboard work and outward for greater repose. Manufactured in three sizes to match as many body types as possible, the skeletal chair represents an attempt to marry the aesthetics of Thonet—which the designers acknowledge—with the latest ergonomic research.[109]

Compared to the Eameses' fiberglass-shell *LAR Chair* introduced in 1950 (cat. 4) and their leather-covered armchair and ottoman of 1956 for office and home (cat. 21), the *Aeron* chair reveals the changes in the signifiers of comfort in American design and even in the nature of office work. Cloth-covered foam padding in some *LAR* variants, and cowhide over amply scaled cushions in the armchair, have given way to a high-performance fiber developed for cars. The design of *Aeron* leaves the thinness of this material undisguised, and exposes the mechanical devices that allow the adjustment of its parts. Its articulated structure announces Chadwick and Stumpf's understanding of the body and the various tasks it must perform. *Aeron*'s occupant can word-process, conference-call, jump up and down, or loll with equal ease. Within months of its introduction, the chair had entered three American museum collections, while a business story on Herman Miller was titled: "Bottom Line: Their Earnings Bad; Aeron Chair Will Sit Them Straight."[110] Although the company's overall profits were weak in 1995, the chair became the most successful seating design in its history.

Tom **Dixon**

123. **Chair:** *Pylon*

Designed 1991
Painted steel
126.5 x 57.3 x 55.5 cm
Produced by Space (London, England), c. 1991;
by Cappellini S.p.A. (Como, Italy), 1992 to the present
D99.137.1, gift of Cappellini S.p.A.

Dixon began his career in London in the early 1980s as one of the "metal bashers," along with Ron Arad and others who relished the New Brutalist look of metal objects roughly welded together. From assembling found materials, Dixon gradually moved to a language of more organic, somewhat African-inspired forms in metal wire and rattan (cat. 94), and in this chair he completed the process of dematerialization. *Pylon* is solely a tracery of wires, like an Eiffel Tower or derrick made by a mad engineer; its back arches up and over the sitter like a futuristic canopy. Monumental in conception, it is surprisingly small in actuality.

When Dixon designed this chair, he was working purely on intuition. In 1992, however, he took a course in engineering to learn how he could make expressionist designs that were structurally sound and to familiarize himself with the latest alloys. One specific result was a thirty-foot steel sculpture in pylon form that he placed on the roof of a chic design shop in South Kensington, London. It is significant that such a monumental sculpture evolved from this chair but, indeed, his first *Pylon* chair was inspired less by seating than creative needs. The design historian Peter Dormer commented that in his designs, "Dixon . . . gives the chair spirit and makes it dance." He "reclaim[s] it from the moralising attitude of the Bauhaus 'fitness for purpose,' or worse, the tendentious 'We know best for you' authority of Utility furniture," the British government-sponsored design of the postwar period.[111]

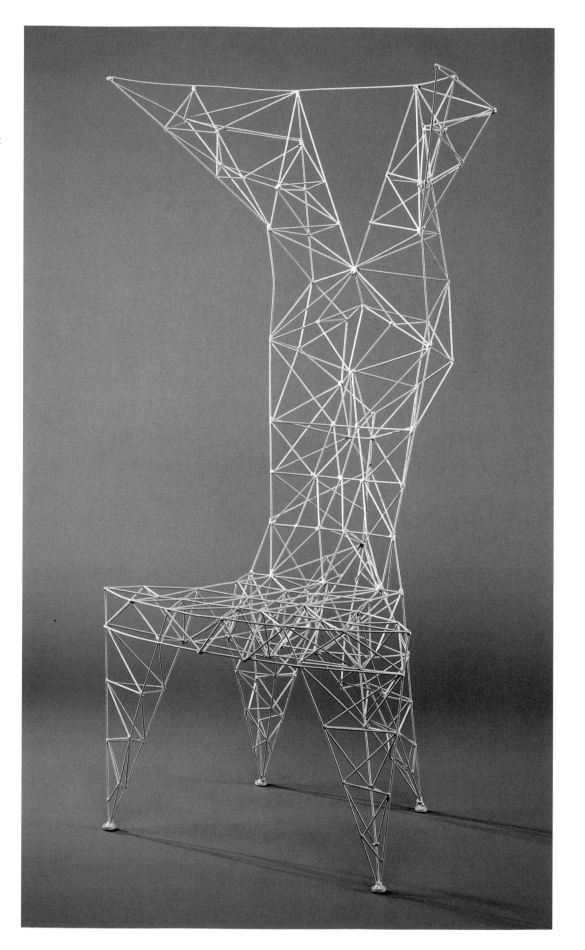

Shigeru **Uchida**

124. **Shelving: *Stormy Weather***

Designed 1991
Presswood, Formica
162 x 163 x 25 cm
Executed by Jean-François Baudouin
(Montreal, Quebec, Canada), 1999
D99.196.1

This vertigo-inducing shelving was inspired by a relief pattern carved on the Agra Fort in Agra, India. Uchida, who saw the Mughal-period relief in a book on worldwide design (fig. 148), was fascinated by the fact that each element is simple and geometric yet the completed pattern looks very complicated.[112] It involves a stairstep of identical squares: the first square in the series is higher than the second by a third of its height, the second square is higher than the third by the same distance, and so on. The smaller squares can be read as both the centers of the larger ones and as the intervals between them. But the system is on its side, as if blown by the stormy weather of the ballad providing the shelving's name. The result is a set of warring directionals that refuse optical resolution. Although this jazzy composition is made solely of right angles, Uchida turns it on the bias in relation to the floor. It is biaxially symmetrical, but it lacks a single horizontal shelf. The vibrating energy of the furniture is heightened by the arrangement of the colors in opposing directions: green versus red shelves, yellow versus blue ones.

The designer challenges our perception, as well as our conventional concept of storing books and other items. Indeed, Uchida's shelving may serve most successfully as a room divider or screen, drawing on the Japanese tradition of veiling interior spaces perceptually with screens. Nonetheless, the shelves are unmistakably Western in their bold scale, bright hues, and dynamic geometries. The designer conceived the work for the 1991 *Kagu*, the annual furniture exposition held in Tokyo, but it has not been put into production to date.

fig. 148 ▲ Line drawing and photograph of relief sculpture at the Agra Fort, Agra, India, from *1200 Line-Drawn Ornaments and Designs: Turkey, India, Japan.*

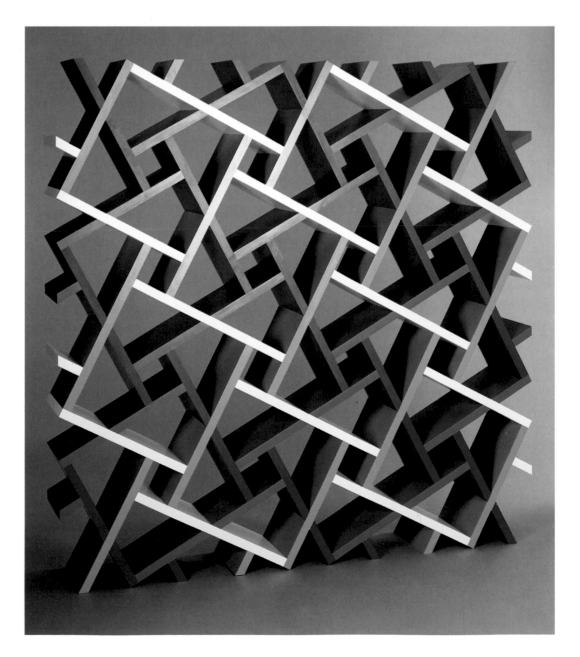

Shiro **Kuramata**

125. **Stool:** *Acrylic Stool with Feathers*

Designed 1990
Acrylic, aluminum with stained alumite finish, feathers
54 x 30.9 x 40.5 cm
Produced by Ishimaru Co., Ltd. (Tokyo, Japan),
1990 to the present
D98.145.1

Kuramata's dematerialization of design reached its apogee in this seating of transparent acrylic. The bird as a metaphor for the soul, the feather as the emblem of lightness—these spiritual associations gather around Kuramata's stool, in which feathers float in eternal suspension. The stool is subtly allusive, as its angled and slablike shapes recall 1980s versions of *Art Deco* designs and traditional Japanese furniture. It is also sensuously beautiful, as it channels the colors and lights of its surroundings. This can be seen to great effect in the stools installed in the Spiral shop, a shining and astonishingly bare home furnishings boutique that Kuramata designed for Tokyo's Axis shopping complex (fig. 149).

In the *Acrylic Stool with Feathers*, Kuramata built on his previous achievement of embedding artificial roses in acrylic for the *Miss Blanche* armchair (cat. 101); here he succeeded in preserving real feathers as if caught in a breeze. Through the elegance of their simple silhouettes, both works transcend kitsch, though they use the dimestore idea of preserving memorabilia in chunks of clear plastic. In fact, Kuramata's suggestion of that idea adds poignancy to his works: they memorialize objects that are valueless except as poetry. The hollow aluminum cylinder at the back of the stool serves as a minimal backrest for the heavy slab, which requires two people to move it. The contrast of these two elemental geometries with the small, gently curling feathers captured within the acrylic is a metaphor, both for Kuramata as a dematerializing artist and for the fragility of existence itself. The latter idea proved all too pertinent to Kuramata the man: not long after completing his designs for this stool and the Spiral shop, he died suddenly of a heart attack at age fifty-six.

fig. 149 ▲ Kuramata, interior of the Spiral shop, Tokyo, 1990.

Toshiyuki **Kita**

126. **Floor lamp:** *91 Holes*
Designed 1991
Mulberry paper, lacquered steel
99.2 x 70 x 27 cm
Executed by Toshiyuki Kita (Osaka, Japan), 1991
D93.199.1, gift of Paul Leblanc

Like the sculptor and designer Isamu Noguchi, Kita was attracted to traditional Japanese lanterns because of the sensuous handmade paper of which they are made. In the 1960s, a paper craftsman introduced him to the soft, translucent material, mourning that there was no market for it since unshaded fluorescent lamps, more economical than incandescent lighting, were more popular in Japan. Kita promised to find a use for the paper, and in 1970 he began his *Kyo* series of lamps with shades in simple geometrical shapes like this semicircular one. They were first marketed in Italy, then throughout Europe, and finally in Japan.

91 Holes is a revision of a lamp designed by Kita, which was mass-produced by IDK Design Laboratory in Osaka from 1983 through 1999. He updated the design in 1991 by piercing holes on one side of one of the lampshades. The number of holes responds to the 1991 exhibition, *91 Objects by 91 Designers*, sponsored by Gallery 91 of New York City and featuring the work of artists and designers. The theme of the exhibition was environmental responsibility at the end of the twentieth century. The *Kyo* lamp series, with its juxtaposed mulberry paper and metal associating nature and the manmade, seemed apropos to Kita. Indeed, designers of both East and West have rediscovered the vernacular Japanese craft of lantern-making from rice or mulberry paper in almost every decade since the end of World War II. In the 1990s, the harmony of body and spirit, humanity and nature, and the contemplative state of mind prized in Buddhist culture were special goals of many observers, and so this lamp bears a weight of cultural longing on its slender frame.

Andrea **Branzi**

127. **Lamp: *Wireless***

Designed 1996
Walnut, rice paper, aluminum, rubber
137.2 x 95.2 x 29.8 cm
Produced for Design Gallery Milano (Milan, Italy), 1996
D97.100.1

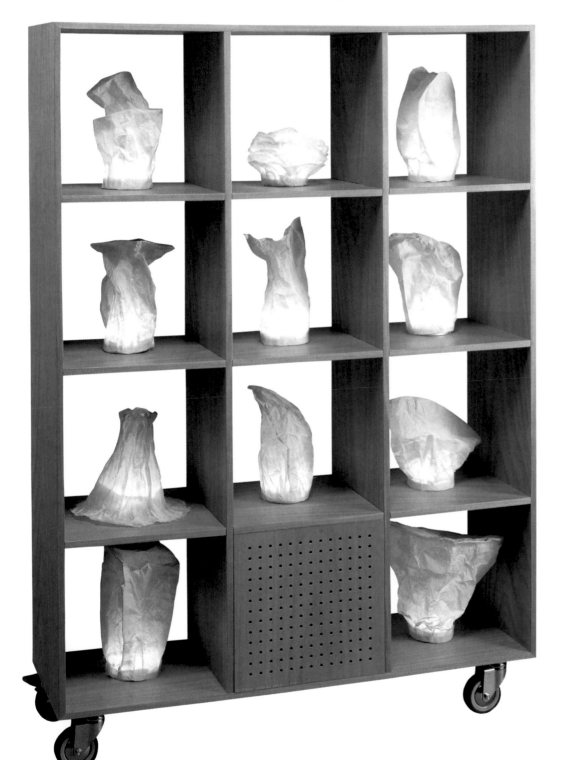

The challenge of defining *Wireless* as a furniture type is revealing, for Branzi's screenlike work combines the ingredients and attractions of lighting, shelving, and sculpture. Its mixed associations—with industry, crafts, and nature—are part of its reticent appeal. Eleven of its twelve polished walnut compartments are open and contain lamps, each covered with a different form molded from handmade rice paper. The light glows from within these wrinkled, irregular, vaselike forms without any wiring, as if by magic. The twelfth, closed compartment hides batteries—the sort used for laptop computers and cellular phones—which allow recharging of the radiant lamps. *Wireless* resembles a gridded pictographic painting by Paul Klee or René Magritte, yet one with soft illumination, architectural scale, and mobility: its wheels and freedom from wiring allow it to be placed at will in a room, and the interchangeable shades permit owners to reconfigure the composition as their needs and aesthetics suggest. The living space, according to Branzi, thus becomes "more flexible, fluid, relational."[113]

Such wireless lighting is a feat of advanced technology, which Branzi feels is "born without a specific cultural destiny," like all such new technologies. He sees his goal as interpreting these technologies, letting them realize their social potential by revealing their possible poetry. Light without wires and the metaphoric possibilities of it enchanted him. He created *Wireless* as an object that corresponds "to a condition of existence in which we all live today: a condition where the 'ties' of the old knowledge systems are breaking, where the 'wires' of the old ideologies have disappeared."[114]

For Branzi, the identification of rice paper and wood with nature is not sentimental or based on an opposition to science. "Those who declare that everything natural is beautiful and good . . . trivialize the great mystery of nature . . . transforming it into a sort of gymnasium for Sunday exercises. So when I bring nature up against technology, I do not seek to reconcile myself with nature, but to reconcile myself with technology, by transferring it into the great plankton of mixed materials in which we live."[115] The air of Asian simplicity in *Wireless* is intended, for Branzi finds that Zen culture offers a middle ground between nature and the rigidity of Western science. At the same time, his design is topical, given the concern in the 1990s for self-sufficient, energy-conserving structures and lighting sources.

Andrea **Anastasio**

128. **Chest of drawers:** *Alba*

Designed 1999
Varnished and lacquered wood, aluminum laminate,
methacrylate
123 x 126 x 48 cm
Produced for Design Gallery Milano (Milan, Italy),
1999
D99.163.1

The formal simplicity of this nearly square-fronted
chest, one in an edition of twelve, is belied by the
play of varied reflections from its smooth surfaces.
The support for the three identical drawers is a
structure hidden at the rear of the case, allowing
the drawers to appear to float, an effect enhanced by
the silvery translucence of their "skins." The drawers
are faced in pink-tinted aluminum laminate (a pale
blue version is also available); the exterior and
interior of the case are mirror-bright aluminum
laminate. This chest attracts the eye with its reflections
of the environment, including passersby, and of
the drawers themselves. But the result is spatial
confusion and optical mystification—delightful,
changing effects evocative of mirrored salons and
boudoirs. The paradox of Anastasio's *Alba* (*Dawn*
in Italian) is its creation of visually seductive and
complex effects with the simplest of rectilinear
forms. This is phenomenological design, like
the "light art" of Robert Irwin (fig. 150), in which
the changing sensuous experience of the work in situ
overpowers any easy intellectual grasp of its parts.

Anastasio first studied art history at the
University of Rome, and earned a master's degree
in philosophy from the University of Venice. His
career in design began in 1989 with glass jewelry,
followed by lamps and vases of blown glass with
an organic aesthetic of Japanese elegance. In its
planar geometry, *Alba* represents a new development,
but its subtle reflectiveness reveals the designer's
predilection for contrasts of surfaces. The illusion
that its shelves are floating aligns this work with
the tendency toward lightness and transparency in
design which marks the end of the twentieth century.

fig. 150 ▲ Robert Irwin, light art installation, *Excursus: Homage to the Square*[3], at the Dia Center for
the Arts, New York, 1998-99.

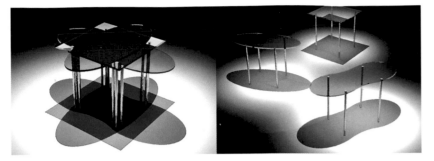

fig. 151 ▲ Domenic Sinesio, Karim Rashid, Inc., computer-generated images showing two alternate configurations of *Aura* tables, 1994.

Karim **Rashid**

129. **Coffee table:** *Aura*

Designed 1990
Glass, Color-Tint Technology, powder-coated
steel rods
48.3 x 91.5 x 69.9 cm
Produced by Zeritalia (Pesaro, Italy),
1997 to the present
D98.179.1, gift of Zeritalia

Aura summarizes the spirit of glass used in much adventurous furniture and architecture of the 1990s. In this triple-decker table, oval, rectangular, and figure-eight slabs of glass compose the design. Each slab is made of two sheets of glass which have been cut identically to computer specifications and sprayed with Colorglass, a patented system of resistant, water-based inks. The oval is in blue, the rectangle in yellow, and the figure eight in pink. Seen from different vantage points, one side of a slab appears different from the other. When stacked, the glass casts different colored shadows, blending according to one's perspective to produce additional optical hues and responding to the environment's changing colored light. Minimal as Rashid's aesthetic is, his technical invention permits manufacture of twenty-seven different compositions. Two alternate configurations are shown here.

Typical of Rashid and his colleagues is the use of the latest industrial materials and the elemental forms of Modernism, but for very different purposes than the interwar Modernists envisioned. For Gropius, Mies, Breuer, and their generation, steel and glass signified industrial technology harnessed to create design types for the improvement of everyone's lives; glass revealed structure in its Platonic geometry. For designers of the 1990s, however, individual perception has supplanted universal, absolute solutions, and technology is but a tool for personal expression. Functionalism is defined more broadly and symbolically: a work must satisfy emotional as well practical needs. The variables of individual response are part of its poetry.

Ingo **Maurer**, Dagmar **Mombach**, and team

130. **Table lamp**: *Samurai*

Designed 1998
Stainless steel, silicone, paper, glass
82 x 79 x 29 cm
Produced by Ingo Maurer GmbH (Munich, Germany),
1998 to the present
D99.140.1

In the continuous flirtation between vanguard art and adventurous design, Maurer is one of the most inventive participants. His medium is light, perhaps *the* medium of the 1990s, and the metaphors of his lamps and lighting systems are as lyrical and engaging as his forms are graphically memorable. The paper-shaded table lamp *Samurai* could be a bouffant skirt from the 1950s, but one upended and pleated by the couturiers Mary McFadden or Issey Miyake (fig. 152), the latter of whom has commissioned Maurer to light his exhibitions. The minutely folded, stiffened paper of the lamp series was developed by Maurer's collaborator Dagmar Mombach; another source was the spirit of traditional Japanese paper lanterns as captured by Isamu Noguchi, an artist whom Maurer knew. From their three names, MAurer, MOmbach, and NOguchi, came the line's whimsical name: *The MaMo Nouchies*.

Maurer has always been willing to play with norms for lighting. His debut design, of 1966, a nod to Pop art, was a huge faux light bulb with a conventional one inside. Among his designs of the 1990s are a Julian Schnabel-like explosion of crockery that forms a chandelier and calls to mind a lover's quarrel; and *Zettel'z* (*Notes*), which evokes Annette Messager's work via eighty-four slips of paper—some printed with love messages, some blank for the buyer to fill in—that radiate from wires around the light bulb and suggest the lovers reconciling. These works testify to Maurer's delight in reconfiguring materials, and in involving his clients. Whether his lighting suggests vanguard art, haute couture, or the traditional costume of Japanese warriors, Maurer's references are international, as is his appeal.

fig. 152 ▲ Issey Miyake, *Rhythm Pleats* dress, spring/summer collection 1990.

Notes

1. This exhibition was based on the Montreal Museum of Decorative Arts' collection of Gehry prototypes for a new line of bentwood furniture for The Knoll Group.

2. "Musée des Arts Décoratifs de Montréal: Functional Program and Diagrams," prepared by George Sexton Associates, Washington, D.C., in association with Marosi Troy Associe, Montreal, and David A. Hanks & Associates, New York City, March 1992. This study provided a series of functional programs for a new building.

3. "Report: The Montreal Museum of Decorative Arts: Future Orientations," Both, Belle, Robb, Ltd., Montreal, 1994. The purpose of this report was to explore alternatives for the future of the MMDA.

4. For a discussion of these commissions, see Mildred Friedman, "Fast Food," in *The Architecture of Frank Gehry* (Minneapolis: Walker Art Center, 1986), 86-105. For a catalogue raisonné of Gehry's projects, including the MMDA, see Francesco Dal Co and Kurt W. Forster, *Frank O. Gehry: The Complete Works* (Milan and New York: Electa and The Monacelli Press, 1998).

5. Edgar Kaufmann, jr., *What is Modern Design?* (New York: The Museum of Modern Art, 1950), 9.

6. "Useful Gifts 1950," *Everyday Art Quarterly* 17 (Winter 1950-51): 1.

7. Kaufmann, *What is Modern Design?*, 7.

8. *Mon Oncle*, 1958. Directed by Jacques Tati. Produced by Louis Dolivet. Starring Jean-Pierre Zola and Adrienne Servante. Set decoration by Henri Schmitt. Specta Films, 1958.

9. Kathryn B. Hiesinger and Felice Fischer, *Japanese Design: A Survey Since 1950* (New York: Philadelphia Museum of Art in association with Harry N. Abrams, 1994), 16.

10. Max Bill and Ettore Sottsass, Jr., "Design and Theory: Two Points of View," in Kathryn B. Hiesinger and George H. Marcus, eds., *Design Since 1945* (New York: Rizzoli and Philadephia Museum of Art, 1983), 3.

11. For illustrations of the Eames House and discussion of it, see John Neuhart, et al., *Eames Design: The Work of the Office of Charles and Ray Eames* (New York: Harry N. Abrams, 1989), 106-21.

12. Harry Bertoia, as quoted in Eric Larrabee and Massimo Vignelli, *Knoll Design* (New York: Harry N. Abrams, 1981), 71.

13. Isamu Noguchi, as quoted in Larrabee and Vignelli, *Knoll Design*, 46.

14. Isamu Noguchi, as quoted in "Akari—Isamu Noguchi," *Arts and Architecture* 72 (May 1955): 14, 31.

15. Sori Yanagi, as quoted in Hiesinger and Fischer, *Japanese Design: A Survey Since 1950*, 60.

16. Hans Wegner, "Furniture," in Hiesinger and Marcus, *Design Since 1945*, 119.

17. Lisa Lovatt-Smith, "Black and White World," *Blueprint* (September 1987): 88.

18. Sottsass contributed a poetic essay to the catalogue for the retrospective exhibition at the Victoria & Albert Museum, Patrick Mauriès, *Fornasetti: Designer of Dreams* (Boston, Toronto, London: Bulfinch, 1991), 8-11.

19. This storage system was well publicized at the time; see "The Storagewall," *Architectural Forum* 81 (November 1944), 90-94; also "The Storagewall," *Life* 18 (22 January 1945), 64-71.

20. Eero Saarinen, "Furniture Design 1947 to 1958," in Aline B. Saarinen, ed., *Eero Saarinen on His Work* (New Haven: Yale University Press, 1962), 66.

21. Julie V. Iovine, "Verner Panton, 72, Is Dead; Dane Designed Stacking Chair," *The New York Times*, 28 October 1998.

22. Alison and Peter Smithson, "But Today We Collect Ads," *Ark* 18 (November 1956), reprinted in Lawrence Alloway et al., *Modern Dreams: The Rise and Fall and Rise of Pop* (Cambridge, MA, and New York: MIT Press for the Institute of Contemporary Art and the Clocktower, 1988), 53.

23. See Lynne Cooke, "The Independent Group: British and American Pop Art, a 'Palimpcestuous' Legacy," in Kirk Varnedoe and Adam Gopnik, eds., *Modern Art and Popular Culture: Readings in High and Low* (New York: The Museum of Modern Art and Harry N. Abrams, 1990), 189-206.

24. For the *Sacco*, see Lesley Jackson, *The Sixties: Decade of Design Revolution* (London: Phaidon, 1994), 196. For the *Sea Urchin* chair, see ibid., 196. For the *Rocks* chairs, see *Designed for Delight: Alternative Aspects of Twentieth-Century Decorative Arts*, ed. Martin Eidelberg (Paris and New York: Montreal Museum of Decorative Arts in association with Flammarion, 1997), 281.

25. Claes Oldenburg, *Store Days* (New York: Something Else Press, 1967), reprinted in *Modern Dreams*, 105.

26. Quoted in Christopher Mead, ed., *The Architecture of Robert Venturi* (Albuquerque: University of New Mexico Press, 1989), 3.

27. See J. R. G., "Fourteen is an Awkward Age," *Industrial Design* 15 (October 1968): 51-53.

28. Arata Isozaki, as quoted in Andrea Branzi, *The Hot House: Italian New Wave Design* (Cambridge, MA: MIT Press, 1984), 4-5.

29. Emilio Ambasz, ed., *Italy: The New Domestic Landscape. Achievements and Problems of Italian Design* (New York: The Museum of Modern Art, 1972), 19.

30. Ibid., 21.

31. Peter Dormer, *Design Since 1945* (London: Thames & Hudson, 1993), 130.

32. *2001: A Space Odyssey*. 1968. Art director John Hoesli; production designers Tony Masters, Harry Lange, Ernest Archer.

33. Gaetano Pesce, as quoted in Alexander von Vegesack, Peter Dunas, and Mathias Schwartz-Clauss, *100 Masterpieces from the Collection of the Vitra Design Museum* (Weil am Rhein: Vitra Design Museum, 1995), 50.

34. Matta, interview with Luc d'Iberville-Moreau, director of Montreal Museum of Decorative Arts, 24 April 1989.

35. Gae Aulenti, as quoted in Herbert Muschamp, "Designing for a World That's Already Filled," *The New York Times*, 30 May 1999: Arts & Leisure, 29.

36. Ambasz, *Italy: The New Domestic Landscape*, 20.

37. Branzi, *The Hot House*, 55.

38. "Quella che Soleri chiama Arcologia: Architettura + Ecologia," *Domus* 474 (May 1969): 2-6. Also see Paolo Soleri, *Arcology: The City in the Image of Man* (Cambridge, MA: MIT Press, 1970).

39. Charles Jencks, *The Language of Post-Modern Architecture* (New York and London: Academy/Rizzoli, 1977).

40. Charles Jencks, *Architecture Today* (New York: Harry N. Abrams, 1988), 10.

41. Ambasz, *Italy: The New Domestic Landscape*, 137.

42. Ibid., 202.

43. Branzi, *The Hot House*, 66.

44. Ibid., 69.

45. David Revere McFadden, ed., *Scandinavian Modern Design 1880-1980* (New York: Cooper-Hewitt Museum and Harry N. Abrams, 1982), 247.

46. Joan Kron and Suzanne Slesin, *High Tech: The Industrial Style and Source Book for the Home* (New York: Clarkson N. Potter, 1978).

47. Guido Drocco, letter to Montreal Museum of Decorative Arts, 3 June 1995.

48. *Boalum* requires an electrical outlet, but a cross between it and a flashlight was marketed from the mid-1990s onward by the American firm Black & Decker. The battery-powered *Snakelight* can be bent around one's neck or shoulder, leaving hands free for the task it lights.

49. Gaetano Pesce, "Design?" *L'Architecture d'aujourd'hui* 155 (1971): 62.

50. Oscar Niemeyer, as quoted in Josep Ma. Botey, *Oscar Niemeyer: Works & Projects* (Barcelona: Gustavo Gili, 1997), 218.

51. Ibid.

52. Giancarlo Piretti, letter to Montreal Museum of Decorative Arts, 3 September 1999.

53. Katherine and Michael McCoy, "Talking with Four Men Who Are Shaping Italian Design," *Industrial Design* 28 (September/October 1981): 33.

54. Masayuki Kurokawa, "Shomei Kiga mo Chiisa na Kenchikumono" (Lighting Fixtures are Small Architectural Objects), *Designers' Workshop* 2 (February 1985): 32.

55. See Giuseppe Raimondi, *Italian Living Design: Three Decades of Interior Decoration 1960-1990* (New York: Rizzoli, 1990), 141.

56. Tom Wolfe, *From Bauhaus to Our House* (New York: Farrar Strauss Giroux, 1981), 5.

57. Andrea Branzi, as quoted in Richard Horn, *Memphis:*

Objects, Furniture, Patterns (Philadelphia: Running Press, 1985), 17.

58. Ettore Sottsass, as quoted in Joe Dolce, "Profiles: Four Designers," *I.D.: The International Design Magazine* 36 (January/February 1989): 56.

59. Barbara Radice, *Memphis: Research, Experiences, Results, Failures and Successes of New Design* (Milan and New York: Gruppo Editoriale Electa and Rizzoli, 1984), 26.

60. *Ruthless People*. 93 minutes. Touchstone Pictures, 1986. Produced by Michael Peyser. Directed by Jim Abrahams, David Zucker, and Jerry Zucker. Starring Danny DeVito and Bette Midler. Set decoration by Anne McCulley. Set design by Um Teegarden.

61. Frank Gehry, as quoted in Martin Filler, "Frank Gehry and the Modern Tradition of Bentwood Furniture," *Frank Gehry: New Bentwood Furniture Designs* (Montreal: Montreal Museum of Decorative Arts, 1992), 100.

62. Conway Lloyd Morgan, *Starck* (New York: Universe, 1999), 79.

63. Hugh Aldersey-Williams, "Milan: After the Manifestos," *I.D.: The International Design Magazine* 36 (January/February 1989): 26.

64. Ibid.

65. Gaetano Pesce, interview with Montreal Museum of Decorative Arts, 12 July 1999.

66. Ibid.

67. Gaetano Pesce, interview with Montreal Museum of Decorative Arts, 11 March 1993.

68. Toshiyuki Kita, *Toshiyuki Kita: Movement as Concept* (Tokyo: Rikuyo-Sha, 1990), 28: "From a mischievous impression, I called it 'WINK.'"

69. The interest in such contrasts, widespread in the art world of the 1980s, was given a scholarly survey in the much-discussed exhibition catalogue *High and Low: Modern Art and Popular Culture* (New York: The Museum of Modern Art, 1990).

70. Branzi, *The Hot House*, 148.

71. Robert Venturi and Denise Scott Brown, as quoted in "Knoll Venturi Collection," (New York: Knoll International, c. 1984), n.p.

72. Massimo Iosa Ghini, as quoted in Karrie Jacobs, "Q. When is a Chair not a Chair? A. When it is an Ideology," *Metropolis* 7 (June 1988): 86.

73. Stephen Hamel, letter to Montreal Museum of Decorative Arts, 6 June 1999.

74. Shigeru Uchida, as quoted in Hiesinger and Fischer, *Japanese Design: A Survey Since 1950*, 162.

75. Alberto Meda, as quoted in Nally Bellati, *New Italian Design* (New York: Rizzoli, 1990), 78.

76. Andrea Branzi, letter to Montreal Museum of Decorative Arts, 8 September 1999.

77. Branzi, *The Hot House*, 143.

78. Germano Celant, *Andrea Branzi Luoghi* (New York: Rizzoli, 1992), 152.

79. Branzi, as quoted in ibid., 9.

80. Oscar Tusquets Blanca, as quoted in Marisa Bartolucci, "Oscar Tusquets: Barcelona's Bourgeois Anarchist," *Metropolis* 11 (June 1992): 37-43, 56-57.

81. Alex Locadia, interview with Montreal Museum of Decorative Arts, 3 August 1999.

82. Forrest Myers, as quoted in *Forrest Myers*, exh. cat. (New York: Art et Industrie, 1988), 8.

83. Ingo Maurer GmbH, letter to Montreal Museum of Decorative Arts, 14 July 1999.

84. Shiro Kuramata, as quoted in Adele Freedman, "Shiro Kuramata: Breaking the Bonds," *Progressive Architecture* 9 (September 1988): 74.

85. Philippe Starck, as quoted in Morgan, *Starck*, 70.

86. Philippe Starck, as quoted in *Nouveaux plaisirs d'architecture*, exh. cat., (Paris: Centre Georges Pompidou, 1985), n.p.

87. Alberto Alessi, as quoted in Morgan, *Starck*, 81.

88. Monaco, Sotheby's, 13 October 1991.

89. Jasper Morrison, ed., *International Design Yearbook 1999* (New York: Abbeville Press, 1999), 5.

90. Francesca Picchi, "Projects: IKEA: Ingvar Kamprad," *Domus* 775 (October 1995): 70.

91. Tedi Bish and Suzette Sherman, "Design to Save the World: A Practical Guide to Green Design," *I.D.: The International Design Magazine* 37 (November/December 1990): 48.

92. Paola Antonelli, "Nothing Cooler than Dry," in Renny Ramakers and Gijs Bakker, eds., *Droog Design: Spirit of the Nineties* (Rotterdam: 010 Publishers, 1998), 12.

93. Renny Ramakers, Foreword, *Droog Design*, 9.

94. Samuel B. Frank, "Reinventing the Architecture of Work," *I.D.: The International Design Magazine* 41 (November 1994): 51.

95. Thomas Weiss et al., *Couleur Locale: Droog Design for Oranienbaum* (Rotterdam: 010 Publishers, 1999), 13.

96. Gehry, "Commentary," in *Frank Gehry: New Bentwood Furniture Designs*, 42-43.

97. David Palterer, interview with David A. Hanks and Luc d'Iberville-Moreau, Milan, 15 April 1994.

98. David Palterer, letter to Montreal Museum of Decorative Arts, 18 August 1994.

99. Marcel Wanders, letter to Montreal Museum of Decorative Arts, 9 September 1999.

100. Ida van Zijl, *Droog Design 1991-1996* (Utrecht: Centraal Museum, 1997), 107.

101. Renny Ramakers, "Spirit of the Nineties," in *Droog Design*, 49.

102. Rene Chun, "Home Design 1997," *New York Magazine* (24 March 1997): 60.

103. Ibid., 61.

104. Philippe Starck, "Manifesto for an Autocracy of Design," in *International Design Yearbook 1997* (New York: Abbeville Press, 1997), 8.

105. Julie V. Iovine, "Milan Report: Soft Forms Ease Winds of Worry," *New York Times*, 22 April 1999, F7.

106. The table and other furnishings were named for friends of Citterio's—which, in light of their impersonal style, may seem ironic.

107. Philippe Starck, "Furniture," in *International Design Yearbook 1997*, 15.

108. Antonio Citterio, as quoted in Caroline Roux, "Antonio Citterio: Milan, Italy: Staying Power," *I.D.: The International Design Magazine* 45 (January/February 1998): 68.

109. See Herman Miller, Inc., Annual Report 1995, "We Think This Chair has a Place in History" (Zeeland, Michigan).

110. Amber Veverka, *Grand Rapids Press*, 27 August 1995, L4.

111. Peter Dormer, commentaries, *New British Design*, ed. John Thackara (London: Thames and Hudson, 1986), n.p.

112. Minako Morita, Studio 80, letters to Montreal Museum of Decorative Arts, 3 and 28 September 1999.

113. Andrea Branzi, letter to Montreal Museum of Decorative Arts, 8 September 1999.

114. Andrea Branzi, as quoted in "Wireless: Design Gallery Milano" (Milan: Design Gallery Milano, 1998), n.p.

115. Andrea Branzi, as quoted in François Burkhardt and Cristina Morozi, *Andrea Branzi* (Paris: Editions du Voir, 1996), 77.

Index

Raymond Meier, New York: fig. 152.

Courtesy Alessandro Mendini, Milan: fig. 109.

Brian Merrett, Montreal Museum of Fine Arts: cat. 89; fig. 99.

Herman Miller Inc., Zeeland, Michigan: figs. 18, 41; figs. 17, 24 (photography by Charles Eames); fig. 21 (photography by West Dempster 234); fig. 39 (Rooks Photography).

Ella Moody, ed., *Decorative Art in Modern Interiors* (London and New York: Studio Vista and Viking Press, 1968): fig. 40 (photography by Henk Snoek); fig. 42 (photography by Martin Hesse).

© Robert Morris / ARS, New York / SODRAC (Montreal) 2000: figs. 111, 121.

Museum of Art and Design, PF-Studio, Helsinki: fig. 11.

Photograph © 1999 The Museum of Modern Art, New York: figs. 72, 74.

Jan Baldwin/Narratives, London: fig. 146.

Ailsa Mellon Bruce Fund, © 1999 Board of Trustees, National Gallery of Art, Washington, D.C.: fig. 20.

Galerie Neotu, Paris: fig. 127.

Courtesy of The Isamu Noguchi Foundation, Inc., Long Island City: fig. 25 (photography by Ezra Stoller © ESTO); fig. 26.

Ambrogio Beretta – Occiomagico; Kazuko Sato, *Alchimia: Contemporary Italian Design* (Berlin: Taco Verlagsgesellschaft, 1988), 16-17: fig. 95.

Photography by Sinya Okayama, Osaka: fig. 129.

© 1970, Claes Oldenburg/Gemini G.E.L., Los Angeles: fig. 89.

Courtesy of Verner Panton Design, Basel: figs. 44, 67; pp. 72-73.

Courtesy of Gaetano Pesce, New York: fig. 135.

© Gaetano Pesce, Pesce Ltd., New York: figs. 71, 112.

Lisa Phillips et al., *High Styles: Twentieth-Century American Design* (New York: Whitney Museum of American Art in association with Summit Books, 1985), 181: fig. 53 (photography by Louis Reens).

Photofest, New York: figs. 1, 13, 70, 108.

Alberto Piovano, Milan: fig. 147.

Giancarlo Piretti, Bologna: fig. 96.

Archizoom Associati Archive, Centre de Creation Industrielle, Centre Georges Pompidou, Paris: figs. 69, 82 (photography by Dario Bartolini).

Poltronova, Montale Pistoia: fig. 66.

Gio Ponti Photo Archives, Milan: fig. 36 (photography by Salvatore Licitra).

Louis Poulsen & Co. A/S, *Lighting Beleuchtung Luminaires* (Copenhagen, 1960), A1: fig. 29.

Design by Karim Rashid. Computer renderings by Domenic Sinesio. Karim Rashid Inc., New York: fig. 151.

Giles Rivest, Montreal Museum of Decorative Arts: cat. 25, 39, 40, 48, 59, 83, 87, 91, 104, 105; figs. 52, 56, 113, 139.

Philippe Ruault, Nantes: figs. 133, 134.

Kazuko Sato, *Alchimia: Never-Ending Italian Design* (Tokyo: Rikuyo-sha Publishing, Inc., 1985), 93: fig. 114.

Maria Schofield, ed., *Decorative Art and Modern Interiors* (London and New York: Studio Vista and Van Nostrand Reinhold, 1977), 75: fig. 90.

Maria Schofield, ed., *Decorative Art and Modern Interiors* (London and New York: Studio Vista and Van Nostrand Reinhold, 1978), 104: fig. 95 (photography by Richard Einzig).

Studio Azzurro Fotografia s.n.c. for Schoner Wohnen, Milan: fig. 106.

Sonnabend Gallery, New York: fig. 111 (photography by Bevan Davies).

Sotheby's, London: cat. 81.

Sottsass Associati E.E.I.G., Milan: fig. 77.

Agence Philippe Starck, Issy-les-Moulineaux: fig. 131; fig. 132 (photography by Jean-Baptiste Mondino); p. 190 (Judith Carmel-Arthur, *Philippe Starck* [London: Carlton Books Limited, 1999], frontispiece).

Stokke Fabrikker AS, Skodje, Norway: fig. 84.

© Tim Street-Porter/ESTO; Maria Schofield, ed., *Decorative Art and Modern Interiors* (London and New York: Studio Vista and Viking Press, 1974), 102: fig. 58.

Strüwing Reklamefoto, Copenhagen; Tobias Farber, *Arne Jacobsen* (New York: Frederick A. Praeger, 1964), 125: fig. 28; pp. 30-31.

Thonet Industries, Statesville, North Carolina: fig. 103.

© Photo Topdeq GmbH, Germany: fig. 140.

Emilio Tremolada, Milan: fig. 126.

Julie Marquart, Venturi, Scott Brown and Associates, Philadelphia: fig. 117.

Vitra Design Museum, Weil am Rhein: fig. 38 (photography by Herbert Gehr); fig. 45.

© Photo Paul Wierink: fig. 141.

David A. Wilkins et al., *Art Past/Art Present* (New York: Harry N. Abrams, 1994), 474: fig. 119.

Yale University Art Gallery, New Haven, Connecticut, Holtzman Trust: fig. 16.

Courtesy of Shoei Yoh, Fukuoka, Japan: figs. 59, 83 (photography by Yoshio Shiratori).

Courtesy of Zanotta S.p.A.: fig. 97.